Hard Money, Hard Times

Edited by
Lars Osberg and Pierre Fortin

James Lorimer & Company, Publishers,
Toronto, 1998

James Lorimer & Company Ltd. acknowledges with thanks the support of the Canada Council, the Ontario Arts Council and the Ontario Publishing Centre in the development of writing and publishing in Canada.

Permission has generously been given to reprint the following copyrighted works. Pierre Fortin's "The Canadian Fiscal Problem: The Macroeconomic Connection" first appeared in *Atlantic Economic Journal* Vol. 23, No. 1, March 1995; James Tobin's "Business Cycles and Economic Growth: Current Controversies about Theory and Policy" first appeared in *Bulletin. The American Academy of Arts and Sciences* Vol. XLVII, No. 3, December 1993; Irwin Gillespie's "A Brief History of Government Borrowing in Canada" was excerpted from *Tax, Borrow and Spend: Financing Federal Spending in Canada, 1867–1990*, published by Carleton University Press in 1991.

Canadian Cataloguing in Publication Data
Main entry under title:
Hard money, hard times

2nd ed.
    Previously published under title: Unnecessary debts.

ISBN 1-55028-613-7 (bound)   ISBN 1-55028-612-9 (pbk.)

1. Debts, Public — Canada. 2. Deficit financing — Canada. 3. Fiscal policy — Canada. 4. Interest rates — Canada. I. Osberg, Lars. II. Fortin, Pierre, 1944—. III. Title: Unnecessary debts.

HJ8033.C3U55 1998   336.3'4'0971   C98-930209-1

James Lorimer & Company Ltd., Publishers
35 Britain Street
Toronto, Ontario
M5A 1R7

Printed and bound in Canada.

*For our children, who deserve the chance
to live in a humane society.*

Contents

Figures and Tables

Acknowledgements

We would like to thank the Social Sciences and Humanities Research Council (Canada) and the Fonds pour la formation de chercheurs et l'aide à la recherche (Québec) for their support of our research over the years. Lynn Lethbridge provided outstanding research assistance while Diane Young and Jim Lorimer speeded this book through the editorial process. Monique Comeau, Jeannie Doyule, Heather Lennox, and Cheryl Stewart also deserve thanks, both for exemplary typing and continual good cheer.

Introduction: Consensus and Controversy in the Debate on Deficit Reduction

In Canada in the second half of the nineties, deficit reduction is rapidly reshaping the political system and reaching into every area of life. Because the federal minister of finance has declared that deficit reduction is an objective which will be met "come hell or high water," the federal government has initiated massive cuts to program spending; however, as the federal government reduces transfer-payments to the provinces, it loses the financial leverage it once had to induce compliance with national standards in areas of provincial jurisdiction, such as health care. As a result, some provinces (e.g., Alberta) have started to argue that, because of the debt crisis, Canada must adopt a medical care system with two tiers — public and private. Thus, in this new, deficit-driven era of provincialism, many argue that the basic rights of Canadian citizens and the fundamental political symbols of our national community are being threatened.

At the same time, despite widespread recognition of the importance of a sound education system for success in the new global economy, provincial government cuts to education make the quality of public schooling increasingly difficult to maintain while rising tuition at cash-starved universities and colleges limits the accessibility of postsecondary education. And while cuts to education and health care affect all Canadians, cuts to unemployment insurance and social assistance are especially hard on the poor, who have little to start with.

Although health care, education and income support programs account for the largest share of government expenditures in Canada, cut-backs are occurring in all areas of government activity. Some would argue that cuts in such areas as environmental protection, basic research or culture and the arts are critical to our future. However, political attitudes to government cut-backs also differ dramatically. Some commentators welcome cut-backs, because they believe the role that governments play in Canadian society should be reduced. Others fear an erosion of our national distinctiveness and a short slide to a nastier, poorer world of polarization, crime and social decay.

Given the political polarization of the debate and the great significance of these issues to all Canadians, the debate on the deficit and debt problems of governments has seen a great deal of sound and fury and descended sometimes into exaggeration and semihysteria. In this atmosphere, it is important to clarify the issues in the deficit/debt debate. It is crucial to recognize where there is agreement and where there is disagreement. Therefore, this introduction starts with a discussion of areas of broad agreement, before outlining the controversies behind the deficit debate. Despite the fact that much of the journalistic discussion of the debt issue focuses on the role of government expenditure, it is only part of the problem. As will become clear below, monetary policy — the Bank of Canada's manipulation of interest rates and the money supply — has played a central role in creating Canada's debt crisis, and monetary policy reform must form an integral part of the solution.

Areas of Agreement

There is no doubt that Canada's national debt is a big number ($583 billion in 1997). However, although the national debt is big, Canada's national income is bigger ($861 billion per year in the third quarter of 1997), and Canada's national wealth is bigger still (about $3 trillion in 1997). In general, for both individuals and countries, debt is a problem only when it is big *relative to ability to pay*. For example, Canadians find it perfectly reasonable to take on debt in order to finance their purchases of homes or automobiles. Such debts become a major problem only if they are large relative to income: for a bank president earning $500,000 annually, a car loan of $25,000 is easily dealt with, but the same car loan would be a crushing burden for a cleaner making $15,000 per year.

The important issue is the debt-to-income ratio. Furthermore, since we are concerned about whether we need to make changes to government policy concerning taxation, expenditures and interest rates, we are concerned with changes in this ratio. If the debt-to-income ratio increases from one year to the next, interest payments on that debt will every year occupy a larger fraction of total government expenditure, and the accumulation of debt will become increasingly more difficult to control. The *trend in the debt-to-*income ratio is the key policy issue.

However, we must also distinguish between short-run fluctuations and long-run trends. During recessions, the debt-to-income ratio usually rises, both because the numerator of the ratio (debt) increases faster and because the denominator (income) falls or increases more slowly. Government deficits tend to rise during a recession, due to declines in tax revenue and increases in social expenditures on unemployment insurance (UI) and social assistance. But despite short-run recessionary increases, the debt-to-income ratio can be stable in the long term if governments take advantage of upswings in the business cycle to reduce the ratio.

The issue that is truly worrying is the long-term trend. Continual increases in the debt-to-income ratio are not sustainable. If this ratio rises continually, interest payments on the debt will eventually dominate government expenditure, meaning that governments will be unable to provide necessary services such as health care and education. Moreover, a debt that is large relative to income feeds on itself, due to compound interest; hence, citizens of all political persuasions are very concerned with the problem of "debt stability."

What determines whether the national debt is compounding to an increasing proportion of national income and becoming an ever more important problem? Despite many areas of disagreement, economists do agree on one fundamental equation. The "debt stability equation" states that:

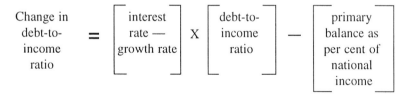

$$
\begin{array}{c}
\text{Change in} \\
\text{debt-to-} \\
\text{income} \\
\text{ratio}
\end{array}
=
\left[
\begin{array}{c}
\text{interest} \\
\text{rate} - \\
\text{growth rate}
\end{array}
\right]
\times
\left[
\begin{array}{c}
\text{debt-to-} \\
\text{income} \\
\text{ratio}
\end{array}
\right]
-
\left[
\begin{array}{c}
\text{primary} \\
\text{balance as} \\
\text{per cent of} \\
\text{national} \\
\text{income}
\end{array}
\right]
$$

Two aspects of this equation are important. First, it is not a matter of "opinion"; the debt stability equation is an accounting identity (see Appendix A for the derivation). Second, there are two terms in the debt stability equation: the primary balance (taxes less program expenditures) and the influence of interest rates compared to growth rates. Much of the public debate on deficits and debt in Canada has focused on part of the primary balance (i.e., government expenditures), and many commentators have ignored the crucial role which interest rates play in compounding the national debt and decreasing the growth rate of national income; however, both parts of the equation are important.

There is broad agreement on the validity of the debt stability equation, and there is also agreement about past events, since they have already happened. In this book, Irwin Gillespie presents a long-term perspective on trends in Canada's national debt from Confederation to the nineties, and Pierre Fortin and Ronald Kneebone examine our more recent economic history. Gillespie makes clear that the issues in the debt debate are not new. Canadian governments have always been concerned about the reaction of international bond markets and the level of Canada's tax burden, compared to other jurisdictions. Canada's economic history has seen the debt load rise and fall several times, and Gillespie discusses the factors behind these historic episodes. Kneebone examines the last thirty-five years and considers the separate factors influencing particular provinces, as well as the federal government.

As both Fortin and Kneebone emphasize, the implications of recent trends in interest rates and growth rates for the stability of the national debt are dramatic. During the sixties and seventies, low interest rates and a high growth rate created a built-in tendency for a decline in the debt-to-income ratio, which also reduced the relative importance of interest rate policy for the national debt. By the mid-1970s, with a ratio between debt and gross domestic product (GDP) of under 10 per cent, the influence of interest rates was minor, and changes in taxation and expenditure decisions largely determined trends in the national debt.

In the nineties, however, the situation is fundamentally different. Interest rates are significantly higher than the national growth rate, and their influence is magnified by a debt that has become rather large, compared to GDP. As Fortin explains, high interest rates, combined with a low growth rate, have created a built-in tendency for government deficits and the debt-to-income ratio to compound each year. Monetary policy, not fiscal policy, has become the crucial determinant of debt stability. As Michael McCracken's chapter demonstrates, the increase in the debt-to-GDP ratio in the nineties is entirely due to the interest rate policy followed by the Bank of Canada.

Areas of Disagreement

Although economists agree on the relevance of changes in the debt-to-income ratio, on the determinants of debt stability and on past trends in interest rates, growth rates, taxes, expenditure and the national debt, they disagree on policy.

What are the areas of disagreement and why do they exist?

The most basic disagreement among economists centres on how the macroeconomy functions. As James Tobin's chapter emphasizes, today's economists hold divergent opinions on the role which government can or should play in influencing macroeconomic outcomes. Those economists who hold a classical view of the economy think of market processes as operating quickly, with few imperfections, to keep the economy in equilibrium. They argue that fluctuations in unemployment and economic output are basically driven by the decisions of individual workers and firms regarding how much labour and how many goods, respectively, will be supplied, which governments can (and should) do little to influence. By contrast, Tobin is skeptical that, unaided, market processes will produce full employment or a desirable rate of growth in output quickly, if at all. He sees an important role for government in mitigating the severity of economic recessions and in maintaining desirable levels of employment and growth.

These disagreements are profoundly important for the deficit and debt issue because, as the debt stability equation makes explicit, the growth rate of national income is one of the key determinants of trends in the debt-to-income ratio. Furthermore, Tobin argues that monetary policy can and should be used to help maintain full employment and acceptable growth in national output, and that central banks should maintain a balance between inflation, output and employment levels.[1] However, heavily influenced by classical economic thinking, the Bank of Canada in 1988 announced its commitment to the *sole* objective of preventing inflation — that is, maintaining price stability — regardless of the implications for the current level of output, employment or the national debt.

This shift in the objectives of monetary policy marked a historic change for the Canadian economy. Previously, Canadian governments had always recognized the considerable interdependencies between the economies of Canada and the United States. With approximately 80 per cent of Canadian exports flowing to markets in the United States and a long history of capital flows and foreign investment, it was long recognized that the macroeconomic stability of Canada is heavily influenced by the country's exchange rate with the United States and by the differential between the two countries' interest rates. In 1988, the Bank of Canada, however, adopted its goal of price stability regardless of economic events elsewhere, or the consequences of its policies on exchange rates and interest rates. From 1988 to 1990, the Canada–U.S. exchange rate appreciated by over 20 per cent, as the value of the Canadian dollar moved from U.S.$.72 to a peak of over U.S.$.89, driven by the inflows of foreign capital that were attracted by the highest differential between the two countries' interest rates in history. High interest rates choked off investment and discouraged consumption, and the high exchange rate priced Canadian exports out of foreign markets. The result was a dramatic worsening of the recession of the early nineties.[2]

In addition to general disagreements about economic philosophy, economists are deeply divided on the wisdom of the monetary policy changes adopted by the Bank of Canada and the federal government in the late eighties. Since these policy changes produced both a large increase in interest rates (compounding the debt much more rapidly) and a sharp fall in the growth rate (resulting in a smaller income with which to pay debt charges, as well as a greater need for UI and social assistance expenditures), the changes had profound effects on the deficits and debts of Canadian governments. In this book, McCracken uses an econometric model of the Canadian economy to answer the question of how big the Canadian deficit and debt would be if the Bank of Canada had followed its historic policy and not allowed interest rate differentials and the exchange rate with the United States to increase so dramatically.

The contributors to this book all recognize the importance of monetary policy for the debt crisis. They differ, however, in their opinions as to what can, or should, be done. Ronald Kneebone argues that, in 1988, the Bank of Canada either ignored the possible effects of its zero-inflation strategy on the national debt and public finances or judged that the benefits of zero inflation exceeded the costs. He also stresses that Canadian governments must share the blame with the Bank of Canada for the debt crisis. Nonetheless, he argues that the solution to the debt crisis lies in expenditure cuts by governments, because he assumes that there will be no future change in the monetary policy of the Bank of Canada, due to the autonomy of the Bank and its policy of promoting like-minded individuals from within. On the other hand, Gideon Rosenbluth argues that Canada can still afford its social programs and that the social waste of unemployment is

Canada's most serious national problem. He concludes that a change in the direction of monetary policy is precisely what is needed, and he argues that such a change is entirely feasible. Marc Van Audenrode also emphasizes the importance of a lack of aggregate demand in maintaining Canada's high level of unemployment, and he takes aim at the Bank's rationalizations for its monetary policies. However, his conclusion is more radical. Given the unwillingness of the Bank to alter its monetary course, he argues that Canada should abandon its independent monetary policy entirely and peg the Canadian dollar to the U.S. dollar. This suggestion deserves serious consideration.

Whichever choice is made, there will be significant implications for Canadian life. Lars Osberg's chapter emphasizes the crucial interdependencies between social policy, macroeconomic policy and the debt. Prolonged periods of high unemployment have grave social consequences — for health, divorce, mental illness and crime — which tend to increase the need for social expenditures. At the same time, high unemployment increases the difficulties facing those trying to get off social assistance. Therefore, "supply-side" policies to retrain or remotivate unemployed workers are pointless unless there is a corresponding increase in demand to ensure that jobs will exist for the retrained and the remotivated.

Overall, our view is that the Bank of Canada's decision to go for zero inflation was based on very flimsy empirical evidence and that the benefits of a zero-inflation regime were grossly overestimated, while the costs of attaining zero inflation were hugely underestimated.[3] However, officials of the Bank of Canada, and their supporters at the Department of Finance, have a vested interest in defending the wisdom of their past decisions, and they tend to select as their successors individuals with similar points of view. These officials guard their autonomy, but we think it is inappropriate that major economic decisions, with implications for so many aspects of Canadian life, are outside the influence of the democratic political process. As the legal mandate of the Bank of Canada recognizes, a complex market economy has a real need for macroeconomic stability. The Bank of Canada is rightly assigned the duty to "mitigate by its influence fluctuations in the general level of production, trade, prices and unemployment, so far as may be possible in the scope of monetary action, and generally to promote the economic and financial welfare of Canada." The citizens of a democracy also have the right to expect that their views will matter in major issues of public policy, such as the balance which is to be struck among these objectives.

As the debt crisis has illustrated, macroeconomic decisions which are made without consideration of all the consequences can produce an economic and political crisis. We therefore believe it is essential that an institution such as the Bank of Canada give serious consideration to alternative viewpoints about policy formation and that public institutions do not become the prisoners of a single (possibly erroneous) school of economic thought. For these reasons, our concluding chapter advocates substantial restructuring of the governance of the Bank of Canada, both to enable the solution of Canada's current debt crisis and to lessen the odds of a similar crisis recurring in the future.

Lars Osberg, Halifax
Pierre Fortin, Montreal

A Brief History of Government Borrowing in Canada[1]

W. Irwin Gillespie

The public debate on Canada's debt problems has seen many alarmist statements asserting that government debt is spiralling out of control, that constitutional amendments are needed to contain the debt explosion and that the globalization of financial markets is a new and dangerous problem for Canadian governments. In this chapter, Irwin Gillespie of Carleton University examines the actual historical record and concludes that these assertions are false.

Over the decades since Confederation, the federal government has often used deficit financing. Wars and depressions have several times pushed up the debt burden, but subsequently it has always been reduced by economic growth, lower interest rates and government restraint. From the 1870s to the 1990s Canadian governments have been conscious of the role played by international capital markets in financing the debt and the need to keep taxation at a level competitive with that of the U.S. Irwin Gillespie notes as well that the increase in Canada's national debt in the late 1970s came about because of tax policy changes in the federal government's three major revenue sources (reductions in personal income tax, the corporate income tax and manufacturers' sales tax) and not *because of increases in program spending.*

Introduction

This chapter reviews the fiscal history of taxes, borrowing and government spending in Canada. It illuminates and explains the tax and borrowing choices that Canadian federal governments have made in financing government spending from Confederation in 1867 through 1990.

This fiscal record is necessary for accurately describing and explaining past governments' taxing, borrowing and spending policies. It is also important for the current debate on government expenditures, deficit financing (borrowing to finance government spending) and the national debt. Discussions of excessive government spending, cancerous deficits and a debt build-up which will have profound effects for our children often ignore or misinterpret the long-term fiscal record.

In the ongoing public debate on deficits, debt and the role of the state, government spending is seen as always increasing, like some uncontrolled leviathan. Some observers describe the deficits and debt build-up since the mid-1970s in moralistic and alarmist terms. The fiscal record undermines this view and demonstrates that the spending of the state has waxed and waned. The fiscal record shows that federal governments have borrowed regularly to finance expenditures since 1868, and that the ratio of debt to national income is lower than it was at the end of World War II. The major cause of the deficits and debt accumulation since the mid-1970s is often asserted to be excessive government spending by profligate politicians. An examination of the fiscal history of this period challenges this simplistic view and establishes the importance of tax policy changes during the seventies.

The debate on the debt crisis of the past fifteen years and concern over hitting the alleged "debt wall" are partly based on the perception that the globalization of capital markets has imposed some new or more significant constraints on the financing of Canadian governments. The fiscal history of Canada demonstrates that there is nothing new about Canadian governments' either actively competing with other jurisdictions for mobile capital and labour or being especially sensitive to good credit ratings in financing part of the national debt in foreign markets. Moreover, some policy solutions to the deficits and debt problem drawn from the U.S. debate, such as instituting enforceable legal "balanced budget" mandates, overlook the fact that, several times, our political system has proven itself capable of reducing the debt-to-income ratio. An examination of the fiscal

Figure 1

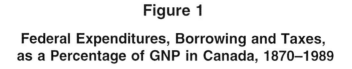

Federal Expenditures, Borrowing and Taxes, as a Percentage of GNP in Canada, 1870–1989

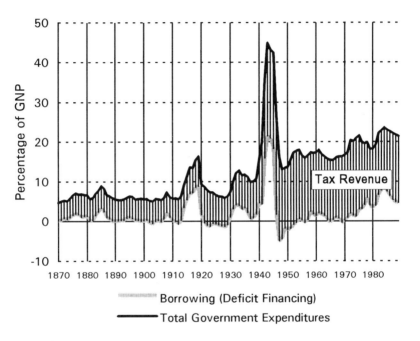

Borrowing (Deficit Financing)

Total Government Expenditures

record offers insights into ways to reduce the size of the debt relative to the capacity of the economy, within Canada's political institutions.

Figure 1 traces the total spending, total borrowing and total tax revenues chosen by Canadian federal governments, as a per cent of gross national product (GNP). The tax indicator, total government tax revenues as a per cent of GNP, is the difference between the spending indicator and the borrowing indicator (the shaded area between the lines). In Figure 2, the tax indicator is shown separately.

These figures offer an interesting picture of the federal government's financing of its spending from 1868 through 1990.[2] The tax indicator was virtually constant at 6 per cent until about 1914; it then rose sharply through World War II before settling down to approximately 17 per cent, around which there has been considerable variation. Within the total tax indicator are considerable variations in specific taxes. During a remarkably fecund period of tax births from 1917 to 1923, the personal income tax, the corporation income tax

Figure 2

Federal Tax Revenue,
as a Percentage of GNP in Canada, 1870–1989

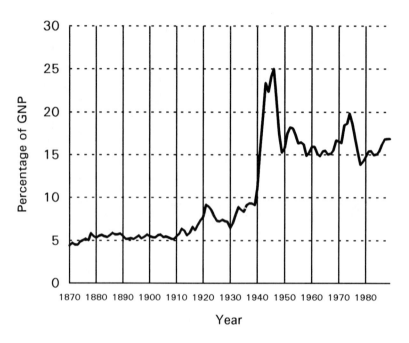

and the manufacturers' sales tax were introduced, and seventy years later, they constitute the three most important taxes in the family of revenue sources.

The total spending indicator, the tax indicator and the borrowing indicator all rose substantially during the two world wars and fell dramatically after the end of World War II. The federal public sector exhibited markedly similar wartime patterns, even though the increase in the tax indicator during World War I lagged somewhat. The two postwar periods reflected a no less remarkably consistent pattern of declining spending and taxing and of substantial surpluses, which were used to reduce the federal debt.

The fiscal record demonstrates that Canadian federal governments have regularly financed a significant part of their spending by borrowing. Even if we ignore the periods surrounding World War I and II, when borrowing reached 8 and 22 per cent of GNP respectively, we find that deficit financing was actively pursued in the depression from the 1870s to the 1890s and in the Great Depression of the thirties, when it reached 4 per cent each time. The seventies and eighties are also characterized by substantial deficit financing, with borrowing increasing to a high of 9 per cent in 1985. And these periods, as Figure 1 indicates, are only the peaks.

In short, borrowing has long been an important instrument of government financing. In the next section, we discuss the evolution of the federal revenue structure from Confederation in 1867 to the summer of 1917, a time when attracting immigrants and persuading the remaining colonies to join the Union were important objectives of federal policy.

Then, we consider the financing of the sustained reductions in the national debt, after each world war. The postwar demand for debt reduction and strong opposition from taxpayers most affected by wartime taxes caused governments to reduce the debt and lower effective tax rates on specific revenue sources. Next, we analyze the increases in deficit financing and the national debt from the mid-1970s to 1990. The initial surge in debt creation was caused, not by federal governments' profligate spending, but by finance ministers' choosing to decrease tax rates of the three major taxes. The conclusions follow in the last section.

Attracting People and Building the Union: Dominion Revenue Policy, 1867–1917

> "all taxation … is a loss *per se* … it is the sacred duty of the government to take only from the people what is necessary to the proper discharge of the public service; and that taxation in any other mode, is simply in one shape or another, legalized robbery."
>
> — The Honourable Sir Richard Cartwright, Minister of Finance, *Budget Speech*, 1878

> "Taxation is the only gateway to progress and in a country … (the way a political collectivity enjoys great public works) is through the gateway of taxation."
>
> — The Honourable George E. Foster, Minister of Finance, *Budget Speech,* 1889

The two main themes in the revenue policy discussions of the budget speeches from 1867 to 1917 were attracting immigrants to Canada and building the Union. Revenue policies that interfered with or inhibited the achievement of these objectives were seen as being politically difficult. The high political costs of interference affected both the choice of revenue sources between borrowing and indirect taxation (the tariff and excise duties on alcoholic beverages and tobacco products), and the choice of tax mix, ranging from the decision *not* to use the potential revenue source of direct taxation, to the choice of taxing some items at reduced rates and exempting others from taxation.

As the Dominion government concentrated on luring immigrants and building the Union, no issue was discussed more frequently, by virtually every minister of finance, than the ability to incur new debt at low interest charges in order to finance expenditures and thus permit a low rate of indirect taxation. Low tax rates were seen as being a crucial factor in encouraging immigration into and discouraging emigration out of the Dominion. Dominion governments feared losing potential immigrants, as well as those immigrants who were newly settled in Canada, to the United States. Thus, governments adopted the principle that their tax levels should not exceed those in the United States. Competition was fierce for these mobile human resources, not to mention for the capital with which these immigrants arrived. Consequently, all Dominion governments were determined to keep tax rates low.

The desire to keep indirect tax rates low led to the demand that the government borrow in order to finance Dominion expenditures. The Dominion government's strong demand for debt finance resulted in a search for low interest rates and a concern to preserve the "good credit standing" of the Dominion. This desire to maintain a good credit rating, in order to have access to international capital funds at low interest rates, constrained the government's borrowing power. The revenue policy problem of Dominion governments involved the choice between incurring additional debt, if it could be lodged without seriously damaging the credit ratings, and imposing additional high indirect taxation, at the political cost of discouraging immigration and encouraging emigration.

Low tax rates were seen as expanding the future revenue bases of the Dominion, since tax rates that were lower than those in the United States would attract immigrants and their capital to Canada. This expansion would enhance the government's capacity not only to pay off the debt, which was incurred to meet total financial requirements, but to pay it off with lower average tax rates per person.

This trade-off between additional debt and additional taxation as a means of financing the spending plans of the government is consistent with the idea that a government will draw upon each of these revenue sources up to the point where an extra dollar of revenue incurs the same additional political cost. The political cost of an extra dollar of debt is the reduced credit standing of the Dominion and the associated higher interest charge. The political cost of an extra dollar of taxation is the reduced net immigration flow. When the government of one country adopts a tax rate that is similar to, or lower than, the tax rate of a neighbouring country, whether to encourage immigration or discourage emigration, it is engaged in horizontal tax competition. Horizontal tax competition emerges very early as a crucial influence on revenue structure and, as we shall see, maintains its dominant role for 123 years. That early Dominion governments perceived this trade-off is evident from many budget speeches and budget debates in Parliament.

Ministers of finance were aware of the relative political costs of additional borrowing compared with additional taxation. They treated borrowing and the associated increasing public debt as a normal condition in a growing young country like Canada. They shaped their revenue policies in response to the interest costs of borrowing associated with a given credit standing of the Dominion and horizontal tax competition, especially with the United States. These determinants of revenue structure carried substantial weight for Dominion governments intent on attracting immigrants and opening up the West.

Dominion spending relative to the size of the economy was remarkably stable during most of the first fifty years of fiscal history. This spending indicator varied between 5 and 9 per cent from 1870 to 1913.[3] The rise to 9 per cent occurred during the 1880s, when national income was falling and the Dominion embarked on one of its "great public works" — the building of the Canadian Pacific Railway. Figure 1 shows the spending variation, including the wartime spending surge which increased the size of the public sector to 14 per cent by 1917. This overall stability of Dominion spending, relative to the size of the economy, masks yearly fluctuations.[4]

Spending was financed from three major Confederation revenue sources: customs duties, excise duties on alcoholic beverages and tobacco products and borrowing (deficit financing).[5] Figure 3 traces

Figure 3

**Confederation Revenue Sources,
as a Percentage of GNP in Canada, 1870–1917**

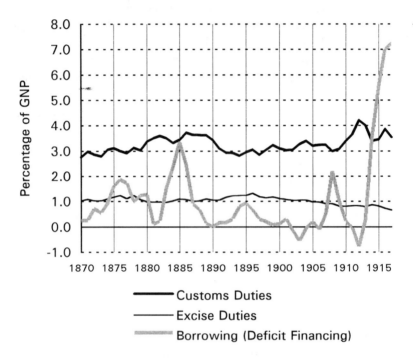

the revenues for these sources, relative to national income, from 1870 through 1917. During this period, the tariff was the primary source of revenue (except in 1885 and the war years), financing between 40 and 66 per cent of total spending. Excise duties accounted for 10 to 22 per cent, and deficit financing, although exhibiting greater variability, accounted for 10 per cent regularly, and occasionally represented as much as 40 per cent of total spending.

Dominion revenues from the tariff, excise duties and the other taxes totalled approximately 5.5 per cent of GNP from 1870 through 1913, a period ending just before the war. The stability of the total tax indicator is consistent with finance ministers' continually expressed desire to keep indirect taxes low to attract immigrants and coax the other colonies into the Union. These objectives provided the context for a demand for deficit financing, which would serve as

an integral component of the governments' total financial requirements.

The Dominion governments borrowed from both domestic and
foreign sources to finance their spending. The domestic sources
consisted of government and post office savings banks and, to a
minor extent, the chartered banks. The foreign sources included
primarily bond issues in the London money market and, to a lesser
extent, British banks. Domestic borrowing was important until the
mid-1880s, after which foreign borrowing became the major source
of deficit financing.[6]

Figure 3 illustrates the variability of the revenue obtained through
borrowing in relation to the size of the economy. Dominion governments borrowed regularly to finance the deficit from 1870 to 1915.
At times, emphasis on borrowing was greater, which suggests that
the relative political costs of using this revenue source were lower
than those of indirect taxation.

Decreasing the public debt was not a policy goal at any time
during the period. Debt issue was a source of revenue, actively
pursued along with customs and excise duties. The data are consistent with a government policy that increased the public debt, especially for the purpose of carrying out the "great works" of the young
Dominion. The six years of debt reduction are merely an aberration
from this policy of debt expansion.[7]

This evidence of a policy of deficit financing and, consequently,
of increasing the public debt, complements the most forceful articu-
lation of that policy, found in the finance minister's budget speeches,
which were delivered in the early 1900s. It is worth noting that the
minister, William Stevens Fielding, defended with passion a policy
of increasing the public debt during years in which he was able to
reduce it due to surpluses in the accounts!

Financing Postwar Debt Reduction

At the end of each world war, Dominion governments repeatedly
generated sizable surpluses in their budgetary accounts. In fact, the
periods from 1921 to 1930 and from 1947 to 1954 show the only two
instances since Confederation of surpluses for more than two consecutive years.[8] The uniqueness of these immediate postwar years is
demonstrated in Figure 1, where the surpluses are measured relative
to the size of the economy. The few remaining surpluses are insignificant.

Figure 4

Federal Borrowing and National Debt,
as a Percentage of GNP in Canada, 1870–1989

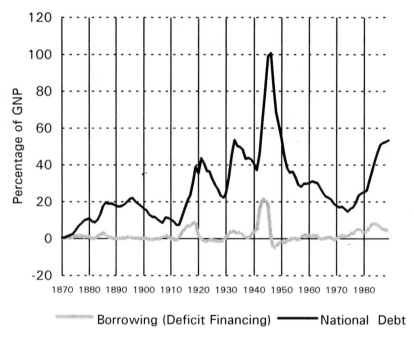

Borrowing (Deficit Financing) ▬▬▬National Debt

After each world war, these surpluses allowed the national debt to be reduced by substantial amounts. Figure 4 traces the debt relative to the size of the economy, from 1870 through 1989, and illustrates the five "waves" of debt creation in Canada's fiscal history. The two most dramatic escalations and descents of the national debt occurred during and immediately after the two world wars.

The debt-to-GNP ratio declines when surpluses allow the retirement of some of the national debt or when the economy grows more rapidly than the national debt. It follows that, even when the national debt grows (through deficit financing), the debt in relation to GNP may actually decline. This factor contributed substantially to each of the four waves of debt reductions.

In addition, Dominion spending, relative to the size of the economy, decreased drastically after both world wars.[9] Towards the end of each postwar period, Dominion spending rose, modestly through

1930 and strongly through 1954. These changes in government spending were influenced, in part, by the pursuit of debt reduction during each of the postwar periods.

Total Dominion tax revenues increased immediately after each war, before declining modestly. From the midpoint of each postwar period, total tax revenues rose.[10] We saw earlier the extent to which total tax revenues, relative to the size of the economy, fell gradually throughout the first postwar period and decreased sharply immediately after World War II, before increasing at the end of the second postwar period.

This changing pattern in total tax revenue is the result of three separate forces. First, Dominion governments chose, after each war, to reduce tax rates on some revenue sources as soon as hostilities ceased. Second, these governments chose to introduce a new sales tax immediately following World War I and to increase its rates during the following years. During the second postwar period, the Canadian government increased tax rates on many of its revenue sources. Finally, the growth of national income following each world war contributed to the increase in government tax revenues. This growth was uneven during the postwar periods, especially during and after the recession of 1921 and in the Korean War period from 1950 to 1952.[11]

Given the regularity with which Canada's Dominion governments created debt to finance their spending, the postwar periods of debt reduction are exceptional. What motivated politicians to choose "painful" taxation in order to reduce the national debt?

After each war, the demand for debt reduction emerged and persisted for an extended period of time. Two separate political forces created this demand. The wartime swell of patriotism, which was reinforced by the exhortations of finance ministers, died in the postwar periods. Holders of war bonds, victory bonds or war savings certificates were likely to redeem them as soon as the war was over, no longer having a "patriotic" reason to keep bonds that paid a rate of interest lower than that of alternative instruments. Given the substantial increase in wartime borrowing by the government, there was a large potential demand for debt redemption from the bondholders themselves.

The second source of demand for debt reduction (at the price of an increase in taxes or a decrease in benefits from government spending, or both) came from voters who insisted on having a public sector capable of managing instability in the economy and political or economic crises. Such a collective good, like national defence and environmental protection, would be provided by the public sector and financed by revenues extracted from voters.[12] For the most part, therefore, such a public good would be provided as part of the total expenditures of the current government.

Voters believe that, at some "magnitude," the public debt poses a threat to economic stability and to the government's ability to cope with instability or crises. For example, the larger the debt is in relation to national income, the more difficult and costly it is to borrow to finance policy initiatives and stabilize the economy. The larger the interest payments on the national debt are, as a fraction of total government expenditures, the more difficult it is for a government to afford emergency expenditures for handling a crisis without diminishing essential government services.

The magnitude at which this perceived threat is believed to occur may take the form of an absolute dollar level, a relative level (e.g., in relation to national income) or even a high rate of increase in the public debt. Such voters will be prepared to support financially a reduction in the debt. As the magnitude of the debt increases, more voters may come to believe in the perceived threat, and eventually this conviction may stimulate a demand for debt reduction so large that a government will ignore it at its own peril. Dominion government expenditures during the two world wars were financed heavily by borrowing, with a consequent rapid increase in the perceived magnitude of the debt.[13]

The early years of the postwar periods saw a reduction in tax rates on revenue sources that had been used most extensively to finance the war effort. The "old tax is a good tax" principle had served to raise effective tariff rates and greatly increase effective income tax rates during World War I and II, respectively. Those increases were met with increasing opposition towards the end of each war period and created a potential demand for tax reduction by the voters most affected. This demand provided the political incentive for postwar governments to lower tax rates significantly on some revenue sources. With the cessation of hostilities, the relative political costs of taxing these revenue sources were sufficiently high for governments to respond with significant reductions in tax rates.

Revenues from three sources were used to reduce the federal debt and to lessen the tax burdens on those voters whose revenue sources had been taxed most heavily during the two wars. First, there was a large reduction in war- and defence-related expenditures, as the war machine was rapidly dismantled. This reduction in spending, especially during these early postwar years, released substantial revenues that could be used to redeem the debt, reduce tax rates or finance increased spending on public services. With the exception of veterans' pensions and, after World War II, the introduction of family allowance payments and federally financed education, revenues were devoted to debt and tax reduction. The behaviour of the early postwar governments is consistent with the absence of any marked increase in voter demand for spending on new peacetime projects.[14]

The second major source of funds stemmed from the introduction of a new tax and increases in effective tax rates on existing revenue sources. The government introduced a sales tax in 1920, at the same time as it was reducing effective tariff rates. Towards the end of the second postwar period, the government raised tax rates on most revenue sources, including the manufacturers' sales tax. The Korean War and defence-related expenditures during the fiscal years from 1950 to 1952 influenced the government's tax strategy. Nevertheless, it is noteworthy that governments during the two postwar periods chose a sales tax to help reduce the debt.[15]

The third source of funds, especially during the second half of each postwar period, was the "revenue buoyancy" of a rapidly growing economy. The increase in revenues due to economic growth is an inherent response of the existing tax structures that can be used to redeem the debt, to reduce effective tax rates or to finance increased peacetime spending. In the mid- and late twenties, tax rates on many revenue sources were reduced, yet the debt was also reduced. During the early fifties, tax rates were increased, government spending increased and the debt was reduced.

Six main elements formed the tax strategy during the two postwar periods. A strong demand for debt reduction, one of the legacies of the wars, led governments to extract budgetary surpluses and pay off some of the debt. Vocal opposition to high wartime taxes led governments to reduce the effective rates of those taxes considerably. The revenues that provided the source for these reductions came from large decreases in wartime government expenditures, a new sales tax, increased tax rates on some revenue sources and revenue buoyancy due to a growing economy.

Of these four sources of funds for financing debt reduction, only the large reduction in defence-related government expenditures is uniquely related to wartime spending. During peacetime, a government determined to reduce the debt can still rely on the sales tax and, with luck, a growing economy. However, any planned reduction in government expenditures would face the opposition of voters whose benefits were being reduced. Peacetime debt reduction, as a political objective, would be much more difficult to achieve than immediate postwar debt reduction.

The Deficit, the Debt and the GST

> The rapidly growing national debt puts Canada's future in jeopardy ... Ottawa must stabilize and reduce the public sector debt as a share of national income (reducing the annual *deficit* alone isn't enough). This is the only moral, financially prudent, thing to do.
>
> — W.A. MacDonald, *Globe and Mail* April 6, 1989

The sales tax, like some heroic knight of romantic tales, has come to the rescue of the damsels, deficit and debt, three times during the past seventy years. Immediately after World War I, the government introduced a sales tax, in part to reduce the substantial wartime debt. Sales tax revenues soared, and the surpluses of the twenties were used for debt reduction. At the beginning of the Great Depression, the government reversed five years of annual reductions in the sales tax rate and increased the rate sharply, to reduce the borrowing that accompanied a collapse of other revenue sources. Sales tax revenues grew substantially, and deficit financing became less important. Finally, several years after World War II, the government increased the manufacturers' sales tax rate to support continued reduction of the substantial wartime debt. Sales tax revenues rose, and the surpluses were used to reduce the debt.[16]

There have been five waves of debt creation in Canada, from Confederation to the present. The first four waves were heavily influenced by federal choices during the financing of wars and depressions. The fifth wave of debt creation began in the mid-1970s and is still rising; the debt-to-GNP ratio has increased from 15 per cent in 1974 to 53 per cent in 1989. The deep recession of 1981–82 contributed to this wave, but there were three additional factors, the origins of which go back to the tax policy choices of the seventies. These policy choices included the reduction in effective corporate income tax rates (on manufacturing and processing profits, on small business and through regionally differentiated tax credits on investments); the proliferation of tax expenditures in the personal income tax base; and the reduction in the effective sales tax rate. The indexation of personal income tax in 1974 did not contribute to this wave of debt creation. A discussion of these tax strategies follows.

Federal government spending, relative to the size of the economy, increased substantially from the mid-1960s through the mid-1970s, tapered off for a few years, rose sharply during the early eighties, and has been declining since 1984. The very high interest rates associated with inflation between 1979 and 1981 forced up government outlays on interest payments, and continued high interest rates during the late eighties have maintained this situation. The deep recession of 1981–82 caused a drop in national income and a rise in federal spending that was linked to automatic stabilizers, such as UI payments. The sharp rise in unemployment from 7.5 to 13 per cent, and its slow decline to its pre-recession range in 1988, kept UI payments and government spending high.[17]

However, the growth in government spending was never more than a minor contributor to increasing deficits and the fifth debt wave. The primary cause of the increase in deficit financing since the mid-1970s was the decline in total tax revenues relative to the size of the economy. The total tax indicator rose at about the same rate as total government spending until the mid-1970s (see Figure 2). The tax indicator then fell sharply between 1975 and 1979, after which it edged up. In other words, total tax revenues had fallen well before the recession of 1981–82 reduced them further.

The first tax strategy that created conditions conducive to growth of the debt was a package of reductions in the effective corporate income tax rate, which was intended primarily to apply to manufacturing and processing firms, but which was eventually extended to other sectors. Finance Minister John Turner initiated this preferential treatment for manufacturing and processing companies in his budget of May 1972 by proposing to reduce the statutory tax rate to 40 per cent and to allow these businesses to depreciate machinery and equipment in a short two years.[18]

Turner continued this preferential treatment in his budget of June 1975 by proposing a 5 per cent tax credit for investments in buildings, machinery and equipment by firms in the manufacturing and processing sectors, among others.[19] Finance Minister Donald MacDonald, in his 1977 budget, extended the effective time and increased the rates of the investment tax credit in regionally depressed areas.[20] Finance Minister Jean Chrétien increased the basic and regionally differentiated rates of the investment tax credit in his budget of November 1978 and made the credit permanent.

This package of reductions is interesting because all these finance ministers expressed concern about the need to maintain international competitiveness, especially with manufacturing and processing firms in the United States. The government's corporate tax choices were responses to horizontal tax competition with the United States, which had introduced institutional changes in the early seventies to enhance the worldwide competitiveness of its manufacturing and processing firms. The effect was to substantially reduce effective corporate income tax rates in the United States,[21] and Canada followed suit.

Finance Minister Turner underlined this policy thrust repeatedly:

> ... tax treatment of companies engaged in manufacturing and processing will now compare very favourably with that in other nations, particularly the United States ... *this radical revision of the corporate tax system as it affects manufacturing and processors will require us to forego revenue* ... but [this] should not be regarded so much as a cost to the federal treasury as a major investment by the nation that over time will repay itself in terms of creating jobs for our workers and increasing prosperity for all Canadians. (Turner 1972, 9; emphasis added)

> The reduction in the tax burden borne by [manufacturing and processing] industries ... will enable them to offset the serious competitive threat posed by the substantial tax subsidies for exports made available in the past year to U.S. corporations. (Turner 1973, 2)

> ... the surtax will not apply to the profits from manufacturing and processing in Canada. I believe it is essential to maintain the reduction in the tax burden on that vitally important sector to enable it to strengthen its international competitive position. *Canadian manufacturers and processors continue to be vulnerable to foreign competition as a result of the extensive use being made of the U.S. DISC tax provisions*, the favourable tax treatment provided to manufacturers in other countries ... (Turner 1974, 18; emphasis added)

Finance Ministers MacDonald and Chrétien acted in a similar manner.[22]

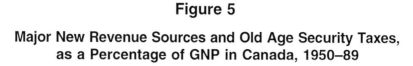

Figure 5

Major New Revenue Sources and Old Age Security Taxes, as a Percentage of GNP in Canada, 1950–89

The effect on corporate income tax revenues is evident in the decreasing importance of such revenues as a source for government funding, a trend which, with considerable variation, began in the early fifties. Corporation income tax revenues, in proportion to the size of the economy, had also been declining since the early fifties (see Figure 5).

The second strategy launched the proliferation of tax expenditures that formed part of the response to the tax reform legislation in 1971. This package of tax choices narrowed the base of the personal income tax[23] and helped to curb the growth in federal personal income tax revenues.

Finance Minister Edgar Benson, as part of the 1971 tax reform, increased the limits on deductions for contributions to pension plans and registered retirement savings plans and introduced an employment expense allowance. Finance Minister Turner increased the exemption for the elderly and the basic personal exemption, and he introduced deductions for postsecondary students, interest and dividend income, the registered home ownership savings plan, and the pension income, as well as the personal tax credit with a minimum and maximum limit (which he subsequently raised). Finance Minister MacDonald increased the limits on deductions for contributions to pension plans and registered retirement savings plans, and for employment expense. He also raised limits on the dividend tax credit, the personal tax credit and the capital loss that could be offset against other income. Finance Minister Chrétien introduced deductions on registered retirement investment funds and increased the maximum deduction on employment expense.[24] The consequent narrowing of the personal income tax base contributed to the relative decline of the personal income tax as a financing source for the government's spending, especially after 1975.[25]

The third tax strategy consisted of two reductions in the effective rate for the manufacturers' sales tax. During the sixties and seventies, many trading countries adopted a value-added tax on consumption, making their exports more competitive than Canadian exports, which carried the added cost of the manufacturers' sales tax. In addition, Finance Ministers Turner in 1974 and Chrétien in 1978 decided that the economy required some fiscal stimulus and chose to provide it through the manufacturers' sales tax. Turner reduced the tax rate on building and construction materials from 12 to 5 per cent, and Chrétien reduced the rate on all other manufactured goods except alcoholic beverages and tobacco products, from 12 to 9 per cent.[26] These tax rate choices contributed to the declining relative importance of sales tax revenues from about 1974 through 1983.

By the mid-1970s, the federal government's three major revenue sources — the personal income tax, the corporation income tax and the manufacturers' sales tax — were declining in relative importance as financing sources for the government's spending. In 1976, the government abandoned the separate Old Age Security Fund and channelled taxes from the fund (comprised of equal percentage points of these three taxes) into the Consolidated Revenue Fund. The three taxes comprise the major component of the total tax indicator in Figures 1 to 3 that declines after 1974.

The tax policy initiative that increased revenues during the seventies — the birth of energy taxes — while not sufficient to offset the decline in the major revenue sources, aggravated the friction between oil-rich Alberta and the federal government; difficult relations continued well into the eighties. This federal government's attempt to share in the windfall to the petroleum sector occasioned by the worldwide increase in oil prices provoked substantial opposition, reflecting the federal-provincial competition for revenue sources, to the expanding family of energy taxes and to the National Energy Program. By the late eighties, all that was left of these taxes was an excise tax on gasoline and on aviation gas and diesel fuel.[27]

With the exception of these energy taxes, decisions on revenue sources adopted by the federal government contributed to the increases in deficit financing during the late seventies. The government made these decisions in response to foreign tax incentives and value-added taxes, the domestic demand for tax expenditures and a perceived need to stimulate the economy and reduce unemployment. The deep recession of 1981–82 strengthened the trend towards deficit financing which, together with the national debt, rose in proportion to national income.

The issue of deficit and debt financing has influenced every finance minister since the Honourable John Crosbie declared, in his ill-fated budget of 1979, that the "fundamental objective of our fiscal plan is to bring about a steady reduction in our deficits."[28] The fiscal plans of Liberals Allan MacEachen and Marc Lalonde and Conservative Michael Wilson have consistently been devoted to reducing deficit financing and stabilizing the ratio of debt to GNP.

As mentioned previously, voters demanding a public sector that is responsive to instability in the economy might, when the public debt reached a certain magnitude, view deficit financing and the public debt as threats to such stability. After the two world wars, this demand for debt reduction was strong enough, when coupled with several other factors, to result in surpluses which were used to reduce the absolute size of the national debt. In the eighties, the rising ratio of debt to GNP and the increasing proportion of federal spending accorded to interest payments could have triggered this demand for deficit reduction and debt control. The stimulus for such a demand is concern about the government's ability to manage instability or crisis situations.

The fifth wave of debt creation is perceived as an issue of political concern. The quotation at the beginning of this section, taken from an article by a corporate tax lawyer at the firm of McMillan Binch, is representative of the strongly held views of many businesspeople on the issue of the deficit and the debt.[29] Moreover, by April 1989, several opinion polls reported that concern about the deficit among Canadians had deepened considerably.[30]

It is of more immediate practical relevance that federal governments, both Liberal and Conservative, turned to that white knight of past rescues, the manufacturers' sales tax, in their search for increased tax revenues that would reduce deficit financing. The sales tax rate has been increased several times since 1983, and sales tax reform has been on the political agenda since 1975.

The Conservative government, mindful of two failed Liberal attempts to transform the manufacturers' sales tax into a wholesale sales tax, employed a consultative strategy before submitting its proposal to convert the manufacturers' sales tax into a goods and services tax. Voter feedback and data on the strength, magnitude and intensity of political opposition guided Finance Minister Wilson as he revised the initial proposals. He consulted with the provinces and then acted independently when agreement seemed difficult. Before the 1988 election, he exempted basic foods, prescription drugs and medical services from the tax base, and finally, in response to a public debate in 1989 and the Blenkarn Committee Report, he reduced the tax rate from 9 to 7 per cent. By adopting such a strategy, the Conservative government achieved the first significant reform of the sales tax since 1924.

Conclusion

One conclusion that emerges from the preceding analysis of government financing policies is that deficit financing has been an active element in the structuring of revenue sources, and not just as a "balancing" item. In addition, the crucial role of borrowing as an important source of revenues is evident in the unique phenomenon of postwar debt reduction and the fifth wave of debt creation.

Since Confederation, federal governments have regularly borrowed significant amounts to finance their total spending. The political costs that led governments to increase borrowing, instead of increasing tax rates on existing tax bases or introducing a new tax, changed over time. Initially, governments pursued a policy of setting low customs and excise duty rates, and engaging in high public spending on "nation-building" activities, to attract and keep immigrants and to coax the remaining colonies into the Union.

These governments expressed concern that high tax rates might encourage immigrants, a potential labour force, to settle elsewhere, thus reflecting the political costs of horizontal tax competition. For the same reason, the government rejected proposals to introduce a new tax on incomes. In addition, government reluctance to tax a source that some municipalities and provinces were already taxing, reflected the political costs of Dominion-provincial competition for revenue sources, which was enhanced by efforts to bring in the remaining colonies. These considerations, which inhibited governments from utilizing tax sources more extensively, also encouraged them to seek higher levels of spending. Thus, the demand for borrowing extensively followed directly from choices among potential revenue sources that were made to facilitate increased spending at a minimum political cost.

During each world war period, deficit financing accounted for the largest share of the financing for the rapid growth in federal spending. In each case, the political costs of borrowing fell relative to the costs of alternate revenue sources. The patriotic fervour aroused by the issuing of war bonds during the early years of each war led to oversubscriptions. Finance Ministers Thomas White and James Lorimer Ilsley responded by focusing more on borrowing than on tax bases. During the later years in each war period, finance ministers resorted to considerable moral persuasion to keep the cost of borrowing low and to dissuade bondholders from redeeming their bonds.

During the depressions that started in 1873 and 1930, deficit financing accounted for a substantial share of total financial requirements. Borrowing in the 1880s reflected an emphasis on keeping the tax burden on a young, growing nation as light as possible. Borrowing during the Great Depression reflected an attempt to keep taxes as light as possible in economically hard times. The policymakers of the thirties differed from their earlier counterparts in that they proclaimed their adherence to the principle of a balanced total budget, while borrowing in order to meet spending objectives without imposing onerously high tax rates.

Federal governments considered deficit financing to be an alternative revenue source. Policy decisions about the way in which total financial requirements would be met were based on a comprehensive evaluation of the various political factors affecting the position of the government of the day. Given such a framework for policy making, it was not unusual that deficit financing was used regularly to meet total financial requirements.

The active use of borrowing as a normal source of financing federal spending is reflected in two additional observations.

First, significant debt reduction in Canada has been a postwar phenomenon. After each war, governments steadily pursued a budgetary policy that enabled them to reduce the twin legacies of war: a greatly enlarged national debt and "enormous tax burdens." These surpluses available for debt reduction, as a share of total financial requirements, ranged from 4 to 23 per cent for the ten years after World War I and from 2 to 36 per cent for the eight years after World War II.

After each war, the patriotic holders of war bonds redeemed them rapidly to finance consumption that had been restricted during wartime and to obtain higher market rates of interest. In addition, voters who judged the postwar debt as a potential threat to economic stability and to the government's ability to manage crises demanded debt reduction (and displayed some willingness to bear the expense of such a reduction). These two forces propelled the demand for a policy of debt reduction and led postwar governments to adopt such a policy.

Even so, major tariff reductions, especially favouring western farmers, were quickly enacted after World War I, and after World War II, substantial reductions in personal and corporate income tax rates passed into law. Such policies reduced the potential surpluses available for debt reduction. Early postwar governments demonstrated mastery in weighing the political benefits of tax rate reductions against those of further reductions in the size of the national debt.

The sources of finance used to implement this dual fiscal policy of debt and tax rate reduction were substantial reductions in war-related defence spending, increases in the sales tax rate and a buoyant revenue system responding to a growing economy.

The second point to note is that the deficits of the late seventies, and the large deficits and rising ratio of debt to national income in the eighties were caused primarily by federal tax policy choices of the seventies and the recession of 1981–82. The government reduced effective tax rates for the three main revenue sources: for corporate incomes, in response to tax cuts in the United States; for personal incomes, through the proliferation of tax expenditures; and for manufacturers' sales, for international tax competition and stabilization purposes. Total tax revenues as a percentage of national income fell, well before the 1981–82 recession.

The recession produced, through the operation of the automatic stabilizers of the fiscal system, a substantial rise in spending, a drop in revenues and a consequent increase in the deficit. During the five to six years that it took for unemployment to return to its pre-recession rate, UI payments continued to reinforce higher spending levels and deficit financing.

This deficit financing and the resulting expansion of the national debt have become issues of current public concern. Finance Ministers Crosbie, MacEachen, Lalonde and Wilson all presented budgets that were devoted, in part, to the reduction of borrowing and the stabilization of the ratio of the debt to national income. Their achievements have been modest. It is not clear whether Canadians would support the substantial increase in tax rates or the significant cuts in government programs that would encourage a minister of finance to reject borrowing as a source of revenue and favour a strategy that would generate the surpluses needed to reduce the absolute size of the national debt.

References

Bird, Richard M. 1970. *The Growth of Government Spending in Canada.* Canadian Tax Paper No. 51. Toronto: Canadian Tax Foundation.

Boadway, Robin W., and David E. Wildasin. 1984. *Public Sector Economics*, 2d ed. Toronto: Little, Brown.

Chrétien, Jean. 1978a. *Budget Speech.* Ottawa: Canada, Department of Finance, 10 April.

———. 1978b. *Budget Speech.* Ottawa: Canada, Department of Finance, 16 November.

Crosby, John. 1979. *Budget Speech.* Ottawa: Canada, Department of Finance, 11 December.

Doman, Andrew. 1980. The Effects of Federal Budgetary Policies 1978–80 on the Distribution of Income in Canada. *Canadian Taxation* 2: 112–118.

Gillespie, W. Irwin. 1978. *In Search of Robin Hood, the Effect of Federal Budgetary Policies during the 1970s on the Distribution of Income in Canada.* Montreal: C.D. Howe Research Institute, Canada Economic Policy Committee.

Gillespie, W. Irwin. 1991. *Tax, Borrow and Spend: Financing Federal Spending in Canada. 1867–1990.* Ottawa: Carleton University Press.

The Globe and Mail. 1990. Editorial, 2 October.

Kohut, John. 1989. Tories Will Face Selling Job after the Budget, too. *The Globe and Mail,* 17 April.

Lalonde, Marc. 1983. *Budget Speech.* Ottawa: Canada, Department of Finance, 19 April.

———. 1983. *The Federal Deficit in Perspective.* Ottawa: Canada, Department of Finance, April.

———. 1984. *Budget Speech.* Ottawa: Canada, Department of Finance, 15 February.

Macdonald, Donald. 1977. *Budget Speech.* Ottawa: Canada, Department of Finance, 31 March.

MacDonald, W.A. 1989. Deficit: The Number 1 Threat to Canada's Future. *The Globe and Mail*, 6 April.

MacEachen, Allan. 1980. *Budget Speech.* Ottawa: Canada, Department of Finance, 28 October.

———. 1981. *Budget Speech.* Ottawa: Canada, Department of Finance, 12 November.

———. 1982. *Budget Speech.* Ottawa: Canada, Department of Finance, 28 June.

Maslove, Allan M. 1989. *Tax Reform in Canada: The Process and Impact.* Halifax: The Institute for Research on Public Policy.

Musgrave, Richard A. 1958. *The Theory of Public Finance.* New York: McGraw-Hill.

Musgrave, Richard A., Peggy B. Musgrave, and Richard M. Bird. 1987. *Public Finance in Theory and Practice.* Toronto: McGraw-Hill.

Peacock, Alan, and Jack Wiseman. 1967. *The Growth of Public Expenditures in the United Kingdom.* Princeton, New Jersey: National Bureau of Economic Research.

Pechman, Joseph A. 1990. The Future of the Income Tax. *American Economic Review* 80, no. 1: 1–20.

Rich, Georg, 1988. *The Cross of Gold: Money and the Canadian Business Cycle 1867–1913.* Ottawa: Carleton University Press.

Samuelson, Paul A. 1954. The Pure Theory of Public Expenditure. *Review of Economics and Statistics* 36 (November): 387–389.

Simpson, Jeffrey. 1989. To Recover from a Bad Decade. *The Globe and Mail*, 20 December.

Toulin, Alan. 1988. The Ominous Rise of Canada's Federal Deficit. *The Ottawa Citizen*, 29 November.

Turner, John. 1972. *Budget Speech.* Ottawa: Canada, Department of Finance, 8 May.

———. 1973. *Budget Speech.* Ottawa: Canada, Department of Finance, 19 February.

———. 1974a. *Budget Speech.* Ottawa: Canada, Department of Finance, 6 May.

———. 1974b. *Budget Speech.* Ottawa: Canada, Department of Finance, 18 November.

———. 1975. *Budget Speech.* Ottawa: Canada, Department of Finance, 23 June.

Wilson, Michael. 1985. *Budget Speech.* Ottawa: Canada, Department of Finance, 23 May.

———. 1986. *Budget Speech.* Ottawa: Canada, Department of Finance, 26 February.

———. 1987. *Budget Speech.* Ottawa: Canada, Department of Finance, 18 February.

———. 1988. *Budget Speech.* Ottawa: Canada, Department of Finance, 10 February.

————. 1989. *Budget Speech.* Ottawa: Canada, Department of Finance, 27 April.

————. 1989. *The Fiscal Plan, Controlling the Public Debt.* Ottawa: Canada, Department of Finance, 27 April.

Winer, Stanley L., and Walter Hettich. 1988. The Structure of the Sieve: Political Economy in the Explanation of Tax Systems and Tax Reform. *Osgoode Hall Law Journal* 26, no. 2: 409–422.

The Canadian Fiscal Problem: The Macroeconomic Connection

Pierre Fortin

In this chapter, Pierre Fortin of the University of Quebec at Montreal examines the role that high interest rates and slow economic growth have played in creating Canada's debt crisis. Canada's public sector debt increased from 5 per cent of GDP in 1974 to 64 per cent in 1994 on national accounts. This paper provides a summary of the relative contributions of changes in taxation, program spending, interest rates and economic growth and of fluctuations to this explosion of public debt. By far the most important source of debt accumulation has been the high domestic interest rates and the anti-inflationary recessions of 1982 and 1990. Higher world interest rates and slower productivity growth have been significant but secondary contributing factors. Unrestrained spending was definitely not a source of debt over the period.

This paper examines the current Canadian fiscal quandary from a macroeconomic perspective. This view is not meant to minimize the importance of the *micro*economic incentive systems that drive the supply and demand for public goods and services and that are in great need of restructuring, in Canada as elsewhere. However, the evidence strongly suggests that macroeconomic factors have dominated the broad fiscal picture in the last twenty years.

Figure 6

Public Debt
Net Public Debt as a Percentage of GDP, 1962–1993

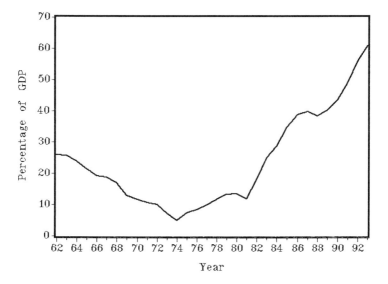

Source: Statistics Canada, Cat. Nos. 13-201 and 13-214.

Figure 6 traces the evolution of the overall public sector net-debt-to-GDP ratio for Canada back to 1962.[1] After a steady decline in the three decades after World War II, the debt ratio began to rise slowly in the late seventies, and then increased sharply in the early eighties. From 5 per cent in 1974, it has increased annually by three percentage points on average over the last two decades, to reach 64 per cent at the end of 1994. The figure indicates only two brief pauses, around the cyclical peaks of 1981 and 1988. Among industrial countries, only Belgium, Greece and Italy now have public debt ratios that are higher than Canada's.

Rising government indebtedness has three major consequences. First, it makes a country poorer over time by crowding out investment, crowding in foreign debt and distorting people's behaviour through progressively higher tax rates. Second, it destabilizes public finances by making them more sensitive to the slightest variation in interest rates. Third, ever expanding interest payments on the debt mean that citizens receive declining amounts of public goods and services in exchange for rising taxes; this situation generates deep frustration and contaminates the quality of democratic life. Traces of all three elements are now visible in Canada.

The Simple Mathematics of Debt Accumulation

What is the source of the debt explosion in Canada? Four factors drive the debt-to-GDP ratio over time: the global tax rate, program expenditure, the average interest rate on the debt and the growth rate of GDP. The annual change in the ratio can be decomposed into components as follows:

$$\Delta(D/Y) = PX/Y - TX/Y + (R - G) \times D_{-1}/Y.$$

In this expression, D is the debt, Y is GDP, PX is program expenditure, TX is tax revenue, R is the average interest rate on accumulated debt, G is the growth rate of GDP and Δ means "annual change." D_{-1} is the amount of debt accumulated up to the end of the previous year.

It is useful to note that the first three terms of this equation form the deficit-to-GDP ratio:

$$DEF/Y = PX/Y - TX/Y + R \times D_{-1}/Y.$$

Thus, the equation for the debt-to-GDP ratio can be rewritten as

$$\Delta(D/Y) = DEF/Y - G \times D_{-1}/Y.$$

This equation says that, for the debt ratio to remain unchanged or to decline, the budget deficit does not have to be zero, but it must not exceed the critical level at which it pushes the debt to increase faster than GDP. Another common formulation of the change in the debt-to-GDP ratio is

$$\Delta(D/Y) = (R - G) \times D_{-1}/Y - OBAL/Y,$$

where OBAL is the operating balance or the excess of tax revenue over program spending (OBAL = TX – PX).

This equation has two key implications. First, it shows that the dynamics of the debt is really driven by the difference between interest and growth (R – G), and more specifically by the product of that differential and the level of accumulated debt. In particular, the sensitivity of the annual change in the debt to variations in the interest-growth differential increases with the level of debt. The

Figure 7

Global Tax Rate
Budgetary Revenue as a Percentage of GDP, 1962–93

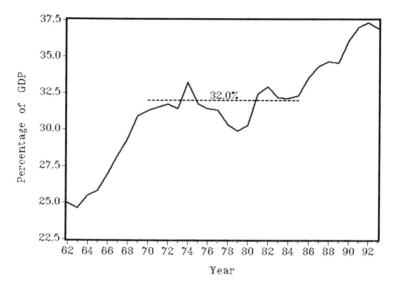

Source: Statistics Canada, Cat. No. 13-201.

second implication is that, if the interest rate exceeds the growth rate, the debt ratio cannot be stabilized unless the public sector generates a surplus. Moreover, that surplus is an increasing function of the interest-growth differential and the level of debt.

This equation also suggests a natural way to organize historical data so as to identify the sources of the rising debt-to-GDP ratio: we can look at trends and fluctuations in the operating balance and the interest-growth differential and assess their respective contributions to debt accumulation.

Trends in the Operating Balance

Figure 7 illustrates three distinct phases in tax rate developments (TX/Y) over the last three decades. The first phase saw the global tax rate increase to 32 per cent of GDP in 1972, from 25 per cent in 1962. This period saw massive public investment in health, education, infrastructures and income security. In the second phase, from 1972 to 1985, the global tax rate remained stable around the 32 per cent level. In the third phase, from 1985 to 1993, the global tax rate

Figure 8

Program Spending
as a Percentage of GDP, 1962–93

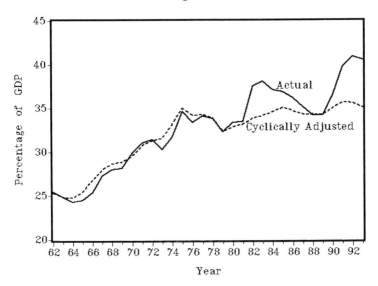

Source: Data from Statistics Canada, Cat. No. 13-201.

increased again, to reach 37 per cent of GDP in 1993. This time, however, taxes were hiked to pay for rising interest payments on the growing public debt. No other areas have reached higher levels of public spending; this situation has clearly contributed to rising levels of taxpayer frustration.

Figure 8 turns to program spending (PX/Y). Here, history is a bit trickier to interpret. On the surface, the ratio of primary spending to GDP seems to follow an inexorable upward trend, from 25 per cent in the early sixties to 40 per cent in the early nineties. However, a more careful interpretation is that, in the last twenty years, the cyclically adjusted (i.e., "structural") program spending ratio, which is displayed as the dotted line in Figure 8, has not increased beyond the plateau at 35 per cent, reached in 1975. The cyclically adjusted ratio removes from the actual ratio the short-term distortions arising from business expansions and recessions.

It is important to smooth the ratio of program spending to GDP. In recessions, the GDP falls, while program spending is inflated by increases in UI and social assistance. This observation, combined with the fact that the 1982 and 1990 recessions have been the most

Figure 9

Operating Balance
Cyclically Adjusted Operating Balance
as a Percentage of GDP, 1962–93

Source: Data from Statistics Canada, Cat. No 13-201.

important and longest in Canada since the Great Depression, explains why the program spending ratio appeared to increase from 1982 to 1986 and from 1990 to 1993. These "bubbles" do not reflect sudden attacks of fiscal extravagance, but are largely mechanical reflections of these recessions and their aftermaths.[2]

Subtracting the cyclically adjusted program spending ratio from the global tax rate gives the cyclically adjusted operating balance, a summary measure of the effects of discretionary fiscal policy on debt accumulation, which is shown in Figure 9. This structural operating balance has been a surplus up to 1974, a deficit between 1975 and 1986, and a surplus again since 1987. The key turning points came in 1974–1975 and 1986–1987. In the seventies, program spending increased permanently by four percentage points of GDP under the Trudeau minority government. In the eighties, the Mulroney government began implementing its fiscal consolidation program.[3]

However, the behaviour of the structural operating balance after 1974 can explain only a small fraction of the debt explosion, for two reasons. First, from 1974 to 1981 the public debt-to-GDP ratio increased by only six percentage points (from 5 to 11 per cent).[4] Second, since 1981, the net cumulative contribution of the structural operating balance to the fifty-two-point increase in the debt ratio (from 12 per cent in 1981 to 64 per cent in 1994) has been virtually zero. The nine points added to the debt ratio by the structural deficits between 1982 and 1986 have been entirely wiped out by structural surpluses from 1987 to 1994.

The conclusion that discretionary fiscal policy alone has not contributed much to the debt explosion in Canada contradicts conventional wisdom. In this case, conventional wisdom is simply inconsistent with the facts. However, we cannot then proceed to the conclusion that fiscal discipline comes easily to the public sector. Given the enormous momentum of debt accumulation in the last fifteen years, it is entirely appropriate to be concerned, first, that the public sector did not react sooner and has not adjusted more, and, second, that it has thus relied much more on tax increases than on spending restraint.

Because it is based on the cyclically adjusted program spending ratio, the structural operating balance removes the effects of the recessions and slow recoveries from 1982 to 1989 and from 1990 to 1994 on fiscal deficits. These cyclical effects have been substantial. From the data presented in Figure 8, the cumulative contribution of the cyclical balance (i.e., the difference between the structural and actual balances) to the increase in the debt-to-GDP ratio is calculated to exceed thirty percentage points from 1982 to 1994, which amounts to about 60 per cent of the total fifty-two-point increase in the debt ratio.

This result underlines the fact that Canada's macroeconomic performance over these years has been dismal, both in absolute terms and in comparison with that of the United States. Put simply, Canada has spent most of the time since 1981 fighting inflation and, particularly after 1987, with more conviction than the United States.[5] The 1982 recession brought inflation down from 12 to 5 per cent, and the 1990 recession finally reduced it to zero. The 1982 recession in Canada was of the same magnitude as that in the United States, but the Canadian recovery was more sluggish. The 1990 recession was three times as pronounced in Canada as in the United States, and recovery was just beginning in Canada in 1994, while it was already almost complete in the United States. It is easy to calculate that if the U.S. economy was currently experiencing as much excess unem-

Figure 10

Real Interest Rate
Average Real Interest Rate Paid on the Public Debt, 1962–93

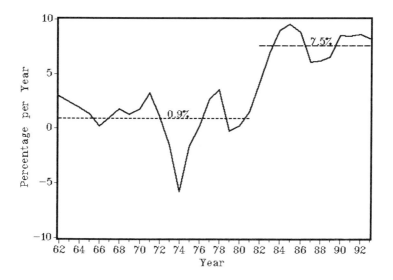

Sources: Data from Statistics Canada (Cat. No. 13-201) and Finance Canada (Economic Reference Tables 1994).

ployment as the Canadian economy, the U.S. fiscal deficit would be as large as the Canadian deficit.[6]

Trends in the Interest-Growth Differential

The difference between program spending and tax revenues is only marginally responsible for the debt explosion since 1981. While the mediocre macroeconomic performance explains 60 per cent of it, we see from the last equation, the remainder of the debt (40 per cent) is attributable to a greater difference between the average interest rate on the debt and the growth rate of GDP.

Figures 10 to 12 show that this interest-growth differential is indeed larger. Figure 10 reports that the average real interest rate paid on the public debt increased from 0.9 per cent in the period from 1962 to 1981 to 7.5 per cent in the period from 1982 to 1993.[7] Figure 11 indicates that the average growth rate of real GDP declined from 4.9 to 2.2 per cent between the same two periods. The combined

Figure 11

Real Growth Rate
Annual Growth Rate of Real GDP, 1962–93

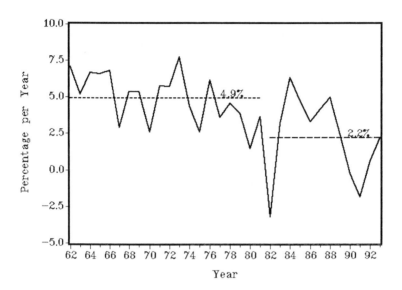

Source: Statistics Canada, Cat. No. 13-201.

picture is that the average interest-growth differential increased by 9.3 per cent, from -4.0 per cent in the first period to 5.3 per cent in the second.

Both structural factors and macroeconomic policy contributed to this sharp turnaround. The slow-down of economic growth and the rise in real interest rates that occurred some time between the mid-1970s and the early eighties are well-known, worldwide phenomena. But domestic macroeconomic policy seems to have made the situation worse in Canada than in other countries, particularly the United States.

Between the two periods (1962 to 1981 and 1982 to 1990), the real interest rate that is under the most immediate control of the central bank — the three-month, short-term rate — increased by 2.25 points more in Canada than in the United States. In addition, the actual real growth rate of 2.2 per cent from 1982 to 1993 lies below the estimated potential growth rate of 3 per cent and underlines the disappointing macroeconomic performance of Canada in that period.

Figure 12

Interest-Growth Differential
Contribution of the Differential to Debt Accumulation, 1962–93

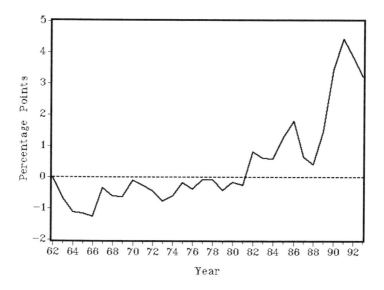

Sources: Data from Figures 6, 10 and 11.

The high domestic interest rate and sluggish growth rate jointly reflect the particularly hard battle fought — and won — by the Bank of Canada against inflation.[8] All in all, since 1981 structural factors seem to account for 75 per cent of the increase in the interest-growth differential, and domestic policy for 25 per cent.

Changes in the debt partially depend on the product of the level of the debt and the difference between the interest and growth rates (see the last equation). As Figure 12 indicates, this difference began to facilitate debt accumulation after 1981. Between 1982 and 1994, it added twenty-two percentage points to the debt-to-GDP ratio, which amounts to 40 per cent of the total fifty-two-point increase.[9] Most conspicuous is the very large contribution between 1990 and 1993 — which has led to the current "debt scare" — aided by a high level of accumulated debt.

Conclusion

The startling, but inescapable, conclusion of this analytical exercise is that the primary cause of the destabilization of Canadian public finances between 1982 and 1994 is not unrestrained spending, but conservative macroeconomic management. Canadian monetary policy has been successful in eliminating inflation, but it has been able to do so only at the cost of raising domestic interest rates substantially above U.S. levels, generating the two worst recessions in sixty years in the country, raising the average unemployment rate to 10 per cent and hence exerting strong upward pressure on public sector deficits and debt accumulation.

The worldwide increase in real interest rates and the slow-down in economic growth have been significant, but secondary, contributing factors. After recovering from surprise, the public sector reacted to offset these two factors, by stabilizing its program spending as a percentage of GDP and by raising the global tax rate.

The primary implication for policy is that the fiscal future of Canada will mainly depend on its ability to recover fully from the recession that began in 1990. The recovery actually started in 1994, when the actual growth rate of 4.3 per cent exceeded the potential growth rate of 3.1 per cent. But the consensus estimate of 8.2 per cent for the output gap in 1994 suggests that to achieve full recovery, Canada needs almost five years of 5 per cent annual real growth.[10] That is, not only must the 1994 momentum be maintained, it must be accelerated. This can only occur if the central bank does not raise short-term interest rates prematurely. The low interest rates and the recovery would directly reduce both the fiscal deficit and the debt-to-GDP ratio.

However, a recovery based on expansionary monetary conditions would not be enough to solve Canada's fiscal problem permanently. The reason is that, once the recovery was complete, the average real interest rate on the public debt would still likely exceed the real growth rate by three points. This rate would add close to two points annually to the debt-to-GDP ratio.[11] Meanwhile, if the ratio of the operating balance to GDP remains unchanged from 1994, it would subtract close to two points per year from the debt ratio. Hence, on balance, the debt would be roughly stabilized as a percentage of GDP. But it would stop falling. Under such conditions, even a mild recession would raise the debt ratio again, which would mean renewed financial problems for the public sector.

The permanent solution therefore requires not only low interest rates and full recovery, but also additional fiscal restraint. The debt reduction strategy, in other words, cannot succeed unless the structural operating surplus of the public sector is increased by, for example, two or three percentage points of GDP. The same effects would result from freezing program spending for two or three years.[12] The alternative of increasing the global tax rate by two or three additional points would be imprudent, given that the tax rate is already 37 per cent — seven points higher than in the United States. In addition to taxpayer frustration, this rate is already generating tax evasion, barter, smuggling, capital outflows, migration and other allocative distortions of rising importance in Canada.

Postscript

Since this paper was written, in late 1994, the federal government has imposed extremely severe fiscal restraint. Between the fiscal years 1994–95 and 1997–98, program spending will have been cut by 12 per cent in absolute value, and by 21 per cent relative to our growing national income (GDP). Meanwhile, the spectre of deflation finally led the Bank of Canada to lower short-term interest rates between mid-1995 and mid-1997. But as unemployment declined to 9 per cent in the second half of 1997, the Bank began to raise interest rates again in a pre-emptive manner to forestall any future increase in the rate of inflation.

The federal deficit, which was 5 per cent of GDP ($37 billion) in 1994–95, will have been almost eliminated in 1997–98. The main cause of deficit elimination has been fiscal restraint. Lower interest rates in 1996 and 1997, and the partial recovery in 1997 have also had a favourable, but smaller, impact on the deficit.

These developments mean that the solution advocated above was rejected by the government. We are not getting moderate fiscal restraint ("freezing program spending for two to three years"), but a deep 21 per cent cut in the federal program expenditure/GDP ratio. The spending cuts have been so large that the government has been overshooting its target. Without any decline in interest rates and without any economic recovery, it did not need to exercise as much restraint to eliminate the deficit. As a result, one of the most popular games in Ottawa now is to determine by how much the government should re-increase spending in its effort to allocate the "fiscal dividend." (Another name for the coming budget surplus.)

We are not recovering fully from the slump since the Bank of Canada has begun to re-increase interest rates while the level of economic activity in Canada remains 6 to 7 per cent below potential, and the unemployment rate is 2 to 3 percentage points above what our labour markets can attain. Canada is running the risk of becoming mired in a permanently underachieving economy.

While unfortunate, these developments once again demonstrate the close connection between interest rates, the state of the economy and the budget.

References

Bank of Canada. 1991. Targets for Reducing Inflation. *Bank of Canada Review* (March): 3-21.

Crow, J. 1988. The Work of Canadian Monetary Policy. *Bank of Canada Review* (February): 3-17.

Drèze, J.H., and C.R. Bean. 1990. *Europe's Unemployment Problem.* Cambridge, Mass.: MIT Press.

Dungan, P., and T. Wilson. 1994. Prices, Wages, Productivity and the Output Gap. PEAP Policy Study No. 94-7. Institute for Policy Analysis, University of Toronto, October.

Fortin, P. 1991. The Phillips Curve, Macroeconomic Policy, and the Welfare of Canadians. *Canadian Journal of Economics* 24 (November): 774-803.

Fortin, P. 1994. A Strategy for Deficit Control Through Faster Growth. *Canadian Business Economics* 3 (Fall): 3-26.

Laidler, D., and W. Robson. 1993. *The Great Canadian Disinflation.* Toronto and Calgary: C.D. Howe Institute.

Four Decades of Deficits and Debt[1]

Ronald D. Kneebone

In this chapter, Ronald Kneebone of the University of Calgary looks at the last thirty-five years of federal and provincial deficits and debts. As he notes, each of the provinces has its own unique history, but on average the provinces moved to control expenditures earlier and more aggressively than the federal government. By the late 1980s, however, all the provinces and the federal government had sufficiently large surpluses of tax revenues over program expenditures to start reducing their debt burdens. These debt reduction plans were derailed by the 1988 to 1992 increase in interest rates and the recession to which that increase contributed. Ronald Kneebone concludes that tight monetary policy can have disastrous effects on government finances and that deficit financing exposes both the provinces and the federal government to substantial risks of an escalating debt burden. Although the reactions of financial markets impose greater constraints on provincial governments than on the federal government, Kneebone argues that all levels of government should budget conservatively to avoid the risk of debt instability.

The Canadian economic union has controlled government deficits and debt reasonably well for most of its history. By the end of fiscal year 1974–75, the federal government had reduced its debt-to-GDP ratio from its high of 111 per cent in 1945–46 to a postwar low of just under 16 per cent and enjoyed a budget surplus of roughly 1 per cent of GDP. The provincial governments, despite a decade-long process of taking on more responsibility for total government spending, had by 1974–75 an aggregate debt-to-GDP ratio of only 5 per cent and a budgetary surplus of 0.5 per cent of GDP. That year was the last to see a budget surplus for the government sector. Since then, two deep recessions, persistently high interest rates, two bouts of very tight monetary policy and certain fiscal policies have increased pressure on both federal and provincial government finances. The finances of taxpayers have also been severely strained by the fact that their governments have pitted them in a race wherein exploding debt interest costs have been matched against fast-growing tax burdens. The net effect of these factors has been a high growth rate of government indebtedness, a steadfast refusal by taxpayers to accept further tax increases and a growing crisis in government finance.

The purpose of this chapter is to discuss the fiscal choices made by the provinces and the federal government between 1961 and 1995. By doing so, I hope to be able to identify some crucial "lessons for fiscal prudence" which the Bank of Canada and the federal and provincial governments need to learn to avoid financial crises. With these lessons in mind, I will explore the implications of recent choices of the central bank and of the federal and provincial governments in the early nineties for public sector finances during the rest of the decade. I begin, in the next section, with a brief overview of the fiscal responsibilities of the provinces and the federal government. In that section, I will also discuss the other major actors who play a role in determining government deficits and debt. Then, I will review the history of provincial and federal deficits and debt between 1961 and 1989 and attempt to summarize the lessons learned from that history. The next section discusses the early fiscal responses of the provinces and the federal government to the 1990–91 recession, and the last section considers the prospects for the future.

The Players

Canada has a federal system of government. The public sector of the Canadian economy is characterized by an independent central bank and eleven independent fiscal authorities, consisting of one federal and ten provincial governments. The provincial governments control roughly half of the total budget for the aggregate public sector. Neither the federal nor the provincial level of government is subject to any statutory or constitutional limit on the amounts it taxes or

Table 1

Federal and Provincial Government Revenues and Expenditures as a Fraction of GDP, Fiscal Year 1991–92

	Revenues			Expenditures	
	Prov-incial	Federal		Prov-incial	Federal
Personal Income Tax	6.1	9.9	Health	6.5	1.1
Corporate Income Tax	0.8	1.6	Social Services	4.1	8.1
Consumption Taxes	4.2	4.6	Education	4.5	0.6
Health Insurance Premiums	1.5	2.3	Debt Service	2.8	6.4
Intergovernment Transfers	3.8	—	Intergovernment Transfers	—	3.8
Total	21.7	20.4	Total	24.0	24.9

Source: Statistics Canada, *Public Finance Historical Data 1965/66–1991/92: Financial Management System*, Cat. No. 68-512.

spends. In particular, there are no constitutional constraints on the size of public sector deficits or debt at either the federal or the provincial level.[2]

Table 1 shows the major revenue sources and the major spending areas of the federal and provincial government sectors in Canada during fiscal year 1991–92. The table shows the important economic role played by the provincial governments. It also illustrates the fact that, in virtually all major tax fields and areas of spending, both the federal and provincial governments play substantial roles. Intergovernmental transfers, equal to 3.8 per cent of GDP and 15 per cent of federal government expenditures, are a crucial element in the Canadian federation. Finally, Table 1 also shows that both the provinces and the federal government make extensive use of deficits to finance their expenditures. In fiscal year 1991–92, the federal deficit was 4.5 per cent of GDP, while the provinces realized a combined deficit equal to 2.3 per cent of GDP.

The implications of the data in Table 1 are threefold. First, these figures show that it is inappropriate to focus on only the federal government when examining the problem of deficits in Canada. Both levels of government rely to a significant extent on deficit financing. Second, any changes in the services provided by the federal government or in the way in which these services are provided must involve the provinces, because they participate in virtually all areas of government. As a result, constitutional and political considerations may well help determine the nature of such changes. Third, the importance of transfers from the federal to the provincial level gives rise to an interesting question. Will the federal government find it politically advantageous to lessen its own deficit problem by reducing transfers, hence passing additional responsibility onto the provinces, rather than by cutting its own programs? Whatever the case, given the extent of provincial responsibilities in the government sector, the provinces are part of the deficit and debt problem, and they must be part of the solution.

Not immediately apparent from the data in Table 1 is the degree of interdependence of government budgets. There are two sources of interdependence: First, cost and revenue sharing, intergovernmental grants and equalization transfers, and provincial income taxes, which are "piggybacked" onto the federal tax rate,[3] are all reasons why the budgetary decisions of one level of government directly affect decisions of the other level. But there is another indirect source of budgetary interdependence. It occurs because the two levels of government spend on and collect revenues from the same private sector. Thus, any fiscal policy change by one level of government must, by affecting the tax base, interest rates and inflation, give rise to what the other level of government sees as an external shock to its budget position. The response of this second level of government to the budget disturbance must affect the private sector and thereby affect the budget of the first level of government. In this way, an interesting dynamic arises that complicates any attempt to forecast the economic implications of fiscal policy changes.

The importance of this interdependency between Canada's federal and provincial budgets is detailed by Wilson, Dungan and Murphy (1994), who use the FOCUS macroeconometric model to simulate the effects of fiscal policy changes. In one simulation, they report that, between 1989 and 1991, several federal tax increases had the effect of *reducing* the federal deficit by $4.25 billion while *increasing* the deficit of the provincial government sector by $1.48 billion — an amount equal to 35 per cent of the federal deficit reduction. Using the same model, Dungan and Wilson (1985) examine fiscal policies under alternative regimes of monetary policy. Although the degree of budgetary independence varies with the combination of fiscal and monetary policies, in every case, improvements in the federal budget are accompanied by increases in provincial deficits.

Dungan and Wilson's simulations suggest that the Bank of Canada is another important player that determines the financial health of fiscal authorities (the federal government and the ten provincial governments). The role of the Bank is crucial, because it controls the levers of monetary policy. In a small, open economy that has adopted a flexible exchange rate, like Canada's, monetary policy is the preeminent tool of macroeconomic policy. By influencing the rate of economic growth, the Bank exerts a powerful influence on the tax revenues and the income-sensitive expenditures of fiscal authorities. In addition, by influencing the level of interest rates, it directly affects the cost of incurring debt. The Department of Finance (1995) estimates that a 1 per cent increase in real output improves the financial position of the federal government by $1.3 billion after one year and by $1.7 billion annually after four years. A sustained reduction of 100 basis points (equivalent to one percentage point) in nominal interest rates is estimated to improve the federal government's fiscal position by $1.8 billion after one year and by $3.6 billion annually after four years. Since real output and nominal interest rates tend to move in opposite directions in response to shocks in monetary policy, these estimates indicate that the Bank's policies can have substantial influence on federal finances.

The last player to have an important role in determining the financial health of fiscal authorities is the financial market. The financial market affects budgetary deficits and government debt by penalizing governments with budgetary policies that financial markets find wanting. This penalty is imposed in two closely related ways. First, as debt grows to levels high enough to introduce the possibility of default, lenders demand a higher interest rate as compensation. Because demanding a higher interest rate increases the risk of default by increasing the cost of carrying the debt, the interest rate premium that lenders demand will increase with the debt. If debt continues to grow, lenders will eventually reach the point where no further interest rate increases can entice them to hold this government's debt; to buy debt at such high interest rates will only guarantee default.

The second way in which financial markets impose penalties on profligate governments is through credit ratings. Credit rating agencies serve financial markets by evaluating and publishing indicators of default risk. A credit downgrade imposes discipline on reckless borrowers not only by signalling the need for interest rate increases, but, more importantly, by causing lenders who are subject to capital adequacy standards to stop lending to such borrowers. As such lenders are typically large, a downgrade requires that the risk premiums rise dramatically to induce the remaining lenders to absorb new debt. Further downgrades lead to increasingly severe consequences as more lenders are required to cut off this borrower. Consequently, default risk becomes an increasing function of the level of debt and results in an increasingly stringent penalty. In this way, credit rating agencies cause financial markets to impose penalties on governments who run large deficits for prolonged periods of time.

We are concerned about government deficits and debt because of their effect on macroeconomic variables such as real interest rates, exchange rates and real growth rates. Since it is the *total* government sector deficit and debt which matters for macroeconomic variables, an obvious implication of the budgetary interdependence between levels of government and the interdependence of fiscal and monetary policies described above is that a coordinated effort at deficit reduction is a logical solution. Unfortunately, recent history suggests that such coordination might be difficult to arrange. In recent years, the federal government and the provincial governments have expressed very different views regarding the urgency with which deficits must be brought under control and the most appropriate way of doing so. For example, Alberta eliminated a large deficit almost solely via expenditure cuts between 1992–93 and 1994–95; the federal government, throughout fifteen years of a fast-growing debt, responded almost exclusively with tax increases and only now has begun to implement sizable expenditure cuts.

These divergent views about the seriousness of the problem and the appropriate solution have led to conflicts between the central players. The dispute between the federal and provincial governments over what the provinces perceive to be unwarranted, large cuts in federal transfers to the provinces — the so-called downloading of the federal deficit onto the provinces — continues to grow. Tensions between provincial governments have stemmed from perceptions that loose fiscal policy by Ontario during the mid-1980s caused the Bank of Canada to impose an unnecessarily strict monetary policy. Since any monetary policy is imposed on all members of a union that share currency, Ontario's fiscal decisions are thought to have had substantial negative consequences for the other provinces. Finally, tension remains between the Bank of Canada on one hand, and the federal and provincial governments on the other; this tension has both caused the Bank to comment that greater fiscal prudence on the part of governments is an important precursor to future interest rate reductions and elicited countercharges that the Bank's high interest rate policies have exacerbated governments' deficit woes.

Deficits and Debt, 1961–89

If we consider the budgetary experiences of governments at both levels over the three decades from 1961 to 1989, we can evaluate the fiscal choices that were made and determine why some governments could maintain reasonably stable finances in the face of economic challenges while other governments could not.

Table 2 contains data on government deficits, primary deficits (expenditures not related to debt servicing minus tax revenue) and debt servicing costs, all as a fraction of provincial GDP for four periods. Table 3 presents data on net-debt-to-GDP ratios at the provincial and federal levels. A comparison of these data, along with an analysis of real growth rates and real interest rates, will show how increases in debt are related to changes in primary deficits and debt servicing costs. But first, it is useful to review the "arithmetic" of the government budget constraint.

At any point in time, total government expenditures, including the cost of servicing outstanding debt, must equal total revenues raised from taxation and from the sale of bonds. Appendix A demonstrates that this requirement implies the following must be true:

Change in debt-to-income ratio = (interest rate − growth rate) x (debt-to-income ratio) − (primary balance as a percentage of national income)

From this simple equation we can see that the debt-to-GDP ratio declines with increases in the growth rate of real output, reductions in the real interest rate and decreases (increases) in the primary deficit (surplus).

Table 2: Budget Measures as

	1961–69	1970–79	1980–89	1990–93
Newfoundland				
Deficit	-4.35	-3.15	-2.02	-1.24
Primary Deficit	-2.68	1.13	3.97	4.64
Debt Service	1.67	4.27	5.99	5.88
Prince Edward Island				
Deficit	-1.31	0.55	0.23	-0.58
Primary Deficit	0.82	3.21	4.05	3.72
Debt Service	2.13	2.66	3.82	4.30
Nova Scotia				
Deficit	-0.05	-0.65	-1.63	-1.90
Primary Deficit	1.45	1.68	2.24	2.68
Debt Service	1.50	2.33	3.87	4.59
New Brunswick				
Deficit	-0.66	-0.62	-1.40	-0.94
Primary Deficit	0.77	1.28	1.90	3.64
Debt Service	1.43	1.90	3.30	4.58
Quebec				
Deficit	-0.67	-1.03	-1.53	-2.11
Primary Deficit	-0.24	0.06	1.42	1.45
Debt Service	0.43	1.09	2.95	3.56
Ontario				
Deficit	0.15	-1.00	-0.81	-2.99
Primary Deficit	0.63	0.22	1.16	-0.83
Debt Service	0.48	1.22	1.97	2.16
Manitoba				
Deficit	-0.09	-0.43	-2.39	-1.67
Primary Deficit	0.63	1.04	1.83	4.21
Debt Service	0.72	1.48	4.22	5.88

a Fraction of GDP

	1961–69	1970–79	1980–89	1990–93
Saskatchewan				
Deficit	0.56	1.23	-1.63	-0.93
Primary Deficit	1.72	2.55	2.46	5.40
Debt Service	1.16	1.33	4.09	6.33
Alberta				
Deficit	-1.65	2.74	1.44	-1.52
Primary Deficit	-1.32	3.52	2.71	0.99
Debt Service	0.33	0.78	1.27	2.51
British Columbia				
Deficit	1.07	0.98	-0.43	-0.64
Primary Deficit	1.16	1.29	0.87	1.46
Debt Service	0.09	0.32	1.30	2.10
All Provincial Governments				
Deficit	-0.18	-0.25	-0.71	-2.11
Primary Deficit	0.33	0.88	1.58	0.80
Debt Service	0.52	1.13	2.29	2.92
Federal Government				
Deficit	-0.00	-1.44	-4.52	-4.31
Primary Deficit	1.89	0.82	0.16	1.53
Debt Service	1.89	2.25	4.68	5.83

Note: All data are on a calendar year, national income accounting basis. A positive value for a deficit figure indicates a budget surplus.

Sources: Revenue and expenditure data from CANSIM matrices 6769–6778 (provinces) and 6671 (federal).

Because the dramatic changes in the federal debt-to-GDP ratio are familiar to most Canadians, it might be useful to start with observations about the federal government's experience. From Table 2, we see that during the sixties, the federal government was a model of fiscal prudence. The budget was usually balanced, and even the economic slow-down of 1961–62 yielded a deficit of only 1.2 per cent of GDP. A modest primary surplus averaging 2 per cent of GDP,

Table 3:

	1969–70	1974–75	1979–80	1980–81	1981–82	1982-83	1983–84
Newfoundland	29.1	31.4	39.4	37.9	35.1	34.9	37.0
Prince Edward Island	32.4	18.9	15.1	16.0	13.6	15.2	13.0
Nova Scotia	13.0	10.8	13.3	15.4	18.6	20.3	20.7
New Brunswick	19.8	14.4	15.1	18.4	17.5	21.6	22.6
Quebec	12.7	15.4	21.9	24.7	21.1	25.1	27.2
Ontario	4.4	5.9	10.2	10.4	10.4	12.2	12.9
Manitoba	1.0	-0.6	6.3	6.5	7.4	10.0	13.0
Saskatchewan	-2.7	-7.9	-8.7	-8.5	-7.9	-5.9	-3.8
Alberta	-5.8	-8.5	-26.5	-25.6	-26.2	-24.2	-24.5
British Columbia	-5.8	-7.6	-5.9	-5.6	-4.4	-1.8	0.3
All Provinces	5.1	4.9	6.0	6.4	5.4	7.9	9.4
Federal Government	21.4	15.7	26.2	27.3	27.5	33.6	40.0

Note: Negative values indicate a net asset position. All debt figures are measured on a fiscal year basis (ending March 31) and represent the difference between financial assets and direct liabilities. GDP data are on a calendar year basis. Debt-to-GDP ratios are calculated using the preceding year's GDP. Provincial debt figures exclude municipal debt and are measured using FMS conventions, while federal debt is measured using national income accounting conventions.

along with high rates of real GDP growth (averaging 5.4 per cent), enabled the federal government to reduce its debt-to-GDP ratio from 31 per cent in 1960–61 to 23 per cent by 1968–69. In the early seventies, the federal government continued the pattern of the sixties: modest deficits offset by small surpluses and a steady primary surplus. By 1974–75, the debt-to-GDP ratio had fallen to approximately 16 per cent.

Net-Debt-to-GDP Ratios

1984–85	1985–86	1986–87	1987–88	1988–89	1989–90	1990–91	1991–92	1992–93
38.6	40.0	39.5	38.1	35.1	35.5	36.7	38.9	44.9
12.5	12.0	11.7	11.8	12.4	12.1	13.3	14.7	17.2
23.0	24.7	24.5	24.2	23.1	27.9	28.4	30.5	36.3
22.4	23.7	23.1	24.8	23.0	21.4	22.6	24.7	26.4
29.3	33.0	33.7	33.4	31.7	31.2	32.6	35.9	39.9
12.8	14.3	14.1	13.6	12.5	11.1	11.7	15.6	20.0
14.5	19.7	24.2	26.4	21.3	20.1	20.2	23.2	25.9
-0.8	3.6	10.7	13.9	15.0	15.6	15.9	26.1	29.1
-25.9	-24.4	-20.8	-18.2	-14.0	-10.0	-7.8	-4.6	1.7
1.5	2.6	3.6	3.2	1.5	0.4	0.8	3.7	5.7
10.3	12.5	14.5	14.8	14.1	13.6	14.4	18.1	22.0
45.9	50.2	53.6	54.0	53.9	54.5	57.8	62.4	67.1

Note: Following Ip (1991), in order to provide a more accurate comparison of provincial finances, the figures for Quebec have been adjusted to remove the net assets of the Quebec Pension Plan.

Sources: Provincial net debt, CANSIM matrices 3202-3211. Federal net debt, CANSIM matrix 3199. Provincial and national GDP, CANSIM matrices 2610-2621.

The late seventies witnessed a dramatic change in the budgetary choices of the federal government. Small budget imbalances, both positive and negative, were replaced by a string of deficits averaging 3 per cent of GDP, primary deficits rather than surpluses, and a steady increase in the debt-to-GDP ratio so that it exceeded 26 per cent by fiscal year 1979–80. The culprit was not slower economic growth that caused tax revenues to fall; real GDP grew by an average of 4.6 per cent per year from 1976 to 1979. Nor were high real interest rates pushing up the cost of carrying the debt; the real interest rate on federal debt averaged just over 1 per cent for the period.[4] Instead, the federal government had made a momentous change in its budgeting philosophy, and switched from budgeting primary *surpluses* averaging 2.2 per cent of GDP between 1970 and 1974 to budgeting primary *deficits* averaging 0.6 per cent of GDP for the rest of the decade.

As Table 3 indicates, most of the growth in the federal debt-to-GDP ratio has occurred since 1981–82. Although the 1982 recession reduced real output by 3.2 per cent, real GDP growth averaged 4.2 per cent from 1983 to the end of the decade. Thus, although the tax base expanded more slowly than it had during the late seventies, this change cannot explain the rise in the federal debt-to-GDP ratio throughout the decade. A more obvious explanation for the deterioration of federal finances during the eighties was the increase in real interest rates brought about by the Bank of Canada. The Bank had attempted to reduce the rate of money growth to levels consistent with the rate of inflation, which would average 3.8 per cent from 1983 to 1990, compared to 8.9 per cent from 1975 to 1982.[5]

Laidler and Robson (1993) describe Canadian monetary policy as becoming "excruciatingly" contractionary in 1980 and at the end of 1981 and suggest that it helped to precipitate the worst recession since World War II. The effect of this policy was not only the temporary fall in real output but, more important to the long-term financial health of governments, a dramatic increase in the real interest rate paid on the federal debt — a rate that peaked at about 10 per cent in 1984 and averaged 6 per cent over the decade. As a result of this rate, costs associated with the federal debt were more than double the average level during the seventies.

The other culprit in the dramatic increase of the federal debt-to-GDP ratio was the failure of the federal government to react forcibly to its growing financial problems by increasing its primary surplus, thereby offsetting the increase in the interest costs of the debt. In fact, as Table 2 shows, the federal government's primary surplus fell from its average values during the sixties and seventies. It was only between 1987 and 1989 that the federal government recorded primary surpluses, and these averaged less than 2 per cent of GDP. Throughout the decade, the federal government increased tax burdens (the tax-revenue-to-GDP ratio increased from 15.5 per cent in 1979 to 18 per cent in 1989), but left program expenditures virtually untouched (these declined from 15.9 per cent of GDP in 1979 to 15.4 per cent in 1989). The resulting increase in the primary surplus from –0.5 per cent of GDP in 1979 to +2.5 per cent in 1989 was virtually identical to the 2.8 per cent increase in the ratio of debt servicing costs to GDP over the same period. Thus, despite significantly increasing the tax burden of Canadians, the federal government had, by 1989–90, merely balanced the growth in its debt service costs and its primary surplus. As a result, the debt-to-GDP ratio doubled over the decade, and the only victory that the government could claim was the levelling off of the federal debt-to-GDP ratio at 54 per cent after seven years of strong economic growth.

During the sixties, the fiscal history of the provinces was similar to that of the federal government; budget deficits were usually small and often followed by surpluses. As evidenced by the low debt service costs in Table 2, provincial debts were also small.

Exceptions to this description were Newfoundland and Prince Edward Island. Throughout the sixties, Newfoundland registered very large deficits, averaging 4.4 per cent of GDP. Primary deficits were also large and grew throughout the decade. By 1969, the expenses of carrying debt had increased by more than three times from 0.8 per cent to 2.6 per cent of GDP. Although Prince Edward Island generally saw more modest deficits, six of the nine years during this period showed deficits, four of which were well in excess of 3 per cent of GDP. In the last two years of the decade, the province responded forcibly to the growth of its debt, caused by the large deficits of the earlier part of the decade, and managed to create substantial primary surpluses. Over the next four years (1969 to 1972), the province recorded primary surpluses averaging in excess of 5.2 per cent of GDP; this favourable situation enabled it to dramatically reduce its debt-to-GDP ratio by the mid-1970s.

The seventies did not yield dramatic changes in the financial conditions of most provinces. Budget imbalances, both positive and negative, generally remained small. Exceptions included Alberta and Saskatchewan, which enjoyed large primary surpluses thanks to increases in oil and gas prices, and which were thus able to significantly improve their net asset positions over the decade. Another exception was Newfoundland, which continued to record large deficits and to pay the price in the form of large and growing debt service costs. In 1974, Newfoundland paid another price for its large deficits when Moody's bond rating service lowered its credit rating to "Baa1," a rating granted to bonds which "lack outstanding invest-

Table 4: Moody's Debt Rating, 1974–95

	Year of Change	To Rating of:	Direction of Change from Previous Rating
Newfoundland	1974	Baa1	Downgrade
Nova Scotia	1976	A1	Downgrade
	1983	A	Downgrade
	1986	A2	Downgrade
	1993	A3	Downgrade
New Brunswick	1976	A1	Downgrade
	1983	A	Downgrade
	1986	A1	Upgrade
Quebec	1974	A1	Upgrade
	1975	Aa	Upgrade
	1982	A1	Downgrade
	1986	Aa3	Upgrade
	1993	A1	Downgrade
	1995	A2	Downgrade
Ontario	1974	Aaa	Upgrade
	1991	Aa2	Downgrade
	1994	Aa3	Downgrade
Manitoba	1974	A1	Upgrade
	1975	Aa	Upgrade
	1985	A1	Downgrade
Saskatchewan	1976	Aa	Upgrade
	1981	Aa1	Upgrade
	1985	Aa	Downgrade
	1986	A1	Downgrade
	1990	A2	Downgrade
	1992	A3	Downgrade

Table 4 (con't)

	Year of Change	To Rating of:	Direction of Change from Previous Rating
Alberta	1979	Aaa	Upgrade
	1986	Aa1	Downgrade
	1992	Aa2	Downgrade
British Columbia	1980	Aaa	Upgrade
	1983	Aa1	Downgrade
	1987	Aa2	Downgrade
	1989	Aa1	Upgrade
	1995	Aa2	Downgrade

Note: Prior to 1988, British Columbia's rating is that applied to the debt of the BC Hydro and Power Authority. Moody's has provided a ranking on Prince Edward Island's debt only since 1986. That ranking has remained at A3 since 1986.

Source: Moody's Bond Survey

ment characteristics and in fact have speculative characteristics as well" (Moody's Bond Record). Only in 1977 did Newfoundland change its fiscal philosophy and begin to budget substantial primary surpluses. Prince Edward Island continued to try to reduce its debt in the same manner.

Table 3 shows that the provinces east of Ontario began the eighties with relatively large debt-to-GDP ratios. The size of these provinces' debts meant that changes in the debt load throughout the decade would be largely a function of changes in the interest rates paid on the debt. When monetary contraction caused real interest rates to soar, the costs of supporting the debt for these provinces exploded to an average well above 3 per cent of provincial GDP. In response, Moody's downgraded their credit ratings soon after the effects of the high interest rates and accompanying recession on their deficits had become apparent (see Table 4). Prince Edward Island's early adoption and Newfoundland's later introduction of large primary surpluses enabled these provinces to absorb the high costs of their debts and actually reduce their debt-to-GDP ratios. Nova Scotia and New

Brunswick managed to introduce primary surpluses that averaged only half the size of those in Newfoundland and Prince Edward Island and were consequently less successful in limiting the increase in their debt-to-GDP ratios. Quebec delayed introducing substantial primary surpluses until 1987; hence, despite strong economic growth following the 1981 recession, it witnessed a sizable increase in its debt-to-GDP ratio.

Provinces west of Ontario began the decade either with small debt-to-GDP ratios (Manitoba) or in net asset positions (Saskatchewan, Alberta and British Columbia). In all these provinces, increases in interest rates accounted for fewer changes in debt-to-GDP ratios. In fact, given the net asset positions of three of these provinces, interest rate increases could have been beneficial. The effects of a major recession and energy and commodity price fluctuations on revenues and expenditures and the fiscal response to these changes provide the main explanations for the debt histories of these provinces in the eighties.

Saskatchewan's finances suffered drastically from the drop in oil and gas prices in 1986, from low potash, uranium and grain prices throughout the decade and from the associated economic slow-down. Despite a concerted effort to turn its finances around by budgeting primary surpluses averaging 4.5 per cent over the last three years of the decade, Saskatchewan moved from a net asset to a net debt position by 1985–86, with the net debt worsening by the end of the decade. A series of credit downgrades followed.

Alberta's net asset position similarly suffered as a result of the falling oil and gas prices and the economic slow-down. The Alberta government failed to recognize that the decline in energy prices was more than a short-term deviation from a long-term pattern of rising energy prices and took little action to remedy its rapidly deteriorating fiscal position. As a consequence, Alberta witnessed a 14 percentage point reduction in i4s asset-to-GDP ratio in only four years.

British Columbia dealt with the volatility of economic conditions during the eighties by simply avoiding deficits. In nonrecession years, the province recorded both deficits and surpluses, but neither exceeded 1 per cent of GDP. Thus, although it too lost revenue due to the lower energy prices and consequently experienced an increase in its debt-to-GDP ratio after 1986, it managed to quickly reduce this ratio to near zero by the end of the decade. Large primary surpluses were not required in British Columbia in the eighties because the province entered the decade in a net asset position and avoided large

Table 5
Fiscal Stance of Provincial and Federal Governments, 1989–90

	Debt-to-GDP Ratio 1989–90 (1)	Actual Primary-Deficit-to-GDP Ratio (2)	Average Real Growth Rate 1987–89 (3)	Required Primary-Deficit-to-GDP Ratio (4)	Predicted Debt-to-GDP Ratio 1990–91 (5)
Newfoundland	35.5	4.43	1.98	1.07	32.1
Prince Edward Island	12.1	4.83	2.26	0.33	7.6
Nova Scotia	27.9	2.05	2.01	0.83	26.7
New Brunswick	21.4	3.77	2.79	0.47	18.1
Quebec	31.2	2.98	3.54	0.46	28.7
Ontario	11.1	2.09	5.37	-0.04	9.0
Manitoba	20.1	4.21	1.66	0.67	16.6
Saskatchewan	15.6	6.67	-0.36	0.84	9.8
Alberta	-10.0	0.30	0.40	-0.46	-10.8
British Columbia	0.4	2.78	5.13	-0.00	-2.4
Federal Government	54.5	2.51	3.86	0.62	52.6

Source: Table 2 and 3 and the author's calculations.

Note: A positive value for a deficit figure indicates a surplus. The real growth rate reported in column three was calculated using the national GDP deflator. The figures in the last column are based on an assumed real interest rate payable on government debt of 5 per cent, an amount that approximates the average rate paid on federal government debt in 1989. The provinces pay higher interest rates on their debt, with the amount varying by province. The calculations are not very sensitive to this refinement. For example, adding 150 basis points to the interest rate paid on Newfoundland books would increase Newfoundland's entry in column five to 32.7.

deficits. In this way, British Columbia was able to minimize the debilitating effects wrought by high interest rates on its finances.

As in British Columbia, the deficit-to-GDP ratio in Ontario did not exceed 1 per cent (either positive or negative), except during recessions; in 1982 and 1983, Ontario's deficit peaked at 2 per cent of GDP. Following the recession, Ontario allowed very strong economic growth to substantially increase its primary surpluses beyond their levels in the seventies. This choice, combined with a relatively small debt at the beginning of the decade which helped protect it from high interest rates, enabled Ontario to allow its debt-to-GDP ratio to increase immediately following the 1981 recession. Then, except for a disconcerting jump in 1985–86 when the Ontario economy was booming, the ratio fell slowly. By the end of the decade, Ontario's debt-to-GDP ratio had virtually returned to the level of the early eighties.

Table 5 presents a snapshot of the deficit and debt situation of both levels of government at the end of fiscal year 1989–90. Columns one and two show data on net-debt-to-GDP ratios at the end of fiscal year 1989–90 and primary-deficit-to-GDP ratios for the 1989 calendar year. Column three gives the average rate of real GDP growth experienced by each province between 1987 and 1989. Over the same period, the real interest rate payable on federal government debt averaged 5 per cent.[6] Assuming that for planning purposes governments were using this interest rate and the recent growth rate as indications of future economic activity, we can use these data to infer how the eleven fiscal authorities intended to deal with their debt-to-GDP ratios and gain some insight into possible outcomes if the 1990–91 recession had not occurred.

Column four shows the primary-deficit-to-GDP ratio sufficient to maintain the debt-to-GDP ratio shown in column one, given the real rate of GDP growth shown in column three and a real interest rate of 5 per cent on government debt. The figures in columns two and four indicate that in fiscal year 1989–90 all eleven governments showed primary surpluses that were more than sufficient to maintain constant debt-to-GDP ratios and hence that were sufficient to reduce their debt-to-GDP ratios over time. Column five shows the predicted debt-to-GDP ratio at the end of fiscal year 1990–91, assuming that the average real growth rate of the previous three years continued and that the real interest rate remained at 5 per cent.[7]

The figures in Table 5 show that if the economy had not entered another recession in 1990 but rather had continued to grow at recent rates, then, even with a high real interest rate, all eleven governments could have reduced their net-debt-to-GDP ratios. In fact, impressive improvements in debt-to-GDP ratios were at hand for a number of provinces. Nonetheless, warning signs are apparent from Table 5.

It is noteworthy, for example, that among highly indebted jurisdictions, the federal government bore the greatest debt. Yet it was
scheduled to make one of the least impressive improvements in its
debt position despite an average growth rate of real GDP over the
previous three years of almost 4 per cent. Another warning sign
comes from observing that Ontario and British Columbia, despite
experiencing extraordinarily high rates of real growth and holding
relatively small debts, were in fiscal positions to forecast only a two
and three percentage point reduction in their debt-to-GDP ratios,
respectively. Finally, from Table 3, we can observe that by 1989–90,
only three of the eleven governments — Newfoundland, Prince Edward Island and Ontario — had reestablished debt-to-GDP ratios that
were below, or within one percentage point, of their levels prior to
the onset of the 1982 recession.

Lessons from the Sixties, Seventies and Eighties

The data in Tables 2, 3, 4 and 5, and Canada's financial history over
the three decades from 1961 to 1989 offer several important and
closely related lessons.

First, tight monetary policy can have disastrous effects on government finances. The Bank of Canada's efforts to reduce inflation in
the early eighties induced a serious recession, but perhaps more
important, the Bank's attempts pushed real interest rates to unprecedented levels that would persist for the remainder of the decade. This
forced governments to choose between dramatically increasing their
primary surpluses via tax rate increases and/or cutting program expenditures to offset their rapidly increasing debt service costs, or
seeing their debt-to-GDP ratios soar and suffering even more trau-
matic adjustments in later years.

The first lesson can be restated as follows: the benefits of having
achieved lower rates of inflation must be measured not only against
the costs of higher unemployment and lower rates of growth, but also
against the costs of decreased government program spending and
higher tax rates.

It is worth noting that in debates about the merits of reducing
inflation, this point is rarely made. In two well-known volumes
debating the issue, *Zero Inflation: The Goal of Price Stability,* and
Taking Aim: The Debate on Zero Inflation, Purvis (1990, 54) and
Scarth (1990, 98) make only a passing reference to this point. It is
also interesting that in summarizing important lessons for monetary
policy drawn from the seventies and eighties, a deputy governor of

the Bank of Canada made no mention of the budgetary consequences of monetary contraction (Freedman 1989).

Second, the decision to finance expenditures with deficits exposes governments to the risk of a very quickly expanding debt, should economic conditions take a turn for the worse — in particular, should interest rates increase and economic growth rates fall for a prolonged period. Under these conditions, a government must respond decisively with increases in its primary surplus before the vicious circle of higher deficits leading to higher debt service payments can gather momentum. If the fiscal authority does not act decisively, its debt-to-GDP ratio and debt servicing costs will grow, thereby increasing the sensitivity of its budget to high interest rates and future economic slow-downs.

Of course, predicting whether a fall in real growth rates or an increase in real interest rates marks the start of a short or a prolonged period of unfavourable economic conditions is very difficult. In addition, the fact that a government must increase its primary surplus by imposing on its citizens the cost of increasing tax rates or cuts in program expenditures, or both, suggests the following restatement of lesson two: Since deficit financing introduces the possibility of the government's having to raise tax rates and cut program expenditures, the potential cost of deficit financing can be very large. The benefits derived from deficit financing must be measured against the risk of imposing these costs on citizens.

Third, the risk of a very quickly expanding debt increases with the level of debt since any increase in the interest rate produces an even larger increase in debt servicing costs. Thus, it is in the interest of governments that opt for deficit financing to avoid large debt-to-GDP ratios and to quickly eliminate increases.

In considering lessons two and three, the experiences of Newfoundland and Prince Edward Island during the sixties and seventies present an interesting contrast. After financing its expenditures with a string of large deficits in the early sixties, Prince Edward Island shifted to very large primary surpluses in the late sixties and early seventies. This shift enabled the government to take advantage of strong economic growth and low interest rates and to quickly reduce its debt-to-GDP ratio throughout the seventies. By the end of the decade, the debt-to-GDP ratio was half its value in 1970, and the province had largely insulated itself from the ill effects of the jump in interest rates that would occur in 1981. Newfoundland similarly chose to finance expenditures with large deficits during the sixties, but it continued the policy until 1977. By this time, its debt-to-GDP ratio had increased to over 35 per cent and debt service costs were now in excess of 5 per cent of GDP. The adoption of large primary surpluses in 1978 came too late. Saddled with a large debt and facing the 1981 increase in real interest rates that would last for the rest of the decade, Newfoundland was doomed to rapid increases in its debt service costs and would require large primary surpluses just to maintain its debt-to-GDP ratio.

The federal government's experience during the sixties and seventies was like a mirror image of Newfoundland's. That is, the government chose to change its strategy from fiscal prudence to fiscal recklessness in the mid-1970s. Learning nothing from Prince Edward Island's and Newfoundland's experiences, the government adopted a policy of large deficits and a growing debt, beginning with its 1975 budget. Between then and 1980, the federal debt-to-GDP ratio increased from 15 to 27 per cent. When the eighties brought persistently high interest rates and reduced rates of growth, it was incumbent on the government to regain control of the deficit and to begin to run substantial primary surpluses. Prudent fiscal policy required primary surpluses large enough not only to stem the tide of rising debt but also to reduce the level of the debt-to-GDP ratio to that at the beginning of the decade. Instead, by the end of the decade, the federal government's debt-to-GDP ratio had doubled, the sizable expense of carrying debt was mounting and the vicious circle of growing debt, growing debt service costs and growing deficits was quickly developing.

Fourth, since deficit financing carries the threat of explosive debts should economic conditions deteriorate, governments must budget for moderate levels of economic growth and interest rates. With this strategy, budgets automatically move into deficit during recession and into surplus during the following expansion, and over the course of a business cycle, the debt-to-GDP ratio remains generally constant. Thus, conservative budgeting provides an alternative to the economic and social disruption that results from changing rates of taxation and program spending. In other words, conservative budgeting allows budget imbalances to act as automatic stabilizers.

Ontario offers an example of a government failing to budget for moderate economic conditions. Although only small budget imbalances appeared from 1984 to 1990, Ontario was enjoying extraordinary rates of real growth, averaging 7 per cent per year. Thus, Ontario was implementing expenditure programs and a tax structure that generated a roughly balanced budget only in a very high growth, low-unemployment economy. If recession hit, either Ontario's deficit would explode or tax and expenditure rates would increase and decrease, respectively. The federal government followed a similar course. From 1984 to 1988, it budgeted deficits averaging 5 per cent of GDP despite enjoying an average real growth rate of 4.7 per cent.

Fifth, good times don't last, and one must plan for the next recession. Many provinces reacted to the 1981 recession appropriately: most allowed their debt-to-GDP ratios to rise and then increased their primary surpluses to reduce these ratios during the following expansion. However, the speed with which some of the provinces reined in their deficits and prepared themselves for the next recession is certainly open to criticism. As Ip (1991) notes, provinces that dragged their feet in reducing the deficit and debt during the period of economic growth — Quebec, which allowed its debt-to-GDP ratio to increase by six percentage points despite enjoying an average rate of growth of 5.4 per cent from 1984 to 1988, especially deserves this criticism — were at a disadvantage when the economy again moved into recession in 1990.

The federal government was the greatest offender in this regard. By not acting quickly and forcibly, the federal government could only halt the growth in its debt-to-GDP ratio by the end of the decade. Failure to act quickly to reduce debt during an expansion leads to "ratcheting" upward of the debt-to-GDP ratio, whereby each recession pushes the ratio higher and each expansion interrupts its growth and leaves it at a new, higher plateau. Since the federal government adopted the policy of budgeting large deficits in 1975, it has reached two such plateaus: at debt-to-GDP ratios of 27 per cent in the early eighties and of 54 per cent in the late eighties. In the next section, we will see that the current government seeks only to establish a new plateau for federal debt at 75 per cent of GDP in the late nineties. Adding twenty to twenty-five percentage points to the debt-to-GDP ratio every business cycle is clearly not a sustainable policy.

Sixth, despite difficult economic circumstances, fiscally prudent budgeting choices are possible. On this point, it is interesting to compare the outcomes of the financing decisions of the federal government with those of Newfoundland and Quebec. At the beginning of the decade, the debt-to-GDP ratio of the federal government was significantly smaller than that of Newfoundland and was similar to that of Quebec. Thus, the threat posed by possible interest rate increases was greatest for Newfoundland but somewhat less for the federal and Quebec governments. Yet subjected to roughly the same interest rate fluctuations as these provinces but benefiting from less volatile revenues due to its more diversified tax base, the federal government doubled its debt-to-GDP ratio and merely checked its growth by 1989.[8] Newfoundland, with the least diversified tax base and the most vulnerability to interest rate fluctuations of the three governments, allowed only a two percentage point increase in its debt-to-GDP ratio and by 1989 had actually whittled that increase away. Although Quebec allowed a much larger increase in its debt-to-GDP ratio than did Newfoundland, it too had managed to make a dent in that increase by 1989. These provinces proved that fiscally prudent behaviour was possible during the eighties; the federal government stubbornly failed to learn this lesson.

Seventh, financial markets will impose significant costs on governments that fail to maintain the levels of fiscal prudence they deem acceptable and will reward those who do comply. However, one of the modes of discipline, credit downgrades, is largely reserved for provincial governments, whose debt the Bank of Canada can refuse to purchase. The federal government escapes credit downgrades because of the perception that the Bank of Canada cannot refuse to purchase federal debt. Table 4 summarizes the credit histories of the provinces between 1974 and 1995.

Did credit downgrades persuade provincial governments to attempt to control their finances when they might not have otherwise? It is difficult to answer this question. Simply being threatened by a downgrade may prompt action, thus making causal analysis difficult. In addition, since bond ratings reflect an appraisal of long-term risks, the rating need not correlate well with a government's current budget position. Furthermore, credit ratings reflect a judgement based in part on nonfinancial factors. Thus the mere election of a government committed to large spending increases, for example, may prompt an immediate credit downgrade, and once again, the relationship between credit ratings and budget policy becomes difficult to observe.

Moreover, Boothe (1993) speculates that the pool of prospective lenders for the Saskatchewan government shrank from between 125 and 140 institutions, when its credit rating was AA+ (excellent), to between 25 and 30, when its rating fell to BBB+ (moderate). Thus Saskatchewan was not only paying a higher risk premium as its debt grew, but also having to satisfy the preferences of fewer lenders. Similarly, in a review of budget papers, Maslove, Prince and Doern (1986) note the frequency with which "preserving the province's credit rating" is given as a rationale for austere measures. Finally, it is also telling that the federal government received no credit down-grades from 1975 to 1989, while it tripled its debt-to-GDP ratio in that period. The anecdotal evidence thus suggests that the budget choices made by governments are indeed sensitive to both actual and threatened adjustments in their credit ratings and that the greater degree of fiscal prudence displayed by the provinces vis-à-vis the federal government is partly due to this influence.[9]

Responses to the 1990–91 Recession

The nineties began with another round of monetary tightening. In the Hanson Lecture of 1988, the governor of the Bank of Canada, John Crow, announced the Bank's intention to pursue a monetary policy designed to achieve a stable price level. The goal was to reduce the rate of inflation, which had averaged 3.8 per cent from 1983 to 1990, and to stabilize prices by an unspecified date.[10] Unlike in the earlier monetary contraction of 1980–81, which in part was determined by U.S. Federal Reserve policy, in this situation, the Bank intended to introduce a "made in Canada" disinflation policy.

Given the poor financial shape of the federal government and of many of the provinces, the Bank's decision to implement a monetary policy that would inflict further damage on government finances is evidence that the Bank either had not yet learned lesson one or was convinced that the benefits of lower inflation were worth that cost.

The tight monetary policy promised by Governor Crow came in early 1990 and brought with it a recession that saw real GDP shrink by 2.3 per cent in 1990–91. This recession was followed by an anemic recovery that barely regained that lost output over the fol-lowing two years. For the federal government, which for the seven years preceding the recession ran deficits large enough to average 4.9 per cent of GDP despite enjoying an average rate of economic growth of 4.2 per cent, this situation spelled financial disaster. The federal government reacted to the recession by increasing tax rates to a degree sufficient to offset the loss in tax base and thereby increase the ratio of total revenues to GDP. Thus, the upward march in the federal tax burden continued from 15.7 to 18 to 20 per cent in, respectively, 1979, 1989 and 1992. This action was woefully insuf-ficient, however, and the federal debt-to-GDP ratio resumed its own upward march from 54.5 per cent in 1989–90 to 67.1 per cent in 1992–93.

With the election of a new government in the fall of 1993 came the rather belated acknowledgement that a fiscal crisis was at hand. By February 1995, Moody's bond rating agency announced that it was reviewing its rating on the federal debt. In the same month, a federal budget was presented. In that budget, the federal government announced plans for program spending cuts of $12.1 billion to be spread over three years (to 1996–97). These cuts were projected to reduce by 3.8 percentage points the ratio of program spending to GDP and constitute the first serious cuts in program spending since the federal government began running large deficits in 1974–75. As a result of these measures, a sizable primary surplus of 3.6 per cent of GDP was targeted for 1996–97, which would reduce the overall deficit from 5.9 per cent of GDP in 1993–94 to 3 per cent in 1996–97. By March 1995, the federal debt-to-GDP ratio was expected to have reached 72.8 per cent.[11] In April, Moody's announced that it was downgrading its rating on the federal debt from Aaa to Aa1.

Although the federal government announced significant spending cuts, it is a measure of the seriousness of its financial difficulties that these cuts are insufficient to lower its debt-to-GDP ratio. Given the government's forecast of 2.5 per cent real GDP growth for 1996, its target of reaching a deficit-to-GDP ratio of 3 per cent by 1996–97 implies a debt-to-GDP ratio of 75 per cent in that year. Should the same growth rate and deficit policy continue for the year after that, the debt-to-GDP ratio will have reached a new plateau of 75 per cent. Given that the budget's forecast of real GDP growth for 1995 (3.8 per cent) is already proving to be optimistic, even the modest goal of stabilizing at this new plateau is unlikely to be achieved.

By the end of fiscal year 1992–93, a number of provinces had managed to absorb the effects of the latest round of monetary tightening without serious consequences for their deficits and debts. Indeed, Newfoundland, New Brunswick, Manitoba and Saskatchewan managed to reduce their average deficit-to-GDP ratios from levels in the eighties. Despite these efforts, the debilitating effects of the recession and high interest rates caused the debt-to-GDP ratios of these provinces to rise. In response to this worsening of debt-to-GDP ratios, all four provinces have taken further steps to reduce their deficits. Handcuffed by very slow growth, Newfoundland has made less progress than the others. Saskatchewan reported a balanced budget for the 1994–95 fiscal year and plans for surpluses until the end of the decade. Manitoba and New Brunswick expect to realize small surpluses beginning in 1995–96 and carrying through to 1998–99.[12]

Prince Edward Island was somewhat less successful at reducing its deficit-to-GDP ratio in the early nineties. It is important to recognize, however, that this province suffered a 4.8 percentage point increase in its unemployment rate between 1988 and 1993 — an amount far greater than the maximum increases suffered by Manitoba (2.4 percentage points), Saskatchewan (1.2) and New Brunswick (0.9). As a result, despite allowing only a small increase in its deficit-to-GDP ratio, Prince Edward Island sustained a sizable increase in its debt-to-GDP ratio. Since then, imposition of a deficit reduction plan has enabled the province to cuts its deficit from $82.5 million for fiscal year 1992–93 to $9.4 million for 1994–95. The government expects a small surplus for 1995–96, and the deficit reduction plan calls for surpluses thereafter to the end of the decade.

Nova Scotia experienced a similar increase in its unemployment rate, but it was less successful at containing its deficit during the 1990–91 recession. As a result, the government added more than nine percentage points to the debt-to-GDP ratio in the four-year period ending in 1992–93. The 1993–94 budget introduced a four-year plan to reduce expenditures. If we assume moderate rates of economic growth, Nova Scotia will likely be left with a small deficit at the end of this period.

The Ontario and Quebec governments were often labelled as spendthrifts between 1990 and 1993. Indeed, inspection of their debt- and deficit-to-GDP ratios in Tables 2 and 3 supports this accusation. However, as we have seen, the 1990–91 recession affected some provinces more seriously than others. While from 1989 to 1993 the national unemployment rate increased by 3.7 percentage points, the provincial rate increased by 5.5 percentage points in Ontario, by 3.8 percentage points in Quebec, but by only 0.6 percentage points in British Columbia. Given the differential outcomes of the recession, a simple comparison between provinces of changes in deficit- and debt-to-GDP ratios can be misleading. If we calculate the ratio of the cumulative increase in each province's deficit-to-GDP ratio to the number of percentage points of unemployment from 1990 to 1993, we obtain a measure of the rate at which each government accumulated debt per percentage point of unemployment. Thus, the increases in the Ontario and Quebec deficit-to-GDP ratios, equal to 2.2 percentage points for every percentage point increase in the unemployment rate, compare favourably with those for the other eight provinces. Outstanding in this regard were Prince Edward Island and Newfoundland, with ratios of only 0.7 and 1.1 per cent, respectively. At the other end of the spectrum was British Columbia, with a ratio of 4.3 per cent.[13] The federal government's ratio was 4.7 per cent.

Criticism of the financial choices of Ontario is appropriate in that the 1990–91 recession only raised its unemployment rate to the national average. Thus, although Ontario's response to the recession did not differ from those of the other provinces, that Ontario ran a deficit equal to 3.7 per cent of GDP in 1993, when its unemployment rate was just under the national average, indicates that the level of spending is to be questioned. When its unemployment rate was below the national average, Ontario could afford social programs that were more generous than those of the average province. The 1990–91 recession demonstrated that the generosity of these programs could be sustained only in a jurisdiction with high growth and a low unemployment rate. The recent election of a new majority government on a platform of paring down social programs signified that the Ontario electorate recognized this problem.[14] Prior to its election defeat, the New Democratic Party government jumped on the balanced-budget bandwagon and forecast three years of shrinking deficits through to 1997–98, when only a small deficit would remain. Since taking office, the new government has made the standard announcement that Ontario's financial situation is worse than the previous government indicated. Thus the future of Ontario's finances is somewhat in the air.

A criticism similar to that directed at Ontario can be directed at Quebec, whose debt-to-GDP ratio held constant from 1984 to 1988, when the province's rate of real growth averaged an extraordinary 5.4 per cent. As these rates of growth are unlikely to be the norm in the future, it is apparent that Quebec, like Ontario, needs to adjust the alignment of its taxes and spending to maintain deficits and levels of public debt that are manageable in the long term. Since the end of the 1990–91 recession, Quebec has made very little progress in reducing its deficit. In an effort to promote job creation, the 1994–95 budget introduced significant tax reductions and promised only to freeze program spending at 1994–95 levels. By the end of fiscal year 1994–95, the deficit, which was budgeted at $4.4 billion but which amounted to $5.7 billion, was very high, at 3.4 per cent of GDP. The budget of May 1995 forecasted shrinking deficits until 1997–98, by which time the deficit-to-GDP ratio should have fallen to 0.9 per cent. This projection, however, assumes a rate of real GDP growth that seems optimistic (3.3 per cent, assuming 2.5 per cent inflation), given recent evidence of a slow-down in the Canadian economy.

From 1987 to 1989, British Columbia benefited from real growth rates averaging in excess of 5 per cent. The province took advantage of this situation and reported three consecutive budget surpluses from 1988 to 1990. This position allowed it to reduce its debt-to-GDP ratio by three percentage points. Despite experiencing another average growth rate in excess of 5 per cent from 1992 to 1993, British Columbia budgeted for deficits, which led to a rapid increase in its debt-to-GDP ratio. In its 1995 budget, British Columbia largely relied on continued strong economic growth in forecasting a small budgetary surplus for 1995–96. Clearly, these budgeting choices are subject to the same criticism of those of Ontario and Quebec; establishing tax and spending levels which rely on extraordinary growth rates is not a feasible long-term policy.

From 1990 to 1992, Alberta continued its long series of budget deficits which stretches back to 1986. Since then, the province's net asset position (24.4 per cent of GDP in 1985–86) had all but disappeared. With the election of Ralph Klein in December 1992, Alberta initiated a bold attack against its deficit problem. By the end of fiscal year 1994–95, the budget deficit of $3.8 billion (4.9 per cent of GDP) recorded for fiscal year 1992–93 had been transformed into a $0.9 billion surplus. Although aided by higher energy prices, much of this turnaround in Alberta's finances is attributable to cuts in government expenditures, which were expected to reach 20 per cent by the end of 1996–97.

Fiscal Prospects

In evaluating the prospects of the eleven fiscal authorities, we must make an assumption regarding the future direction of monetary policy. It is reasonable to expect that, as low inflation becomes entrenched in the economy and as fiscal deficits continue to fall, current monetary policy will likely result in lower real interest rates. These rates will benefit governments by lowering their debt servicing costs. However, since any change in monetary policy is likely to be minor, fiscal authorities should not expect real interest rate reductions to exceed those resulting from the Bank's following its current policy. This belief is partly based on the conclusions of Laidler and Robson (1993), who, in reviewing the politics of monetary policy since 1988, conclude that the Bank's autonomy in directing monetary policy remained intact despite a number of challenges. It is also based on the observation that the replacement of John Crow by Gerald Thiessen as governor of the Bank of Canada has not produced a noticeable change in the Bank's monetary policy.

Despite the expenditure cuts announced in the 1995 budget, the federal government's finances remain in dire straits. The plan to reduce the deficit to 3 per cent of GDP by the end of fiscal year 1996–97 is, by any measure, adequate only as a very short term policy. Even if this goal is achieved, it will merely continue the pattern of the past twenty years wherein each economic downturn adds twenty to twenty-five percentage points to the federal debt-to-GDP ratio. Thus, the policy will do nothing to reduce the debt and thus nothing to increase the federal government's ability to absorb the effects of future recessions. Since adding so many percentage points to the debt-to-GDP ratio every business cycle is obviously not a sustainable policy, we can expect to see further tax increases, expenditure cuts and transfers of responsibilities onto the provinces.

Six provinces — Prince Edward Island, New Brunswick, Manitoba, Saskatchewan, Alberta and British Columbia — have either realized or budgeted for balanced budgets by the end of the 1995–96 fiscal year. Newfoundland and Nova Scotia have introduced plans to reduce their deficits substantially, although not enough to balance their budgets. With the exception of British Columbia, which continues to rely on high rates of growth to balance its budget, these provinces have largely returned to the levels of fiscal prudence of the sixties and early seventies.

Unfortunately, real interest rates, debts and debt servicing costs are much higher today than they were in those decades. Returning to levels of debt enjoyed in the past calls for extraordinary measures. For example, a province with a 25 per cent debt-to-GDP ratio, a 6 per cent real interest rate on its debt and primary surpluses equal to 2 per cent of GDP will need to enjoy an annual rate of real GDP growth of 3 per cent for a remarkably long period of time — just over ten years — to reduce its debt to 10 per cent of GDP.[15] An increase in interest rates or a decrease in the growth rate or in the primary surplus will lengthen this adjustment period. Nonetheless, these provinces seem to be on this road to recovery.

This assessment is shared by financial markets. The spread between interest rates paid on New Brunswick government bonds and on Government of Canada bonds shrunk from 101 basis points on March 31, 1991, to 55 basis points on March 31, 1994. Less dramatic but still substantial changes over the same period were realized by Alberta (62 to 30), British Columbia (61 to 33), Saskatchewan (86 to 73) and Manitoba (63 to 51). Over the same period, the spread between rates on Ontario and Canada government bonds increased from 58 to 66 basis points.[16]

Unfortunately, the main concern regarding provincial finances surrounds the three largest provinces: Ontario, Quebec and British Columbia. These provinces account for the bulk of provincial borrowing and are thus mainly responsible for the negative consequences of provincial deficits on interest and exchange rates.

Although the budget policy of the Ontario government of Mike Harris remains to be seen, the government's first action upon taking power was to cut $1.9 billion of expenditures. However, even this dramatic step leaves a deficit estimated by the *Globe and Mail* on July 22, 1995, at $8.7 billion for fiscal year 1995–96. If we assume a 6 per cent rate of growth for Ontario's nominal GDP (roughly 3.5 per cent real growth) for 1995, the province will still show a very large deficit, equal to 2.7 per cent of GDP. Even to hold its debt-to-GDP ratio constant at its current level, as opposed to reducing it to allow some budgetary flexibility for the next recession, Ontario must impose substantially larger costs on its citizens in the years ahead.

Quebec shows the least dedication to deficit reduction. It continues to rely on optimistic forecasts of GDP growth just to balance its budget sometime in 1998–99. Similarly, although reporting a balanced budget, British Columbia has achieved it only with the aid of a high growth rate. As is the case in Quebec and Ontario, British Columbia's fiscal position will deteriorate if growth rates falter. All three provinces have a long way to go before they can return to the levels of fiscal prudence displayed in the sixties.

We set out in this chapter to compare the fiscal choices made by the provinces and the federal government from 1961 to 1995 in the hope that we would arrive at an understanding of why some governments maintained control of their finances better than others. By looking at differences in the economic conditions faced by each province, by comparing their fiscal policy choices as measured by changes in their primary deficits, and by detailing the debilitating effects on their finances wrought by two periods of monetary contraction, we have gained much insight into the financial operations of governments. However, there remains the crucial question of why fiscal authorities differed in the policy choices they made. Why did Alberta choose to eliminate its deficit solely via spending cuts while

Saskatchewan did so relying more heavily on tax increases? Why did Prince Edward Island decide in the late sixties to discontinue its earlier policy of large deficits and to vigorously attack its debt by running very large primary surpluses? Why during the same period and under similar economic conditions did Newfoundland continue to run up its debt? Why did the federal government not demand that the tight monetary policy that had pushed up their borrowing costs and led to (or, at minimum, worsened) the 1981 and 1990 recessions be changed? Failing that, why did it not respond to that policy by more vigorously restricting the growth in its debt-to-GDP ratio? Why did the federal government delay making this choice until the spring of 1995, when it chose the latter course of action, thereby committing Canadians to far larger tax increases and program cuts than would have been necessary had it reacted more quickly?

Trying to answer these sorts of questions takes us beyond the scope of this chapter and into the realm of political economy. Although some researchers have attempted to investigate such questions (see, for example, Laidler and Robson [1993] and Kneebone [1994]), much needs to be done. The statement made by Bruce and Purvis (1989) that "[in] our view, the unprecedented peacetime rise in government debt relative to output is an extraordinary fact of political economy that begs an explanation" remains true in 1995. As a starting point in such explanations, it is important to recognize that the public sector is not a monolith composed of a central bank and many fiscal authorities, working in harmony. Such cooperation has not been the hallmark of intergovernmental relations in Canada. Instead, the total government sector consists of separate government units with competing goals and agendas. In addition, within these smaller government units are agencies and individuals whose motivations vary widely. Recognition of such conflicts explains why governments respond differently to similar changes in their budgets and why the right mix of fiscal and monetary policy is so difficult to achieve. Understanding the political economy of monetary and fiscal policy making is crucial. If this understanding facilitated greater coordination of monetary and fiscal policy, the benefits would undoubtedly be huge.

Epilogue

During the two years since I wrote this chapter, much has happened and it is useful to place the arguments I made in the present context.

The theme of the paper was that the policies adopted by the Bank of Canada and those adopted by the federal and provincial governments combined to cause the large debts incurred by Canadian governments over the past twenty years. The Bank of Canada either did not understand the implications of tight monetary policy for government deficits and debt, or chose to put very little weight on this consideration relative to the weight it placed on the benefits of reducing inflation. The federal government, and to a lesser extent the provincial governments, were slow to understand the implications of tight money on their deficits. Thus, despite an era of strong economic growth during the 1980s that gave them the opportunity to react decisively, governments were slow to adjust their spending and tax regimes to effectively short-circuit the "vicious circle" of growing deficits and growing interest costs. The federal government did not respond in a serious way until the budget tabled in the spring of 1995 — after it became known that Canada's foreign denominated debt was to lose its triple-A credit rating.

During the past two years, two favourable economic changes have occurred that bear upon the issue of government deficits and debt. First, the economy has been growing strongly. This is partly the result of a substantial loosening of monetary policy by the Bank of Canada. Second, due to this looser monetary policy, tighter fiscal policy, the relative absence of constitutional crises and a favourable assessment of Canada's economic prospects by international investors, interest rates have fallen to thirty-year lows. In fact, Canadian interest rates are now significantly lower than those in the United States.

These events have combined to reduce the gap between the growth rate and the interest rate payable on government debt, making reductions in debt/GDP ratios easier to obtain. Add a concerted effort by most governments in Canada to cut their spending, and we have witnessed a dramatic improvement in government finances.

As of March 31, 1997, seven provinces (Prince Edward Island, Nova Scotia, New Brunswick, Manitoba, Saskatchewan, Alberta and British Columbia) reported budgetary surpluses. It is expected that the federal government will be in a surplus position by March 31, 1998. This means Ontario and Quebec will be the main sources of government deficit, but even these governments forecast a rapid reduction in their deficits. Within the next few years, then, Canadian governments are expected to have returned to levels of fiscal prudence not seen since the early 1970s — albeit with much higher tax rates and debt servicing costs. To return to the levels of taxation in existence in the seventies would require a substantial reduction in debt servicing costs, which in turn requires the pay-down of the debt accumulated during the past twenty years. As I noted two years ago, this means many years of budget surpluses. Nonetheless, evidence from the past two years suggests that the monetary stance of the Bank of Canada and the fiscal stance of the federal and provincial governments are such that we are on a path that *can* lead to tax cuts in the future.

Having described that hopeful scenario, it is useful to note some clouds on the horizon. The first comes from the most recent *Monetary Policy Report* issued by the Bank of Canada (November 1997). It states that the Bank projects the Canadian economy will reach capacity output towards the end of 1998. Since it is well known that monetary policy acts upon the economy only with a long lag, the implication of this statement is that we can expect the Bank of Canada to start moving short-term interest rates upward. Indeed, on the day the *Report* was issued, the Bank increased short-term rates by one-quarter of a percentage point. The purpose of this and future interest rate hikes is to discourage too rapid a rate of economic growth so a steady rate of inflation-free economic growth can be maintained. It is also designed to halt the recent fall in the value of the Canadian dollar; a fall that imports inflationary pressures and may encourage speculative behaviour. Clearly, this is a dangerous tightrope to walk since too high an increase in interest rates may stall economic growth with subsequent negative consequences on government deficits.

A second cloud is the strong U.S. economy. It is almost certain that the Federal Reserve Bank will need to increase U.S. interest rates in the near future. Despite the fact that Canadian interest rates have shown signs during the past two years of moving independently of U.S. rates, it is unlikely that Canadian interest rates would be able to avoid following suit. Again, this has negative consequences for government deficits.

A third and final cloud is the discussion among federal politicians about the appropriate way to spend the so-called "fiscal dividend." The concept of a fiscal dividend is a nebulous one. The government of Alberta identifies it as the interest payments saved by having paid-down its debt. Thus in the past three fiscal years, the government of Alberta has reduced its net debt by $3.6 billion and used the money it would otherwise have had to pay on that debt, some $400 million, to increase program spending. Federal politicians seem to be defining the fiscal dividend much less restrictively as funds that would have, had they not been spent, produced a budget surplus.

This is a dangerous approach because it presumes that the goal of the federal government should be to maintain a zero deficit. As I noted two years ago, one of the key "lessons" Canadian governments should have learned from their experience with deficits over the past twenty years is that a prudent fiscal plan is one that seeks to balance the budget over the business cycle. This requires budget surpluses during periods of strong economic growth to offset the impact upon the debt of the budget deficits that result during periods of slow economic growth. With Canada enjoying strong economic growth, the federal government should be running budget surpluses. What's more, given the magnitude of the federal government's debt problem, these should be large surpluses. In my opinion, there is no fiscal dividend for the federal government to spend, and there won't be one for a number of years.

The past two years have been witness to very favourable conditions for deficit and debt reduction. The combination of loose monetary policy and tight fiscal policy has caused the provinces and the federal government to get their deficits under control. I fear, however, that some governments — the federal government in particular — are relaxing the reins too soon. This is especially worrisome because it is occurring just as the Bank of Canada is preparing to tighten monetary policy. There is potential, therefore, for us to return to the days of tight money and loose fiscal policy: the same recipe that produced the current high debt load and high level of taxation.

References

Bank of Canada. Table G6. *Bank of Canada Review*. Various issues.

Boothe, P. 1993. Provincial Government Debt, Bond Ratings and the Availability of Credit. In *Deficits and Debt in the Canadian Economy*, edited by R. Harris. Policy Forum Study 29. Kingston: John Deutsch Institute for the Study of Economic Policy.

Bruce, N., and D. Purvis. 1989. Implementing a Prudent Fiscal Strategy over the Medium Term. In *Policy Forum on Macropolicy Issues in the Medium Term*, edited by J. Mintz and D. Purvis. Policy Forum Series 14. Kingston: John Deutsch Institute for the Study of Economic Policy.

Canada. Department of Finance. 1995. Budget Plan. Ottawa: Department of Finance, 27 February.

Dungan, P., and T. Wilson. 1985. Altering the Fiscal-Monetary Policy Mix: Credible Policies to Reduce the Federal Deficit. *Canadian Tax Journal* 33: 304–18.

Freedman, C. 1989. Monetary Policy in the 1990s: Lessons and Challenges. In *Monetary Policy Issues in the 1990s*. A symposium sponsored by the Federal Reserve Bank of Kansas City.

Ip, I.K. 1991. *Big Spenders: A Survey of Provincial Government Finances in Canada*. Policy Study 15. Toronto and Calgary: C.D. Howe Institute.

Kneebone, R. 1994. Deficits and Debt in Canada: Some Lessons from Recent History. *Canadian Public Policy* 20: 152–164.

Laidler, D., and W. Robson. 1993. *The Great Canadian Disinflation*. Policy Study 19. Toronto and Calgary: C.D. Howe Institute.

Maslove, A., M. Prince, and G. Doern. 1986. Federal and Provincial Budgeting. Vol. 41. *Report of the Royal Commission on the Economic Union and Development Prospects for Canada*. Toronto: University of Toronto Press.

Purvis, D. 1990. The Bank of Canada and the Pursuit of Price Stability. In *Zero Inflation: The Goal of Price Stability*, edited by R. Lipsey. Policy Study 8. Toronto and Calgary: C.D. Howe Institute.

Scarth, W. 1990. Fighting Inflation: Are the Costs of Getting to Zero Too High? In *Taking Aim: The Debate on Zero Inflation*, edited by R. York. Policy Study 10. Toronto and Calgary: C.D. Howe Institute.

Wilson, T., P. Dungan, and S. Murphy. 1994. The Sources of the Recession in Canada: 1989–1992. *Canadian Business Economics* 2, no. 2: 3–15.

4

Recent Canadian Monetary Policy: Deficit and Debt Implications

M.C. McCracken

What would have happened to unemployment, output and Canada's national debt if the Bank of Canada had followed a different monetary policy during the late eighties? If interest rates had not been raised so dramatically from 1989 to 1991, the recession of the early nineties would probably have been less severe. To quantify the impacts of monetary policy decisions on the Canadian economy, Michael McCracken, Canada's foremost private sector economic forecaster, uses the Informetrica model of the economy to calculate how the Canadian economy would have performed if the Bank of Canada had followed a policy of keeping interest rates in line with those in the U.S. Michael McCracken estimates that faster economic growth would have substantially reduced unemployment and the private capital stock would have been $16 billion greater by the end of 1995. In addition, Canada's debt burden would have fallen slightly, instead of rising substantially.

The normal pattern has been for Canada's real interest rates to follow those of the United States closely, with only minor deviations for a few months at a time. However, at the end of 1988, the Bank of Canada adopted an independent monetary policy, raising interest

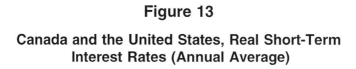

Figure 13

**Canada and the United States, Real Short-Term
Interest Rates (Annual Average)**

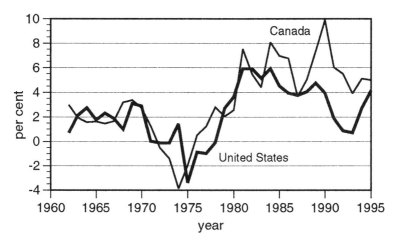

rates in a period in which U.S. rates were fairly stable. The gap
between U.S. and Canadian real interest rates widened, compared to
earlier periods, and this policy, combined with other factors, pushed
the Canadian economy into recession. Unemployment rose, as did
the exchange rate.

Between 1989 and 1995, Canada's monetary policy deviated substantially from U.S. monetary policy. This deviation can be most
easily seen by comparing real interest rates (nominal interest rates
less the rate of inflation) in the two countries over the last thirty years
(see Figure 13).

With increases in demand in 1987–88, the Bank of Canada had
been concerned about its objective of price stability. In early 1988,
it raised interest rates in line with U.S. rates (both countries had
lowered interest rates in the aftermath of the stock market collapse
in October 1987). The Bank maintained a differential between Canadian and U.S. nominal interest rates of about 175 basis points.

These moves were deemed insufficient to slow the economy and
raise unemployment, and, in 1989, the Bank increased restraint,
raising short-term interest rates by about 2.5 percentage points (250
basis points). The differential with U.S. interest rates rose to roughly
300 basis points (see Figure 14). This strategy suppressed activity in

Figure 14

Canada and the United States, Short-Term Interest Rates (Monthly Values)

the areas of housing, consumer durables and investment, especially in Ontario.

In 1990, Canadian short-term interest rates were raised again (to an average of about 13 per cent), while U.S. rates declined by 90 basis points. The differential widened to about 470 basis points. By this time, economic growth had stopped in most regions, and the unemployment rate had begun to rise.

Monetary restraint continued in 1991, with a differential between Canadian and U.S. interest rates of about 250 basis points. At the same time, the Bank of Canada, in conjunction with the Department of Finance, announced long-term targets for price stability. The targets for the Consumer Price Index (CPI) were 3 per cent by the end of 1992, 2.5 per cent by mid-1994, 2 per cent by the end of 1995, and "clearly less" than 2 per cent in the long term.

Economic growth declined in the first quarter of 1991, snapped back in the second quarter, with the uncertainty about the Gulf War removed, and essentially levelled off for the rest of the year. By the end of 1991, the national unemployment rate was 10.4 per cent.

In 1992, despite very low inflation rates and the higher unemployment rate, the Bank of Canada continued its policy of monetary restraint, only slowly reducing interest rates through August 1992.

With downward pressure on the Canadian dollar in September 1992, the Bank increased interest rates markedly to prevent a devaluation of the dollar, further weakening the economy. The unemployment rate at the end of 1992 was 11.5 per cent.

From 1993 to 1995, economic recovery was under way, with easing of nominal interest rates, although real interest rates remained high. The pace of recovery was modest, particularly given the depth and length of the recession. The unemployment rate declined due to both falling participation rates of the labour force and increased employment. The exchange rate declined through 1995, helping the recovery by increasing exports and reducing imports.

While most analysts presume that the main reason behind the adoption of this restrictive monetary policy between 1989 and 1995 was to decrease inflation by creating high unemployment and enhancing the dollar's value, there are other possible explanations. For example, the Bank may have wanted to mitigate any second-round inflationary effects of introducing the Goods and Services Tax (GST) at the beginning of 1991. There was concern in some circles that this new tax might trigger a jump in inflation. An initially higher CPI may have kindled demands for higher wages, which, in turn, would have raised labour costs, pushed up prices and driven up inflation. One way of minimizing this risk was to ensure a sluggish economy at the time the GST was introduced. On January 1, 1991, the government introduced the GST with few visible shocks to the rate of inflation and with a single adjustment to the CPI of 1 to 1.5 per cent.

An alternative hypothesis is that the higher interest rates, and particularly the rising value of the dollar, were the result of an "implicit agreement" between Canada and the United States that required a higher Canadian dollar as part of the Free Trade Agreement, introduced in 1989. This explanation is supported by the concerns expressed in 1986 by U.S. congressmen and other officials that the Canadian dollar was "too competitive." Not surprisingly, the existence of any such agreement has, to date, been vehemently denied by all parties. In any case, high interest rates and the high value of the Canadian dollar seem to have led to overcautiousness on the part of Canadian business, allowing U.S. business, backed by a more accommodating monetary policy, to move first and most advantageously to take advantage of the expanded market opportunities and options to rationalize production.

The restrictive monetary policy did reduce the rate of inflation, as measured by changes in the CPI (see Figure 15). At the end of 1992,

Figure 15

**CPI Less Food, Energy and Indirect Taxes,
and Bank of Canada CPI Target Range
(Monthly, Year-Over-Year Change)**

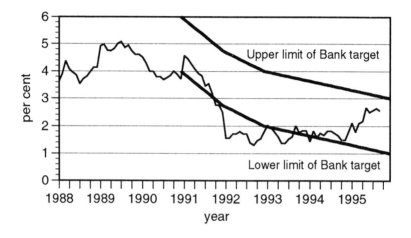

inflation was 2.1 per cent, almost at the bottom of the target range
(2 to 4 per cent). And the CPI remained at or below the bottom of
the target range, even excluding the effects of indirect tax cuts on
cigarettes in 1994.

However, this policy of high interest rates has accomplished its
objective at great cost. The Canadian economy suffered severe hard-
ship from 1989 through 1995, performing very poorly compared to
the economies of other G-7 countries, and generating a rise in the
unemployment rate to a peak of 11.9 per cent in November 1992.
Since then, unemployment has improved slowly, with the rate averaging 11.2 per cent in 1993, 10.4 per cent in 1994 and 9.5 per cent
in 1995.

High real interest rates relative to economic growth have forced
both federal and provincial governments to impose further fiscal
restraint to keep deficits from exploding and the rise in the debt ratios
from accelerating. The decline in business investment, particularly
in nonresidential structures, is greater than that in the 1981–82 recession. As well, in the residential construction sector, housing starts
fell from almost 246,000 in 1987 to about 156,000 in 1991. After a

brief and modest recovery in 1992 and 1993, housing starts declined again in 1994 and 1995. The estimated number of starts for 1995 (112,000) is the lowest since 1960 and is well below the level of growth in the number of households.

Charting an Alternative Path

In this paper, we address the question, What would have happened if Canadian interest rates had remained in line with U.S. rates between 1989 and 1995? The technique for examining such an alternative is to use an econometric model of the Canadian economy, in which specific assumptions can be changed and compared to a historical track of the economy. (The model used here is TIM, the Informetrica model.) The emphasis is on the difference between the two paths, with the net result of the policy changes being represented by the difference between, for example, the levels of GDP in the alternative policy case and in the base case.

The use of an econometric model ensures that the assumptions underlying a different policy are made explicit. Although journalists can generate, on a daily basis, grand assertions about inflation, unemployment and prospects for economic growth, it is unclear how these predictions are made, how important specific assumptions are, and, indeed, whether these predictions "add up" in an accounting sense. In an explicit econometric model, the results are replicable, and the model ensures consistency with accounting identities as well as with economic theory. The user of the model is forced to consider whether the results conform with common sense, to delineate each influence and to judge the net effects.[1]

The development of an alternative scenario is not merely a mechanical exercise. If Canada had pursued a different monetary policy from 1989 to 1995, it is likely that the exchange rate would not have increased to the same degree, and the government may not have introduced other strategies that have had adverse effects on economic activity. In particular, higher interest rates have made balancing both federal and provincial budgets difficult. In turn, both the federal and the provincial governments pursued more restrictive fiscal policies during this period.

Lower interest rates might have demanded less fiscal restraint, which would have led to fewer job losses and more economic growth. This assumption about fiscal policy is contentious; some analysts argue that greater, rather than less, fiscal restraint would have been needed, given a less restrictive monetary policy. If lower inflation through the creation of higher unemployment was the objective, then tighter fiscal policy would have had to substitute for monetary restraint. Other approaches to reducing inflation, through productivity increases, would have been consistent with a looser fiscal policy. Given the different possibilities, we have chosen to separate the effects of the assumptions about fiscal policy from assumptions about monetary policy and exchange rate consequences. The result is two separate scenarios — Monetary Reasonableness (MR) with unchanged fiscal policy and Monetary Reasonableness with Fiscal Easing (MR + FE).

The definition of "unchanged" fiscal policy could take a number of forms:

1. Maintaining the level of the primary balance (taxes minus program expenditure) that was reached in 1988 through 1995 in nominal terms or in real terms.

2. Maintaining the rates of taxation and the real expenditures per capita at their 1988 levels.

3. Maintaining the primary balance each year at its actual level (the base case).

4. Maintaining the institutional rules, rates of taxation and per-capita real spending at their actual levels for both the alternative scenario and the base case.

The first two rules assume that all fiscal moves after 1988 were driven by monetary policy considerations. Adoption of this interpretation means that, if monetary policy had been easier, we would have seen much more fiscal easing than actually occurred. The last two rules essentially minimize the interdependencies between monetary and fiscal policies.

For one of the scenarios or alternative paths, we have chosen to maintain the same rules and rates as those in the base case over the period (Option 4). This path focuses the analysis primarily on those consequences directly linked to monetary policy. The rules governing the UI fund remain; thus, contribution rates decline when the fund's balance improves.

A second scenario or alternative path (MR + FE) increases expenditures or reduces taxes to ease some of the strain that governments experienced in the base case. The amount and timing of the fiscal easing is linked to apparent deviations in behaviour by governments, represented by the historical relationships in the model. Most of the easing takes place after 1992. This fiscal shock is much smaller than the shock that would have occurred if fiscal policy had been maintained at 1988 levels (Option 1 and Option 2).

In the above scenario, we:

- increase federal transfers to provincial governments,
- increase provincial, municipal and hospital spending on goods and services while increasing transfers from the provinces to accommodate this increased spending and
- eliminate the federal wage freeze.

This particular package reverses some of the federal restraint in areas in which the federal government had cited "fiscal need" to justify the cuts. Provincial fiscal balances improve from larger federal transfers. It is assumed that the provinces maintain their spending in line with demographic needs, while ensuring that the other levels of government for which they are responsible meet the underlying needs. These projections are based on estimates of the lower levels of spending recently seen in a number of areas as a result of fiscal restraint.

In the remainder of the paper, we first discuss the channels through which interest rates affect the Canadian economy. Then, using an alternative policy for the period from 1989 to 1995, we illustrate the quantitative implications of lower interest rates. We also consider the effects of federal and provincial governments using the additional fiscal freedom that results from lower interest rates to follow a less restrictive fiscal policy.

Less restrictive monetary and fiscal policies would have substantially improved the economic outlook over these years. The economy would have become stronger, with less unemployment. The fiscal position of governments would have been improved. Business investment would have been more vibrant. External trade would have made a larger contribution to the Canadian economy and lessened the build-up of net foreign debt. What may be surprising to some is that inflation during this period would have been only marginally higher.

Effects of Interest Rate Changes

Interest rates influence the Canadian economy through a number of channels; in particular, they affect those sectors that are traditionally financed by debt and are discretionary purchases, such as business investment, housing and consumer durables. Higher interest rates lead to delays and cancellations of spending plans in these areas of the private sector. In addition, they directly raise regulated prices in domestically oriented industries that require large amounts of capital, such as electric power, transportation and communications, by increasing the interest payments on these industries' debt. These higher prices erode real incomes of consumers by pushing up prices for almost all goods and services.

Higher rates of interest also increase interest payments on outstanding government debt, often leading governments to curtail expenditures or raise taxes. If governments apply deficit financing to the higher interest payments, they incur greater debt and even higher interest payments in subsequent periods. When interest rates exceed the growth rate of the economy, an unstable situation can develop, unless governments run large primary surpluses.

Of course, someone receives the higher interest income associated with higher interest rates. The "creditors" in society (those with net financial assets) must receive more income, while the "debtors" (those with net financial liabilities) will direct greater proportions of their income to interest payments. This redistribution of income probably serves to reduce real economic activity, since the income of those with a higher propensity to save increases, while the discretionary income of debtors, who probably have a lower propensity to save, decreases. It is likely that the debtors are also poorer than the creditors; thus, income is redistributed in the direction opposite to that of many other government policies.

Effects of Exchange Rate Changes

In an economy with a flexible exchange rate, higher interest rates usually lead to an increase in the value of the currency. Exchange rates move for a number of reasons, including interest rate shocks, major changes in the flow of foreign direct investment or fluctuations in commodity prices that affect the current account balance.

The most direct result of a jump in the exchange rate is the reduction of revenue in Canadian dollars for those exports with prices that are set in world markets. It is not that the world price changes; rather, its conversion into Canadian dollars produces a lower yield.

Exporting thus becomes less profitable and less attractive. Investors may postpone or cancel projects in the resource sectors, and companies in the export sector may go bankrupt.

At the same time, Canadians can buy goods and services supplied internationally more cheaply. These lower import prices, while beneficial to consumers, put substantial pressure on Canadian industries competing with imports, squeezing profit margins and diminishing their financial incentives to expand. The net consequence of a higher exchange rate is to dampen real economic growth and to lower prices directly through the imported goods component of the CPI and indirectly through the increased pressure on Canadian business.

Less real economic activity also results in higher unemployment, which increases downward pressure on wage rates in Canada. The reduced compensation lowers real incomes of consumers, raises unemployment and welfare rolls, and further suppresses investment in business. Although the lower wage costs will eventually translate into improved international competitiveness, these improvements take years to develop, and the net consequences do not offset the adverse effects on competitiveness of the initial rise in value of the currency.

Effects on Government Balances

Higher interest rates and a rising currency value also have negative implications for the fiscal balances of governments. Government revenues decrease as the tax base shrinks, due to a weaker real economy, less inflation, reduced wage income and lower corporate profits. Expenditures on social assistance and UI increase. Since most governments are net debtors, interest payments on debt rise, both on any new financing and on the rollover of existing debt.

An Alternative Policy

What would have happened if the Bank of Canada had not adopted a much more restrictive policy in 1989, but rather had maintained the somewhat restrictive policy in place between 1981 and 1988?

For the purposes of this study, we have created the MR policy. The objective of the MR policy is to maintain the differential between Canadian and U.S. real short-term interest rates from 1989 to 1995 at the average recorded in the previous eight years (83 basis points). Since the Canadian and U.S. economies would likely show different inflation rates, we have chosen to define this differential in real terms. That is, we subtract the rate of inflation from the nominal

Figure 16

Impact on Short- and Long-Term Real Interest Rates
(MR Case Less Actual)

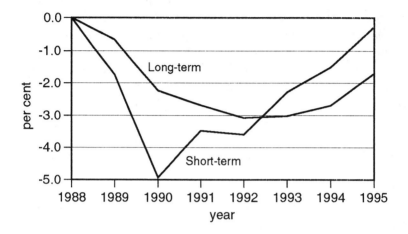

short-term interest rate for each country to calculate the alternative policy path.

As a consequence, real short-term interest rates are substantially lower throughout the period, by about 1.7 percentage points in 1989, 4.9 percentage points in 1990, about 3.6 percentage points in 1991 and 1992, 2.4 and 1.4 percentage points in 1993 and 1994, and only 0.3 percentage points in 1995 (see Figure 16). Real long-term interest rates are also lower, by almost 3 percentage points in 1991 to 1994. Nominal interest rates decline somewhat less, because inflation is slightly higher.

In this environment, the Canadian exchange rate does not rise between 1989 and 1992. We have allowed the exchange rate to adjust to the lower interest rates and to other changes over the period, based on the equation in the model. By 1992, the exchange rate is about U.S.$.09 lower, or about U.S.$.737 per Canadian dollar, compared to the observed average of U.S.$.827. By 1995, the dollar is only $.055 lower in nominal terms (about U.S.$.68), and the real exchange rate is only $.016 lower than in the base case. In the combined case, with the MR + FE policy, there is little difference in the patterns of the interest and exchange rates (see Figure 17).

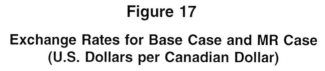

Figure 17

Exchange Rates for Base Case and MR Case
(U.S. Dollars per Canadian Dollar)

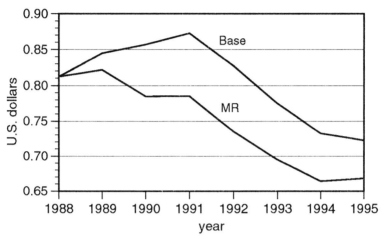

The MR scenario, without a strong dose of monetary restraint, exhibits higher real output in each year from 1989 to 1995. Unemployment is lower, productivity is higher and corporate profits improve. The capital stock at the end of the period is also larger, leaving a positive real legacy. Governments have smaller deficits, reflecting the lower interest payments, higher revenues and lower welfare payments. The only economic measure that does not improve is the rate of inflation, with annual CPI increases higher by 0.8 to 2.5 per cent in the first few years, although the inflation rate is actually lower from 1994.

National employment improves each year, starting at 61,000 jobs in 1989, rising to 236,300 jobs in 1992 and continuing above levels of the base case by well over 100,000 jobs through 1995. With the MR + FE case, employment shows greater improvements, ending up more than 400,000 above base levels in 1995.

The total output of goods and services is higher in all years. In the MR scenario, the maximum percentage increase occurs in 1991, when GDP is higher by 2.5 per cent or $13.9 billion (in 1986 constant dollar terms). In the MR + FE case, GDP is almost 3 per cent higher in 1994, at $17.7 billion (see Figure 18).

Figure 18

Impact on GDP
(Per Cent of Base Case)

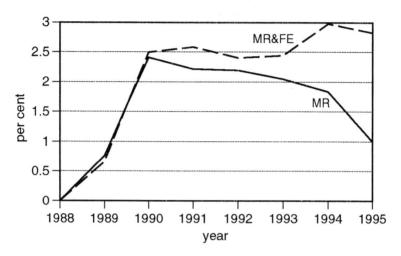

With lower interest rates and a lower dollar, almost all components of demand are stronger. In particular, business investment strengthens throughout the period, with the level about 4 per cent higher between 1992 and 1994, reflecting a greater number of housing starts, more nonresidential construction (up 7 per cent) and more investment in machinery and equipment. The lower dollar also encourages exports to grow.

With the MR + FE policy, the assumption that governments do not have to make severe cut-backs means that higher levels of both government and consumer expenditure strengthen the GDP.

Lower interest rates and an improved current account balance also reduce interest payments to nonresidents. As a result, Gross National Income (income accruing to Canadians) improves slightly more than Gross Domestic Income (income generated within Canada's borders) by an additional 0.5 per cent from 1992 in both the alternative cases.

The increase in exports and improved domestic activity are particularly helpful to manufacturing, increasing its real GDP by more than 7 per cent by 1992. The capital stock is increased over the entire period, through higher levels of business investment. At the end of 1995, the capital stock is 1.27 per cent higher. When we use the MR

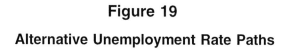

Figure 19

Alternative Unemployment Rate Paths

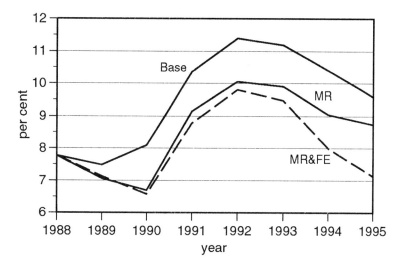

+ FE alternative, capital stock is slightly higher, at 1.35 per cent by 1995.

As a consequence of increased production, employment is higher by 1.8 per cent, or 236,000 jobs, in 1992 in the MR case. Canada could not have remained untouched by U.S. or worldwide recessions, but a reasonable monetary policy would have reduced their effects on Canada. The unemployment rate is lower throughout the period (see Figure 19); an average decrease of 1.5 percentage points in 1992 is sufficient to reduce the unemployment rate to about 10 per cent, from its 11.4 per cent average for 1992. In the MR + FE case, employment increases by 406,000 jobs or 3 per cent by 1995, and the unemployment rate drops by 2.5 percentage points from the average of 9.5 per cent in 1995.

With lower unemployment and a lower exchange rate, wages and prices are higher throughout the period. Reduced UI premiums help contain total labour compensation, and higher productivity contributes to an increase in unit labour costs of about 5.8 per cent by 1992, even though the CPI level is 6.2 per cent higher. Much of the upward pressure on prices is attributable to higher import prices as a result of a drop in the exchange rate of about 12 per cent. In later years, there is less of a decline in the dollar's value (8 per cent by 1995),

Figure 20

Alternative Inflation Paths

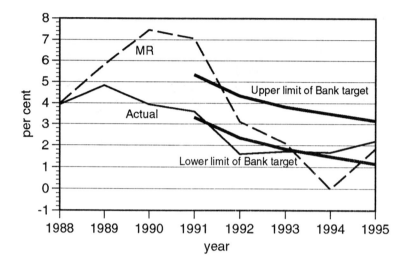

and inflation shrinks below the base case rates evident in 1994 and 1995.

Although the CPI level is higher throughout the period, the increase in the rate of inflation (measured as the percentage change in the CPI) grows through 1990 with the falling dollar and then slows to less than 1 per cent in 1993. Thus, the inflation rate in 1992 would be 3.1 per cent, which is well within the Bank of Canada's target range of 2 to 4 per cent for this year, instead of 1.6 per cent (see Figure 20). There is little difference in the path of inflation predicted by the MR + FE policy, since we did not choose to loosen fiscal reins with measures that influence prices (e.g., indirect tax reductions or increases in subsidies).

Real disposable income per capita is slightly reduced in the MR scenario, as a result of much lower interest income and higher consumer prices. (It should be recalled that the consumer sector is a net creditor.) A reduction in the personal savings rate (particularly reflecting lower interest receipts on pensions and registered retirement savings plans) and lower interest on consumer debt are sufficient to allow a modest expansion in consumer expenditure. (The reduction in real disposable income could be offset by lower personal income

Figure 21

Impact of Federal, PLH* and Pension Fund Balances (MR Case Less Base Case)

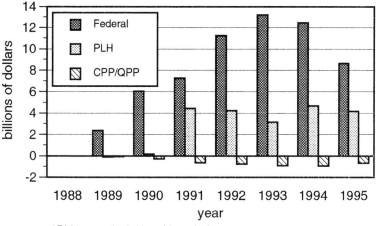

*PLH - provincial local hospital

taxes, given the improved fiscal position of governments.) In the MR + FE case, the net effect on real disposable income per capita disappears by 1995.

Corporate profits were devastated between 1989 and 1992. The MR policy produces lower interest rates, a lower dollar and improved real performance, which combine to improve corporate profits substantially over this period. These improvements prompt the increased investment discussed earlier and provide a stronger revenue base for the federal and provincial income tax systems. Although corporate profits in 1995 are lower, higher capital cost allowances, as a result of increased investment in previous years, improve corporate cash flow. Indeed, after-tax corporate cash flow is higher by $0.7 billion or 0.9 per cent in 1995 in the MR case, compared to the base case.

Government Balances

The fiscal position of governments, particularly at the federal level, improves in all years (see Figure 21). The federal balance benefits from higher revenues, lower shared-cost expenditures on social assistance and lower UI benefits. With lower UI benefits and higher contributions, the balance of the fund improves. This improvement

Figure 22

Federal Debt-to-GDP Ratio

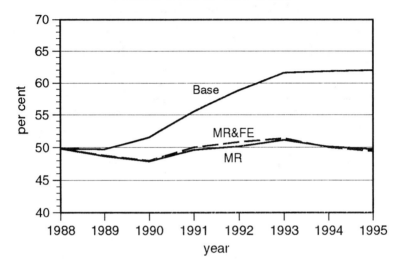

allows the government to set a lower contribution rate in subsequent years while maintaining the UI fund's balance.

Provincial, local and hospital balances improve only modestly, since the higher price level raises nominal expenditures on goods and services and indexed transfer payments. Interest payments are lower. Revenues improve, but their tax share of corporate profits is much lower than at the federal level, limiting the degree of improvement from this source.

For the public pension system, lower interest income from lower interest rates and higher pension plan benefits from higher inflation offset the increase in contributions from more people being employed. The net effect is a modest worsening in the pension fund balance.

Much of policy has focused on reducing the ratio of federal government borrowing to GDP. Improved federal fiscal balances result in less borrowing by the federal government. At the same time, a larger economy resulting from more people working increases the denominator in this ratio. In the MR case, the federal government's debt-to-GDP ratio is lowered by almost 12.5 per cent by the end of 1995 (see Figure 22). Even when some of the improved balances are used in the scenario, it is still possible to lower the debt-to-GDP ratio.

Indeed, the federal ratio improves even more in the MR + FE case, since the increased activity from Provincial Local Hospital (PLH) spending raises GDP and federal revenue, both of which lower the federal debt-to-GDP ratio. In addition, the debt ratio for all governments shows a greater decline, with the increased growth improving the denominator (GDP) by more than the increase in the numerator due to slightly larger deficits over the period.

It is important to note that the MR policy would have stabilized the federal debt-to-GDP ratio at 1988 levels. Instead, a substantial increase actually occurred between 1988 and 1995.

Summary

The Bank of Canada followed a restrictive monetary policy between 1989 and 1995, in pursuit of zero inflation. This study estimates the economic costs in terms of lost jobs and output that are directly attributable to higher interest rates and the associated increase in the exchange rate, independent of the consequences of the more restrictive fiscal policy, weaker world markets, the Free Trade Agreement, the GST, or other federal or provincial policies.

The "counterfactual" path of the economy is predicted by assuming a less restrictive monetary policy (lower real interest rates) and a lower exchange rate during this period, while holding other assumptions unchanged. By comparing the counterfactual case with the actual track of the economy over this period, the lost "opportunity" is revealed.

The benefits of the MR policy include higher output, more employment, improved government balances, enhanced exports and higher productivity. Although the inflation rate is slightly higher (averaging less than 1 per cent per year), from 1992, it remains within the target range promulgated by the Bank of Canada and the Department of Finance in early 1991.

By 1992, GDP is 2 per cent higher, there are 206,630 more jobs and the unemployment rate is 1.3 per cent lower. Government balances improve throughout the period, with a lower deficit for all governments. Debt-to-GDP ratios stabilize.

To translate the notion of a less restrictive monetary policy into quantitative terms, short-term real interest rates are assumed to be lower by 173 basis points (or 1.73 percentage points) in 1989, 493 points in 1990, 348 points in 1991 and 362 points in 1992. From 1993, the interest rate reductions are smaller: 236 basis points in 1993, 144 points in 1994 and 30 points in 1995. The choice of these reductions is based on maintaining Canadian and U.S. real interest rates at the average differential that prevailed between 1981 and 1988. (The use of the term "less restrictive" is intentional. Monetary policy in the United States has also been judged to be restrictive over much of this period.)

The exchange rate for the Canadian dollar is lower, as a result of the lower interest rates and other economic changes: U.S.$.0227 in 1989, U.S.$.0724 in 1990, U.S.$.0887 in 1991 and U.S.$.0903 in 1992. After 1992, the effects are smaller: the decrease is U.S.$.081 in 1993, U.S. $.0676 in 1994 and U.S.$.0546 in 1995.

Even better economic performance would have been possible if governments had "shared" some of their fiscal improvements through fiscal easing. Although many possible fiscal packages are conceivable, we assumed, for illustrative purposes, that the federal government did not freeze its employees' wages or cut back on transfers to the provinces under Established Programs Financing. At the same time, we assume that provinces, municipalities and hospitals do not cut back in their basic spending, especially from 1993 to 1995.

The fiscal changes alone by 1995 add 1.8 per cent to output and lower the unemployment rate by 1.6 per cent, with few effects on the inflation rate. Fiscal positions of governments are still substantially improved relative to the base case, and debt ratios are even lower.

The essential message of these simulations is that the Canadian economy could have followed a different path from 1989 to 1995, which would have kept more people working, business investment higher and fiscal positions of governments under less strain. The governor of the Bank of Canada, with the concurrence of the minister of finance, chose a restrictive monetary policy, with the benefit of a reduction of less than one percentage point in inflation, at the expense of higher unemployment, lower output and large increases in debt ratios.

The trade-off seems to have been an expensive one, particularly if we include some of the qualitative elements, such as soured federal-provincial relations, rising despair among some groups and the loss of confidence by citizens in their governments. To date, there has been no evidence of the benefits from lower inflation that offset the economic and social costs associated with the restrictive policies.

5

The Debt and Canada's Social Programs

Gideon Rosenbluth

———————

When government deficits are so large, can Canada "afford" its social programs? Gideon Rosenbluth, a past president of the Canadian Economics Association, argues that by any meaningful measure, Canadians are now richer than they were when our social programs were first introduced. He notes that government revenues increase when the economy grows and that expenditures on transfer programs, such as UI or social assistance, fall with growth. Consequently, the key issue in getting the deficit under control is to raise the level of economic activity and reduce unemployment. Since lower interest rates would stimulate the economy by encouraging consumer expenditure, business investment and exports, and also reduce the cost of servicing the national debt, Gideon Rosenbluth argues that the Bank of Canada should make use of its control over interest rates to stimulate growth and reduce the deficit.

Since about 1975 federal and provincial governments have restricted expenditure on social programs. They have claimed that these restrictions have been necessary in order to reduce government deficits and to stave off a disastrous financial crisis. We have been told that we must "get our fiscal house in order" and that we can no longer afford the luxury of social programs at the standards that prevailed twenty-two years ago.

Figure 23

Real GDP and GNP per Head At 1986 Prices (Consumer Price Index)

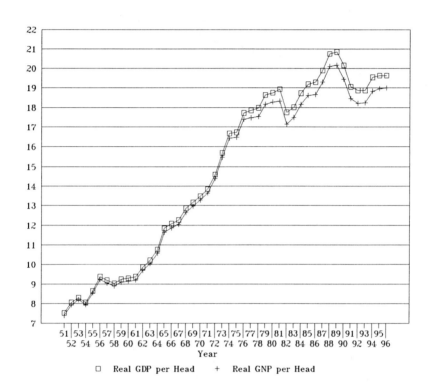

This paper explains why this view is mistaken. Economic analysis of the relevant facts leaves no doubt that as a means of reducing government debt in relation to the size of the economy, restricting expenditure on social services, health and education is neither efficient nor equitable. The efficient and equitable way to reduce the debt-to-income ratio is to cut interest rates and to add other government measures that will combat unemployment and raise the growth rate of the economy.

Is the Economy Worse Off than Before?

If we say that we can no longer afford something, we suggest that our economy produces less income for us than it did before. Figure

23 investigates whether this statement is true. The top graph measures real GDP per head of population. Gross domestic product is the value of all goods and services produced by the economy in a year. "Real" means we have eliminated the effect of price changes on these values. The figure shows that in the eighties and nineties real GDP per head began to rise and fall with the business cycle. But if we compare equivalent points in the business cycle, peak to peak or trough to trough, we continue to see an upward trend.[1] Thus, in terms of what the economy produces, we can certainly afford social programs in the nineties at the level of those in the seventies or early eighties.

However, some of our economic output yields income, not for Canadian residents, but for foreign owners and creditors of Canadian businesses, as well as for foreign creditors of Canadian governments, about whom we hear so much nowadays. The lower line on the chart, which shows real GNP per head, subtracts this income accruing to foreigners and adds income paid to Canadians (including businesses and governments) from their involvement in foreign businesses and from loans to foreigners. Although the increase is smaller, and although we see again the stalled recovery in 1995 and 1996, the basic story is the same. In terms of real income received by residents (which includes governments), we were on average better off in 1993 than in 1982 or 1975, and better off in 1994–96 than at any time before 1987.[2]

We conclude that residents of Canada have more real income per person now than they had before, even after payment of interest on the government debts, about which everyone complains. So it is unreasonable to claim that we can no longer afford services we could afford in the seventies.

This conclusion is reinforced if we consider that the rise in income per head took place in the face of rising unemployment, and therefore in the face of a widening gap between the economy's actual output and income, and the output and income it would yield if unemployment were reduced. The top line in Figure 24 indicates that unemployment rates have shown a strong upward trend over successive cycles and have remained high in the current recovery. The graph again makes it clear that the recovery stalled in 1996, but our estimate for 1997 (based on incomplete monthly figures) suggests that business improved in 1997.

If our federal and provincial governments had followed policies that reduce unemployment instead of policies that increase unem-

Figure 24

Ratios of Deficit to GDP and Unemployment Rate

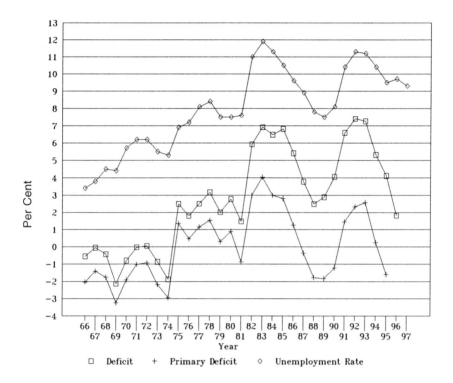

ployment, the economy would have had even greater scope to maintain and enhance social services. Instead, these governments have been creating unemployment and saying, in effect: We could afford unemployment benefits when there were fewer unemployed, and we could afford social services and welfare payments when there were fewer people needing them. In other words, the greater the need, the less we are prepared to help.

How is it possible for the economy to be better off, when unemployment rates are up? The upward trend of real GDP per head is the product of rising trends of real GDP per employed person, largely due to advancements in technology, and employment per head of population. The increase in this latter category reflects the entry of women into the labour force in large numbers. As women have

Table 6
Federal Direct Debt as a Proportion of GNP
(Gross Debt Less Sinking Funds)

Period	Average Debt-to-GNP Ratio (Per Cent)
1932–39	75
1940–46	110
1947–55	85
1988–93	56

Sources: M.C. Urquhart et al. *Historical Statistics of Canada*; Department of Finance, *Economic and Fiscal Reference Tables*.

entered the labour force, both the number of employed and the number of unemployed have increased in relation to the total population.

The standard argument for the need to reduce government deficits ignores the increasing productiveness of the economy and instead, in its least objectionable version, appeals to statistics such as those in Figure 25.

The Debt-to-GDP Ratio

Figure 25 shows the total net debt of all levels of Canadian government — federal, provincial and local. Net debt is the amount these governments owe minus the amount owed to them. Net debt is measured here as a proportion of the GDP. There are many different definitions and measurements of government debt, but, fortunately, this one has been found acceptable and relevant both by those economists who think we have a debt crisis and by those who do not.[3]

From this figure, we see that government debt was falling until 1974, when it reached a low of just under 5 per cent of GDP. It rose gradually to just over 10 per cent of GDP in 1981, and then it increased dramatically, exceeding 60 per cent in 1993. Note the countercyclical pattern: the debt rose most quickly during recessions and declined twice in the eighties, at the peaks of our booms.

Table 6 puts this pattern into a wider historical context. While present debt levels seem high, they are in fact low, compared with the debt levels of the thirties, forties and early fifties, the period that

Figure 25

Government Sector Net Debt
Per Cent of GDP

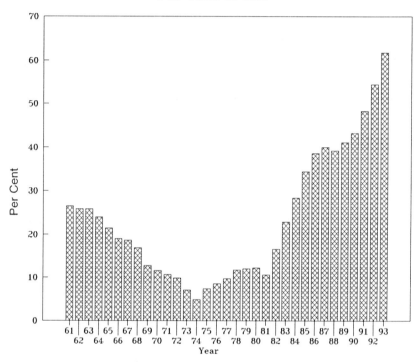

includes both the Great Depression and World War II. By ignoring history, the current trend of the debt-to-GDP ratio can be made to look vaguely threatening. We are urged to believe that unless the rise in this ratio is stopped at once, nobody will lend money to our governments or lenders will charge extortionate rates of interest, the burden of interest payments on the taxpayer will become unbearable and similar stories. The federal government's 1994 discussion papers (Government of Canada 1994) suggest these ideas, as do the speeches of our ministers and of the governor of the Bank of Canada.

We can agree that in the long run this growth has to be stopped, though not for the "reasons" outlined above. In the long run, a high debt ratio means a high level of government interest payments financed from taxes, and we can imagine the growth of the debt ratio pushing tax rates to levels where they begin to impede the operation of the economy. Such a possibility is far in the future, though Conservative, Liberal, and Reform politicians would have us believe it is already here. Nevertheless, we can agree that the rise in this debt ratio should be stopped. The question is *how*? Appendix A presents the mathematics that we need to answer this question.

First of all, let's note that to reduce the debt-to-GDP ratio, it is not necessary to reduce the debt. We can reduce the ratio by slowing down the growth rate of the debt or by speeding up the growth rate of the GDP. We refer here to *proportionate* growth rates, that is, growth rates expressed as a percentage per year.

How do we slow down the growth of debt? The amount by which government debt rises each year is the government deficit — that is, the difference between expenditure and revenue for the year. So, the proportionate growth rate of debt is the ratio of deficit to debt.

To see how we can reduce this ratio, we have to look at the two parts into which the deficit is conventionally divided. One is the net interest payments on the outstanding debt (interest paid by governments less interest received), and the other is the rest of the deficit, called the "primary deficit." It consists of expenditures other than debt interest (often called "program expenditures"), minus revenues other than interest receipts.[4]

Hence, the ratio of deficit to debt is the sum of two parts: the ratio of primary deficit to debt, and the ratio of interest payments to debt. The ratio of interest payments to debt is, of course, the rate of interest that governments are paying on their debt.

To sum it all up, then, policies that reduce the growth of the debt-to-GDP ratio must either reduce the primary deficit, or lower interest rates, or raise the growth rate of GDP, or achieve some combination of these outcomes.

Let's deal with the primary deficit first.

Reducing the Primary Deficit

Reducing the primary deficit is the only route contemplated by the federal and provincial deficit slayers. Cutting expenditure programs and raising tax rates are the only ways they see to reduce the primary deficit, and they consider raising tax rates taboo. That leaves no alternatives to cutting expenditures. This approach follows from the Conservative/Liberal view that the deficits are due to the "extravagance" of earlier governments.

However, every first-year economics student knows that there is another way primary deficits are caused, and therefore another way to reduce them: through the operation of the so-called automatic stabilizers of the economy.

Most tax revenue is linked, in one way or another, to the level of economic activity. For example, in 1994, income tax accounted for 51 per cent of federal revenues, taxes on the purchase of goods and services constituted 21 per cent and contributions to UI made up 14 per cent. So, without changing tax rates or any of the rules governing taxes, revenues increase as business improves and unemployment declines, and they fall as economic activity declines and unemployment increases.

On the other hand, some major expenditures increase when unemployment rises and decrease when it falls, without any change in the programs or rules governing these expenditures. For example, between 1989 and 1992, when the unemployment rate rose from 7.5 to 11.3 per cent and real GDP per head fell by nearly 10 per cent, UI benefit payments rose from $11.4 billion to $18.6 billion, while provincial and municipal welfare payments rose from $7.4 billion to $13.1 billion. The same countercyclical pattern applies to health expenditures (since poverty is bad for your health), to social service expenditures and even to education expenditures (since more people upgrade their skills or learn new skills when there are fewer jobs). The same pattern also applies to government programs designed to bail out businesses in trouble.

Tax and expenditure rules that produce these effects are called "automatic stabilizers," because the resulting larger deficits in recessions make the recessions less severe than they would otherwise be, by pumping purchasing power into the private economy.

Figures 26 and 27 show that these effects dominate the annual changes in government revenue and expenditure. Fluctuations in annual changes in real per-capita government revenue coincide with those in real per-capita GDP, while corresponding changes in government expenditure show the opposite pattern. By measuring everything in "real" terms and per head of population, we have eliminated the compounding effects of the continuous rise in population and the price level. The government expenditures shown here exclude interest payments on government debt since, as we have just discussed, we want to separate program expenditures, which are governed by the automatic stabilizers, from interest payments, which are not. Correspondingly, interest received by governments has been excluded from receipts.

Figure 26

Real Per Capita GDP and Government Revenue Year-to-Year Percentage Changes

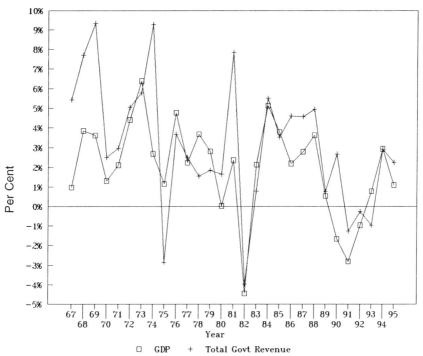

Figures 26 and 27 show a pattern that the theory of automatic stabilizers would predict if there were no changes in the budgetary rules governing revenues and expenditures. But, of course, every federal and provincial budget has made such changes every year. The figures therefore demonstrate that, over the period shown, which is the period in which the debt ratio has grown, budgetary decisions have been of little importance compared to the action of the automatic stabilizers in determining fluctuations in the deficit.

If we turn back to Figure 24, we see the resulting behaviour of the primary deficit and the total deficit between 1966 and 1994, starting about a decade before deficits began to be seen as a major problem. We again combine the accounts of all levels of government, and rely on Statistics Canada's National Accounts for consistent estimates of the combined deficit, net interest payments and the primary deficit.

Figure 27

**Real Per Capita GDP and Government Expenditures
Year-to-Year Percentage Changes**

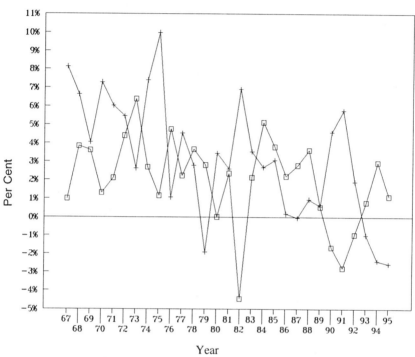

Year

GDP Per Head   +   Govt Spending Per Head

It is again clear that business fluctuations were the main influence on changes in the primary deficit over this period. We had no primary deficits or total deficits before 1975, at which point there was a dramatic change from a budgetary surplus to a deficit, coinciding with a sharp increase in unemployment. The cycles in the unemployment rate with low points in 1969, 1974, 1981 and 1989, and with high points in 1972, 1978, 1983 and 1992 are reproduced in both the primary deficit and the total deficit. This correspondence indicates that the unemployment rate, our indicator of business conditions, was indeed the major influence on the primary deficit.

But Figure 24 also tells us something about the combined effect of the changes in expenditure programs and tax rules made by eleven governments, federal and provincial, over successive budgets.

Notice that the primary deficit shows a slight upward trend over its successive cycles, but that the unemployment rate has a much stronger upward trend. These phenomena have two implications.

First, for a given level of unemployment, primary deficits are now lower than they used to be (compare those in 1976, 1981 and 1989). That shows that changes in rules and programs have been towards greater "restraint," not towards greater extravagance, which is often alleged. In fact, since 1975, eleven governments have complained about deficits and practised "restraint."

Second, restraint has been ineffective: it has contributed to the upward trend in unemployment and has not produced a downward trend in the deficit. This finding is not surprising, since restraint in government expenditure has reduced employment. It has produced "automatic destabilization," to coin a phrase.

The lesson is that primary deficits have resulted from the rising level of unemployment acting on the automatic stabilizers, moderated but not offset by increasing government "restraint," which has itself contributed to unemployment. Clearly, the efficient strategy for reducing the primary deficit is to reduce unemployment. The alternative strategy of cutting programs in order to reduce the deficit will only worsen our social problems.

How can we reduce unemployment?

Reducing Interest Rates

One important strategy for reducing unemployment is to lower interest rates. Readers will recall that this strategy also lowers the debt-to-GDP ratio, by decreasing the other component of the deficit, the interest payments. Net interest payments are shown in Figure 24 by the vertical distance between the primary deficit and the total deficit. Except for the deep depression years of 1982–83 and the "stagflation" years of the late seventies, net interest payments have been larger than the primary deficit. From 1987 to 1990, the primary balance was a surplus; thus, net interest payments exceeded the total deficit. In 1994 net interest payments accounted for the entire deficit.

The beneficial effects of lower interest rates are summarized in Figure 28. The interest cost of governments is lower, and that reduces the growth rate of the debt-to-GDP ratio. Less obviously, the GDP and its growth rate are higher: at lower interest rates, there is a greater pay-off to businesspeople who borrow money to build houses or apartments or to expand their businesses, and it is cheaper for house-

Figure 28

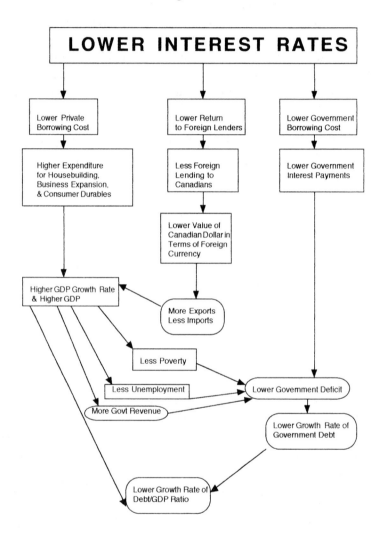

holders to borrow to buy appliances, furniture and cars, as well as houses.

The increase in economic activity resulting from business expansion and household purchases of cars, appliances, and so on reduces unemployment and thus shrinks the deficit through the automatic stabilizers. The higher growth rate of GDP is an added factor reducing the debt-to-GDP ratio. There is a further effect that raises GDP:

at lower interest rates, our bonds become less attractive to foreign investors, and our governments have less incentive to borrow in New York. These developments mean that there is less foreign currency wanting to be exchanged for Canadian dollars, so the value of the Canadian dollar falls in foreign exchange markets. Hence, Canadian exports become cheaper for foreign buyers, and imports become more expensive for Canadians. As a result, there is a further improvement in Canadian output through greater exports and the substitution of domestic products for imports, and hence a further reduction in unemployment and in the deficit.

The economy pays a price for increased jobs through a cheaper dollar. The higher cost of imported goods and services means a drop in real purchasing power for those who buy them, and in the Canadian economy, everyone buys some imports or imported components.[5] But it is a reasonable presumption that foreign goods and services make up a greater proportion of expenditure for the rich than for the less well off, so that the impact of a cheaper dollar as a stimulus to employment is "progressive" (in the technical sense). In this respect, it differs sharply from conservative proposals for stimulating employment, such as the abolition of minimum wages, attacks on labour legislation and employment standards, and more tax concessions to business.

But haven't interest rates dropped considerably in the last few years, and can they be lowered further? Yes, they have come down, but there is plenty of room for further reductions. Figure 29 shows that long-term, Government of Canada bonds were yielding 15 per cent interest at their 1981 peak and 11 per cent at their 1990 peak. The interest rate fell to between 7 and 8 per cent in 1993, rose to 8 and 9 per cent in 1994, and fell again to 6.5 per cent in 1997.

What is more, to appreciate the implications for economic activity, one must look at the *real* interest rate; that is, the amount by which the interest rate exceeds the inflation rate. The reason is that the real cost of money to the borrower and the real return to the lender are reduced by the amount that prices rise between the time money is borrowed and the time interest is paid. As the figure shows, with inflation running at just over 1 per cent in 1997, the real interest rate is between 5 and 6 per cent, which is high by historical standards. The figure shows that, before the eighties, real rates were typically at 2 or 3 per cent, and often lower. There is therefore plenty of scope to lower rates. How?

Figure 29

Long-Term Federal Bond Yield
Nominal and Real

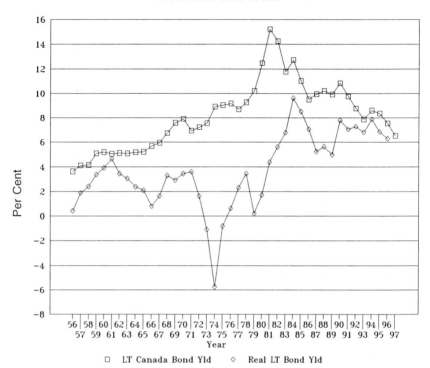

The federal government's agency in charge of interest rate policy is the Bank of Canada, although the Bank sometimes tries to deny that it can exert much influence on interest rates. It no longer influences them by regulation; it only intervenes in the market for loans, in which interest rates are determined. It can intervene by buying and selling federal government bonds and treasury bills and also by participating in the weekly auction of treasury bills.[6] In recent years, the Bank has confined its intervention to treasury bills and stayed out of the market for longer-term bonds. If the Bank wants interest rates to rise, it sells treasury bills in its portfolio. The increased supply offered for sale tends to depress prices, and a fall in prices of treasury bills means a rise in their yield (i.e., the rate of interest that a purchaser will earn). Conversely, to lower interest rates, the Bank buys treasury bills and bids high in the auctions.

The different credit markets are connected, since lenders and borrowers can substitute one kind of loan for another. So, if the Bank lowers treasury bill yields, it exerts downward pressure on the interest yields of federal and provincial bonds, corporate bonds, bank loans, mortgages, guaranteed investment certificates, annuities, and so on. Of course, this indirect influence on bond rates is weaker than if the Bank intervened in these markets directly, as it has done in the past. In staying out of the bond market, the Bank has abandoned a powerful policy tool.

Can Canada Reduce Interest Rates?

The current version of conservative deficit-phobia asserts that debt and deficit ratios have to be reduced in order to achieve lower interest rates. It would follow that we cannot reduce interest rates in order to achieve a lower debt ratio. The lower debt-to-GDP ratio would be a *precondition* for lower interest rates.

The theory is that lenders view the ratios of debt-hanging and deficit-to-GDP as measuring the possibility that the borrowing government may default on its obligations or may create inflation in order to reduce the real burden of its debt. The interest rate therefore has to include a "risk premium" that rises as the debt or deficit ratio rises (Macklem, 1994).

This proposition is implicit in the official federal government statement that "high deficits and debt undermine investor confidence in the ability of the government to meet its financial obligations, leading to higher interest rates which affect all borrowers, resulting in reduced spending and business investment, and slower growth and job creation" (Government of Canada, 1997, page 8).

The major error in this theory is that it ignores the existence of the Bank of Canada, whose holdings of government debt are determined by monetary policy, not the profit motive. Even if other potential lenders were to have doubts about the government's solvency, the Bank can counteract their influence by expanding its loans to the federal government. Moreover, the Bank is empowered to lend to provincial governments, but has chosen not to exercise this power for many years. The role of the central bank is to make high or low interest rates a monetary policy choice.

Government spokespeople know, of course, that there is a Bank of Canada, so one may wonder how they can cling to their theory that interest rates are determined by debt ratios. The answer is to be found in the implicit assumption that if expansionary monetary policy (Bank purchases of treasury bills or bonds) threatens to drop interest rates below a level determined by the debt ratio, all private lenders will drop Canadian debt like a hot brick, and the Bank's task would become unmanageable.

It is, however, unreasonable to suppose that for each class of government security there is a unique interest rate below which no private lender will want to hold it. In other words it is not realistic to suppose that there is a unique price for the security above which all private holders will sell. Holders of some issues of Canadian bonds will require a higher price to make it profitable to sell rather than holding their bonds until they mature. The profitable price depends on the coupon rate and maturity date. Others will not sell a domestic bond without a rise in price because investing in foreign loans exposes them to a foreign exchange risk that is avoided by keeping their money at home. In addition, the extent to which Canadian lenders can switch to foreign securities is still restricted by regulations such as the foreign content limit on RRSPs. But the most important point is that lenders, both foreign and domestic, differ widely in the amount and quality of information they possess concerning the risks entailed by different debt instruments — foreign and domestic, in their interpretation of this information, and in their attitude to risk.

Consequently, as interest rates drop (that is, as security prices rise), some foreign lenders will sell some or all of their holdings of Canadian government debt while others will not sell. The higher the price in relation to other investment opportunities, the more will be offered for sale.[7] Therefore the Bank of Canada can indeed raise the price by intervening in the market to buy and hold more government debt. The lower the interest rate, the more of the debt the Bank must hold.

Finally, it is not clear that debt and deficit ratios are in fact major determinants of the interest rates at which private lenders are willing to hold Canadian debt. For reliable evidence one has to find or construct comparisons in which debt and deficit ratios differ while monetary policy does not.

Comparisons of interest rates paid by the federal government and the ten provinces show that provinces with higher debt ratios tend to pay slightly higher interest rates, although there are important exceptions to this rule. On the other hand, the federal government, which has a higher debt ratio than any province and is the only government that can influence the rate of inflation, pays lower interest rates on its debt than any province (Rosenbluth, 1992, 1995). Clearly, other important factors are at work.

A statistical analysis of the deficit and debt ratios for the consolidated account of all Canadian governments shows that year-to-year changes in the debt ratio do not influence changes in the interest rate on federal or corporate bonds. However, changes in the deficit ratio do have a small independent influence [8] (Rosenbluth, 1995). This result presents a puzzle. At present debt levels there is not a significant probability that any Canadian government should be unable to meet its obligations. Moreover, the *deficit* ratio is not a logical indicator of solvency. One may therefore conclude that holders of some Canadian debt are not well informed or are not totally rational. This conclusion is not surprising, since it accords with the large fluctuations in international securities and currency markets that have recently been observed. What is surprising is that in the face of mounting evidence of the imperfect functioning of these markets, conservative policy should continue to promote deregulation of the international movement of securities and cash.

We conclude that reducing interest rates is a monetary policy choice not dependent on getting our fiscal house in order. On the contrary, a low enough level of real interest rates would raise the rate of economic growth, improve the balance of government revenues and expenditure, and so ultimately reduce the debt-to-GDP ratio.

This conclusion raises the question of why the policy of reducing nominal interest rates from the dizzying heights of 1981 (Figure 29) was not carried further and why it was reversed in 1984, 1987–90, and 1994. The major reason is the Bank of Canada's single-minded focus (with the government's approval) on preventing price increases. This policy is based on (or at least defended by) the proposition that no greater disaster could befall the Canadian economy than inflation.

Inflation

Inflation, an extended period in which prices rise quickly, occurs when the demand for goods and services rises faster than the rate at which they can be produced. There is no doubt that lower interest rates increase the economy's total demand for goods and services. Indeed, as we have just seen, higher total demand is our objective. The important point, however, is that rising prices are not inevitable if employment and output can be expanded.

BOX 1

Unemployment surpasses the "frictional and structural" level when the demand for goods and services at existing prices falls below what can be produced by the existing labour force (apart from those unemployed for frictional or structural reasons).

If we had reliable statistics on the number of unfilled job vacancies, we could estimate the amount of unemployment due to inadequate demand as the difference between the number of unemployed and the number of vacancies. The number of unfilled vacancies would be our measure of frictional and structural unemployment.

If U represents the number of unemployed and V the number of vacancies, the proportion of frictional/structural unemployment would be V/U and the proportion of unemployment due to inadequate demand would be 1-(V/U). Thus if V/U declines, the proportion of unemployment due to inadequate demand rises. Regrettably we do not have a count of unfilled job vacancies, but Statistics Canada's Help Wanted Index can serve as a "proxy," an imperfect substitute indicator. It measures the number of vacancies advertised in newspapers.

If V is proportional to the Help Wanted Index, call it W, a fall in W/U signals a fall in V/U. Even if we make the more general assumption that V is a linear function of W with a positive intercept (V = a+by; a0; b0), a decline in W/U *as U increases* would indicate a decline in V/U. This is a very reasonable assumption.

We have already seen that unemployment had a rising trend (Figure 24). Figure 30 shows an index of the ratio of the number of vacancies advertised to the number of unemployed. It exhibits the obvious cyclical swings, but it also shows a clear downward trend, and like Figure 24, it shows the stalling of the recovery in 1996 and its resumption in 1997. The downward trend suggests that a growing proportion of the rising unemployment is due to deficiency of demand in relation to the supply of labour. If we compare the ratios in 1973, 1979, 1985, and 1994, each two years after a cyclical trough, we see a continual decline.

As a result, those who maintain that lower interest rates would be disastrous have to rely on the assumption that employment and output cannot be expanded fast enough. How can they maintain that assumption in the face of high and rising unemployment and excess capacity? The answer is that they assume that all unemployment is "frictional" or "structural." Frictional means that the unemployed are not satisfied with jobs that are readily available and that they prolong their unemployment by searching for a job that suits them. Structural means that the jobs are not located where the unemployed are or that available jobs require skills that the unemployed do not have.[9]

However, the statistical evidence indicates that an increasing proportion of the rising level of unemployment is neither frictional nor structural, but is due to inadequate total demand for goods and services (see Box 1). Lower interest rates therefore can be expected to have the beneficial effect of raising output and reducing government deficits without causing high inflation.

Of course, inflation is a matter of degree, and increasing aggregate demand may exert some upward pressure on prices even when there is some slack in the economy. The present policy of high real interest rates must therefore be based on the further assumption that the presumed evil of slowly rising prices outweigh the certain misery and destruction of human capital entailed by the unemployment and poverty resulting from high interest rates. No one who has lived through the thirties, forties, fifties and sixties can regard this set of assumptions and underlying values as reasonable.

The Bank of Canada's preoccupation with inflation has led to a "ratchet" theory of asymmetrical impotence, propounded by the Governor of the Bank in a speech to the Montreal Board of Trade in January 1995. The Governor said that the Bank's purchase of government securities in order to lower the interest rate would be *seen* as inflationary, and the interest rate demanded by lenders would increase in line with these expectations. In other words, the Bank can raise interest rates by monetary contraction (selling securities), but it cannot lower them by monetary expansion (buying securities).[10] There is no evidence that the markets behave in this strange fashion.

When the recovery stalled in 1995 the Bank of Canada changed its mind, and three-month treasury bill rates fell from a high of 8.2 per cent in March 1995 to 2.9 per cent in December 1996, before rising, gradually, to 3.6 per cent in November, 1997. The governor explained the Bank's new policy in March 1997:

Figure 30

Help Wanted Index Per Unemployed
Index, 1966=100

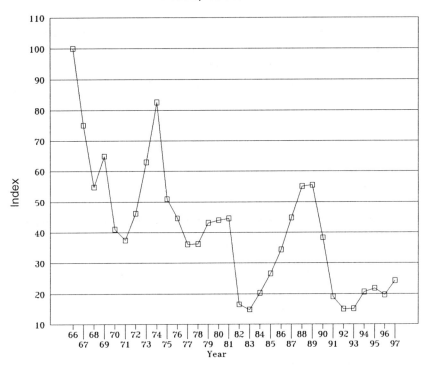

Because of the lags involved, the contribution of the easier monetary conditions to a stronger expansion in output and employment should continue for some time. Thus, we expect the economy to expand at rates in excess of growth in potential output through 1997 and 1998. In other words, we anticipate that the margin of unused capacity in our economy will shrink substantially over the next couple of years... One would expect inflation to start accelerating only after a period in which the level of aggregate demand had exceeded the economy's capacity to produce on a sustained basis. That is by no means the situation we face in Canada today. In fact, we have a fairly large margin of spare capacity. (Thiessen, 1997).

Evidently the Bank of Canada now agrees that unemployment, not inflation, is the major problem facing the economy, and that low interest rates are an effective policy to raise output and employment. We now consider additional tools for combating unemployment and excess capacity.

Reducing Unemployment

Other government policies for reducing unemployment and increasing output are well known. Lower interest rates reduce the unemployment that reflects insufficient demand for goods and services. Government expenditures have the same effect, but, of course, how much they increase output and employment depends on how and where the money is spent.

For example, the effect of government expenditure in creating jobs and output is greatest when the recipients respend their money within the Canadian economy, rather than salting it away in Swiss bank accounts or spending it in the Bahamas. Consequently, income support payments for people living in poverty are very good for job creation. In contrast, tax concessions to the banks (on the grounds that the development of their computer programs constituted scientific research)[11] benefited their stockholders, who tend to be rich and respend much less of their gains within the country.

What about the other types of unemployment — structural and frictional unemployment? The first thing to note is that reducing the unemployment that is due to insufficient demand will also reduce structural and frictional unemployment. We learned that lesson in World War II and in the postwar reconversion period. People will retrain and relocate more readily when they are assured of jobs.

Government policy can do more to reduce frictional and structural unemployment. There is much talk about retraining, but both federal and provincial programs in this area have been hit by governments' preoccupation with expenditure slashing and have not been very effective. And as for relocation, present policies still place the bulk of the cost on the unemployed.

Conclusion: Policies to Reduce the Debt Ratio

Fear of inflation and the notion that we must "get our fiscal house in order" are rooted in mistaken analysis and in antisocial values, and have the effect of rationalizing the current attacks on social programs.

A realistic program for reducing the debt ratios must insist that the Bank of Canada lowers interest rates, and that Canadian federal and provincial governments pursue policies that create employment.

At the time of writing (December 1997) the prospects for policy reform are mixed. Lower deficits in the federal and many provincial government accounts have resulted from lower interest rates, the slashing of social programs and improvements in our export markets. The "improved" fiscal balances have led to talk of a "fiscal dividend" and there is widespread agreement that some of this dividend should be used to repair the social safety net and to create employment. However, there has been no change in the mistaken view that it is essential to pay down the debt, and that reducing taxes is more important than spending on social programs, health and education.

It is possible, therefore, that the fallout from the current recession in Asian economies will again lead to calls for greater fiscal restraint as unemployment rises.

Moreover, the expansionist posture of the Bank of Canada is by no means secure. The Bank continues to react to slight reductions in the foreign exchange value of the Canadian dollar by raising short-term interest rates, leading to immediate increases in the rates at which banks make business loans or grant mortgages.

While there are encouraging signals, it is clear that policymakers have not been fully converted to the correct view of Canada's recent economic history: The debt ratio should be brought down by expansionary monetary and fiscal policy, not by slashing valuable programs of public expenditure.

References

Floyd, J.E. 1995. Are Canadian Interest Rates Too High? *Canadian Public Policy*: 143–158.

Government of Canada. 1994. *Agenda: Jobs and Growth.*

Macklem, T. 1994. Some Macroeconomic Implications of Rising Levels of Government Debt. *Bank of Canada Review* (Winter): 41–61.

Moore, T. 1994. What is Government Debt? in *Public Sector Assets and Liabilities — A Historical Overview.* Statistics Canada, Catalogue 68-508.

Rosenbluth, G. 1995. The Influence of Government Deficits and Debt on Interest Rates: Canada 1970–1995. Paper presented to the annual meeting of the Canadian Economics Association, Montreal, Quebec, June.

Thiessen, G.G. 1995. Financial Markets and the Canadian Economy. Bank of Canada, January. Mimeograph.

Some Myths about Monetary Policy[1]

Marc Van Audenrode

Marc van Audenrode of Laval University starts from the position that the main economic problem facing Canada today is the dramatic lack of jobs. Unemployment in Canada is high, he argues, because the Bank of Canada has chosen to focus on the elimination of inflation, regardless of the effects of this policy on output and employment. He attacks the four myths that now guide monetary policy in Canada and suggests that since the Bank of Canada is incapable of reforming its own policies, its independent control over monetary policy should be abolished and Canada should adopt a fixed exchange rate policy with the United States.

Nothing in my areas of interest and research as an economist predisposes me to write an essay on monetary policy in Canada. Yet monetary policy is the subject of this work. I have studied the Canadian labour market for several years, and I am now convinced that the main economic problem Canada faces is its dramatic lack of jobs. When you face that reality every day, the official political line maintained by the Bank of Canada, propagating over and over the "Great Fear of Inflation," simply sounds ludicrous and calls for a response, which I will try to formulate in this essay. Of course, the fact that I am not a specialist on monetary policy implies that the arguments I will develop will often be based on common sense and not on complex theories. I believe, however, that the point of view of an economist whose primary area of interest is outside monetary policy is worthy and can enlighten the debate.

The most surprising aspect of monetary policy, to a nonspecialist, is the secrecy it is shrouded in. In contrast, every aspect of labour market policies is constantly scrutinized. But those who are in charge of monetary policy and the leaders of financial institutions tell us that any question related to monetary policy is either already answered or not to be asked.

My essay could actually be very short. In the preamble of the act establishing the Bank of Canada, it is written that:

> Whereas it is desirable to establish a central bank in Canada to regulate credit and currency in the best interests of the economic life of the nation, to control and protect the external value of the national monetary unit and to mitigate by its influence fluctuations in the general level of production, trade, prices and employment, so far as may be possible within the scope of monetary action, and generally to promote the economic and financial welfare of the Dominion ...

Among all these missions and responsibilities, the Bank of Canada has chosen exclusively to concentrate on the stability of prices. Twenty years ago, the Bank of Canada announced that it would bring the level of inflation down to zero in the country. After two terrible recessions, worse here than in any other country in the OECD (Organization for Economic Cooperation and Development), the Bank finally succeeded. In doing so, however, it also succeeded in making Canada first among OECD countries in unemployment, real interest rates, and, as I will argue, public deficit. Clearly, all these efforts were not worth it. We were promised light at the end of the tunnel, but the tunnel turned out to be quite long. After all those years fighting inflation, we spent almost a decade fighting to regain control of our public finances, which had spun out of control as a direct result of Canada's monetary policy. And we are not sure we will see the end of that tunnel before we face another train, since the Bank of Canada is already talking about tightening its policy to fight the return of inflation. One can even *wonder whether this light* we were promised really existed, or whether it was just a delusion. Worse, it could have been a cruel hoax designed to radically change the balance of political and social power at a time when industrialized countries were undergoing the most dramatic social advances of their modern history.

In the real world of output and employment, it is hard to escape the nonsense about the fight against inflation. For anyone lucky enough to have done so, however, I will further develop my arguments. I will present a series of myths related to monetary policy. These myths can be heard on radio, seen on television or read in the newspapers. They consist of unproven affirmations, said to be true without requiring any debate or proof. Sometimes, they are even considered unquestionable. Unfortunately, although these myths are untrue, they guide the way we see monetary policy.

Myth 1: In the Mid-1990s, Inflation Poses a Threat to the Canadian Economy

Is it true that inflation is a threat? The efforts made by the governor of the Bank of Canada in his presentation of the Bank's annual report for 1994 to the Senate Finance Committee and its November 1997 *Monetary Policy Report* were particularly enlightening. They would actually have been amusing if they had not had serious ramifications for Canada's economic future. Despite the near-perfect price stability Canada had experienced at that time for many years, the governor goes to great lengths to argue that inflation is still threatening. To do so, he invokes, in turn, the rise in prices of raw material, the rise in taxes and, especially, the impending return of Canada to its full production capacity.

Those efforts to justify a continued fight against inflation at a time when real interest rates in Canada had returned to the level which had triggered the 1990 recession are particularly worrisome. Any first-year economics student knows not to dissect the Consumer Price Index. The index's role is precisely to take into account the fact that, when there is no generalized inflation, some prices rise while others go down.

The attitude which emphasizes only the few prices that rise and ignores those that decrease is particularly worrisome because of what it reveals about the Bank's view of the economy. The rise in raw materials prices had nothing to do with inflation; as explained in first-year economics classes, it simply resulted from a movement of the demand curve for these goods, triggered by economic expansion in the world in 1994. This increase was simply a correction to the world prices of raw materials after years of decline. When the Bank of Canada says that these price increases are dangerous and inflationary, it is saying that it will never again accept rapid economic growth, because no growth can occur without increases in prices and because the Bank has shown it will not tolerate price increases under any circumstances. It is obvious that, if the Bank of Canada does not rapidly change its policy, Canada will soon be hit by another recession, which will be deeper, longer and more painful than the previous ones. But Canadians are getting used to that by now.

This doomsday scenario is made all the more likely by the fact that the Bank now believes that the Canadian economy is getting close to its potential; i.e., that Canada is now close to a point where any increase in production could lead to inflation. According to the Bank, Canadian unemployment will soon hit the NAIRU (nonaccelerating inflation rate of unemployment). Recently, Steve Poloz, at the time head of the Bank's Research Department, declared that the Bank estimated the natural rate of unemployment in Canada to be no less than 9 per cent. Sherry Cooper (1997), an economist from Nesbitt Burns, goes even further when she claims that full employment has already been reached in many regions of Canada. No empirical evidence supports that affirmation. Before the recession of the early nineties, Canada's unemployment was around 7.5 per cent. There is no reason to believe that this level can no longer be achieved. No major structural change has happened since then which could justify such an increase in the natural rate of unemployment. To the contrary, many changes have had the opposite effect. These changes include the reduction in the generosity of most social programs (the increase in social spending over the last few years is exclusively due to the increase in the number of claimants); a large decrease in minimum wages, in real terms and compared to the average industrial wage; and finally, the demotion of Canada's UI system from the status of a Rolls-Royce to that of a Lada. On the other hand, the increase in payroll taxes, which the government instigated during the recession to finance the UI system and which could be blamed for higher unemployment, has now been stopped. Payroll taxes could be further reduced if unemployment decreased.

All these changes indicate that, if anything, the Canadian natural rate of unemployment should be below 7 per cent now, rather than above 9 per cent. But this is clearly not what the Bank believes and even less what it aims at. I am sure that those who voted for the creation of the Bank of Canada did not mean by economic stability a situation without jobs, growth or inflation — as the Bank seems to understand its mandate today.

Of course, when inflation disappears, so does the considerable power central banks have accumulated over the last decades. Without inflation, the key role central banks have played in the world financial system vanishes, and they go back to the tasks they once had; i.e., being print shops.

Central banks are public administrations. They are likely to suffer the same problems other public administrations are known to suffer. The worst fate of public administration is to become unnecessary. Niskanen (1971) and Buchanan (1980) contend that public administrations often pursue their own objectives and not the objectives the government had in mind when creating them. In good times, the ultimate goal of any public administration is its own growth; in bad times, the objective is its own survival. Public administrations want to survive, regardless of whether they are still needed: this is also true for central banks, as shown by Acheson and Chant (1973).

There is no reason why the Bank of Canada should be immune to this plague. It is surprising to see and hear that the same people who can be extremely harsh with governments and public administrations can also be very accommodating with central banks. One fact remains, however: the success of the Bank of Canada in its fight against inflation is also its political death warrant. The only way left for the Bank to retain some of its past glory is to threaten Canadians constantly with the return of inflation.

Myth 2: Interest Rates Are High Because of Government Deficits and There Is Nothing the Bank Can Do

Being a central banker is an especially nice job, because there is always a large supply of scapegoats you can blame for your mistakes. In Canada, the chief scapegoat for all of the country's financial and monetary problems is the federal government, with the provincial governments a close second. I will argue that the large deficits Canadian governments are struggling with are the consequence, and not the cause, of high real interest rates.

In economics, it is crucial to understand the direction of causation. In lay terms, causal analysis provides the answer for the question of the chicken and the egg: which came first? Determining the direction of causal relationships between macroeconomic phenomena is the basic question of economic policy. Thus, economists have developed many tests of causality. These formal tests are complex and often hard to implement, yet all proceed from the same intuition: one event cannot be caused by a later event.

At the end of the eighties, public finances in Canada were back under control. This fact was acknowledged by the OECD, an organization which is not known for promoting fiscal softness. In its 1990 report on Canada, the OECD recognized that Canada's risk of embarking on a spiral of increased budget deficits leading to increased interest payments and higher debt had been considerably reduced. The OECD even wrote that the Canadian budgetary policy had become sustainable (1990).

This conclusion should not come as a surprise. It can be shown that the proportion of program spending[2] by the federal government decreased, from 19 per cent of GDP in 1984 to 14 per cent in 1994. When public finances were back under control, Canada experienced a dramatic increase in real interest rates, an increase willfully implemented by the Bank of Canada as part of its adoption in 1980 of a long-term plan to bring the level of inflation to zero. Since then, real interest rates have been higher in Canada than in the United States, despite the fact that, at that time, the problem of public deficit and debt was much more worrisome in the United States than it was in Canada.

It is difficult to disentangle how much of the high interest rates paid by the Canadian government since 1990 is due to monetary policy and how much is due to differences in risk between the U.S. and Canadian governments. However, the interest rate paid by the Canadian private sector is clearly not subject to that differential risk factor, and, therefore, the comparison of the interest rates paid by the private sector is a good indicator of the implications of monetary policy. If the interest rate paid by the Canadian government since 1990 had been lower by an amount roughly equal to the differential between the private short-term rates of the two countries, today's federal debt would be lower by almost $80 billion, while the deficit would have been cut by more than $10 billion.

Despite that enormous additional burden, the Bank has, when it has wanted to, been able to bring interest rates down. When the Bank fails to convince people that governments are responsible for high interest rates, it resorts to another tactic: self-pity. It insists that it is small and that its means are limited, compared to the gigantic power of financial markets. The problem with this position is that the Bank cannot have it both ways: it cannot take credit for a successful policy — the fight against inflation — and then claim that it does not have the means to conduct that policy. Either the Bank of Canada exerts some control on Canadian interest rates and, therefore, can be credited for the successful fight against inflation, or it does not and, therefore, the disappearance of inflation in Canada is just a Divine gift.

Public debts in Canada can largely be attributed to past high interest rates, both directly — because of the high interest payments on the debt that they imposed — and indirectly — because of the increase in transfer payments and decline in tax revenues caused by the recession that they induced. There is no evidence to the contrary — that high deficits would have caused high interest rates. By fighting inflation at any cost, Canada nailed itself to the ground in its fight to control public finances.

Myth 3: The End of the Tunnel

The ultimate justification for fighting inflation has always been that today's costs and the suffering that the fight imposes on us are small compared to the benefits provided by a healthy economy, free from the plague of inflation — economic heaven on earth.

Canadians have been expecting these large benefits for twenty years, and they might well have to wait longer! There is no consensus among economists on what the benefits of living with zero inflation are. There is even less consensus on how large these benefits could be. It is also worth noting that the official "spin" given by the Bank to its own policy has changed over time. Its attitude towards the policy has clearly been downgraded from "unconditionally supportive" to "neutral." While in 1990, Jack Selody wrote in a Bank publication, "… the benefits of price stability — or, conversely, the costs of inflation — are many and large whereas the costs of attaining and maintaining price stability are transitory and small by comparison," the 1994 annual report stated, more moderately, "Price stability is not an idea unique to the Bank of Canada, but a goal shared by all the major industrial countries in the world." No further reference was made to the large benefits to be reaped from zero inflation, nor to the huge costs resulting from inflation; instead, "we do it because others do it." Everybody's grandmother has explained, long ago, why such an argument might not be compelling. In addition, even if many other central banks share the general goal of price stability, most balance this objective with a concern for the real economy. None has pursued zero inflation with as much relentlessness and dogmatism as the Bank of Canada. The latest step in the Bank's retreat from

full-fledged support of a zero-inflation world has been to argue that
the benefits of zero inflation are so diffuse and pervasive that they
can hardly be measured. Trust us, we are the doctors...

This distinction between the general objective of price stability —
which everybody, including myself, shares — and the relentless
pursuit of zero inflation at any cost is particularly important. Everybody knows the costs of hyperinflation, but to this day, nobody has
convincingly established that there were costs associated with annual
inflation of 5 to 6 per cent. In the meantime, it is becoming evident
that the costs of recessions, which are inevitably associated with the
fight against inflation, are permanent. Today's costs are merely ap-
petizers, coming right before a main course of other sacrifices — and
not to be followed by a juicy dessert. Several arguments can be used
to justify why the costs of fighting inflation are permanent.

First, it is becoming more obvious every day that a money illusion
exists.[3] The main reason why public opinion supported the fight
against inflation a few years ago is that many homeowners did not
want to pay 15 per cent interest on their mortgages any more. For
our purposes, the main consequence of the money illusion is the
downward rigidity of nominal wages. If nominal wages seldom can
be reduced, so too real wages in a situation of zero inflation. While
many workers might agree to nominal wage increases which are
below the level of inflation, few will agree to lowering their nominal
wages. This fact has recently been documented in studies by Fortin
for Canada (1995) and by Akerlof, Dickens and Perry in the United
States (1995). A low level of inflation gives some breathing space to
struggling firms. With zero inflation, real-wage rigidities lead to
unstable jobs, lay-offs and massive destruction of specific skills.
These costs are permanent.

Second, and more worrisome, stringent monetary policy can lead
to underinvestment in human capital. The decision by an employer
to train employees is an investment decision: it depends on the cost
of training and the benefits the investment is expected to generate.
As with any investment, high interest rates reduce the value of the
future benefits. When interest rates are too high, firms invest less in
general, and even less in human capital, in particular. Similarly, if
the restrictive monetary policy leads to a major recession every seven
to eight years, it increases the uncertainty associated with the benefits
of training. Why should anyone train a worker that may be laid off
a few years later? There are, however, even more unfortunate effects:
when firms invest less in their workers' human capital, they have

less incentive to retain these workers during recessions. Less human capital leads to less labour hoarding, which in turn leads to higher employment instability and greater, more frequent losses of specific human capital.

Underinvestment in human capital is permanent. Those who suffered from lack of training have now grown older, and, even if a major change in policy restored employers' confidence and incentives to invest in training, employers would probably choose to focus on younger workers; the return on their investment for these employees will last much longer than that for older workers, who are closer to retirement.

Third, and finally, we have not yet estimated many of the long-term costs of many other phenomena generated by the fight against inflation. High real interest rates may have already prevented a whole generation of Canadians from owning homes, and by the time they will be able to afford a mortgage, they will have become too old to maintain it. The snowball effect that high interest rates have imposed on the national debt has taken away most of the federal and provincial Parliaments' discretion in determining public spending. In a way, the Bank of Canada has placed itself above the democratic will of the Canadian people and imposed upon governments its own preferences concerning the way to conduct social and economic policy. The Bank of Canada has made sure that the only choice of the elected party, regardless of political affiliation, would be massive cuts in program spending.

Myth 4: We Don't Care about That Scientific Methodology Stuff

The people at the Bank of Canada and other Canadian financial institutions are so sure about the *truth* that, despite claiming their arguments are strongly grounded upon scientific evidence, they ignore the elementary rules of scientific methodology.

In a recent piece, Sherry Cooper (1997) argues that several Canadian regions have already reached the level of their "natural rate" of unemployment — a concept she clearly equates with the concept of Non Accelerating Inflation Rate of Unemployment (NAIRU), the level of unemployment below which inflation starts picking up in an economy. Yet to show that, she uses a methodology that demonstrates most U.S. states have been below their natural rates of unemployment for months. As far as I know, inflation hasn't picked up in the United States. To argue that Canada is getting close to the natural rate of unemployment on the basis of that evidence contradicts an essential rule of scientific research: one counter example proves a theory is wrong.

In a similar vein, the latest important policy document from the Bank of Canada is full of puzzling statements. Since arguing about the ghosts of inflation in an economy which, for the vast majority of Canadians, is still far from prosperous and even farther from over-heated, the Bank of Canada has now invented the concept of "virtual" ghosts of inflation. In the Bank's November 1997 report, it is stated that "... the Bank's current estimate is that the economy may very well be producing at full capacity towards the end of 1998 ..." (pp. 22–23), or "Once the Canadian economy reaches full capacity, infla- tion pressures could mount unless ... " (p. 28), or again "... it seems likely that further action to reduce the monetary stimulus will be required ..." (p. 29).

Economic theory is about facts, theories and evidence. Mays, coulds and seems are from the realm of politics. By starting to use so openly the language of politics, the Bank of Canada undermines a key proponent of an independent institution in charge of monetary policy: the need to isolate those who determine monetary policy from day-to-day political pressure. When the Bank of Canada becomes so concerned about its political agenda that it starts to behave like a politician, it oversteps its mandate and ceases to be an independent institution whose credibility is grounded in its objectivity.

Myth 5: Shhhh ... You Are Making the Financial Markets Nervous ...

Of all the myths I have addressed, the most insidious one is probably the conspiracy of silence. Nobody can question or discuss the choices of monetary policy. Simply hinting at the need for a change in policy can make the financial market nervous, which in turn leads to higher interest rates and which weakens the Canadian dollar.

On the one hand, I cannot understand why the public, which shows so much distrust towards economists in general, takes their word at face value when these economists call themselves bankers. One gets the impression that the public and the media believe that everything said by those in charge of financial markets is not only true, but also desirable for everybody. Those in charge of financial markets are bond retailers, whose primary responsibility is their clients and whose objective is to make profits in buying or selling bonds. This objective is often met at the public's expense. For example, the higher the interest paid on the debt by the government, the greater the profit made by a banker. This situation is clearly not in the interest of the average taxpayer, who must assume that cost. The speeches given by those in charge of financial markets are not motivated by general economic interest, but rather are guided by the interest of their clients. It has to be so, otherwise they would be betraying their duty to their clients. One has to keep that simple fact in mind when advocating the application of every economic policy proposal put forward by these individuals.

On the other hand, financial markets do not really need solid reasons to be nervous. They can take care of that by themselves. Everything can become an excuse for financial markets to be nervous, because nervousness leads to speculation, and speculation leads to profits. In France, financial markets recently launched a powerful attack against the French franc, after European Union president Jacques Delors announced he would not run for the French presidency. These attacks, which required strong interventions from the Banque de France, occurred despite the fact that, at that time, political analysts generally agreed that M. Delors's declining to run almost ensured victory for M. Balladur, a man who had proven as a prime minister that he was everything financial markets might dream for in the chief executive of an important European country.

It is also troublesome to see that bankers' analyses of comparable events differ across countries. The Canadian explanation of any mishap in financial markets inevitably implies Quebec's separation, some electoral deadline and the high public debt. The U.S. analysis often focuses on some political or marital trouble for President Clinton, while the French explanation invariably involves the selfishness of the Bundesbank or the carelessness of the U.S. Federal Reserve. When can we expect UFO sightings to become the main explanation for all our financial troubles?

We must question Canadian monetary policy. We must offer alternatives to the current options. This is crucial, not only to our economy, but also to our democratic process. We must refuse the current axiom that financial markets have imposed upon industrialized countries — after having imposed it on developing countries: duties for everybody, except financial markets, which have only rights. We must hold financial markets liable for their actions and for what they are doing to our economies. In short, we must make them aware of their civic duties. We must refuse to let the Bank of Canada exonerate itself from any responsibility by accusing the government or by saying that its only mandate is the fight against inflation. The remarkable success of the Federal Reserve in fine tuning the U.S. economy proves that it is possible to keep inflation under control without hurting growth. This example should serve as a model to the Bank of Canada.

Conclusion

Over the last few years, Canadian governments, both federal and provincial, have shown their determination in bringing public finances back under control. Some discrepancies still exist regarding how this goal must be achieved and at what speed, but governments no longer ignore that goal. This shift constitutes a major political change, compared to what was generally accepted fifteen to twenty years ago. The other, more recent, change in the general budget orientation has been that, in addition to blaming the victims of the recession (the unemployed and people on welfare), the government has started attending to the true source of its financial troubles. The last federal budget initiated a large reduction in the size of government and promised to start its withdrawal from many areas into which it had ventured without any reason.

All these efforts and these changes in the way people see governments will, however, remain fruitless without a significant change in the country's monetary policy. Regardless of magnitude, the imposed cut-backs will not be sufficient to allow governments to regain control over their finances as long as real interest rates on the debt are excessive and the economy is functioning at a level far below its capacity. There are physical limits to the magnitude and the importance of the cuts a government can implement — the ultimate cut being the prime minister firing her- or himself as the last federal civil servant. To avoid hitting that wall, monetary policy has to change. It was a chimera to believe that Canada could solve its problems by doing the same things that had created the problems. It was an illusion to believe that pushing the unemployed and welfare recipients into starvation offered a solution. It is a fantasy to believe that firing civil servants facilitates the achievement of these goals.

The Bank of Canada has to change its policy. It has to do so before it plunges Canada into a new recession and annihilates all the sacrifices Canadians have made in recent years to bring public finances back under control.

The Bank of Canada has to follow its charter. It has to recognize that it cannot pick and choose among the duties the Canadian people have vested in it. Its actions have to be consistent with the general economic interest and not only with the objective of price stability. The corporate culture at the Bank precludes us from hoping that such a change will occur soon. Therefore, I propose an alternative: the Bank of Canada has to announce today that it renounces its zero-inflation policy to pursue instead a policy of fixed exchange rates with the United States. To make that decision more credible, it should secure formal support from the Federal Reserve for that policy.

There are at least four major advantages of such a policy. First, the stability of the exchange rate is favourable to free trade. One cannot, at the same time, support free trade and agree to large variations in exchange rates. One cannot, at the same time, encourage Canadian firms to invest and trade with the United States and tell them that they must do so without knowing what these transactions will be worth a few years from now. The fluctuating policy that the Bank of Canada has imposed on the Canada-U.S. exchange rate for the last two decades must be revised. One cannot advocate free trade and fight stability of the exchange rate.

Second, by pegging its currency to the U.S. dollar, Canada, a small, open economy, would benefit from U.S. monetary policy. For many years now, real interest rates have been much lower in the United States than in Canada, and the Bank of Canada refuses to see this discrepancy as evidence of the failure of its policy. A credible policy for a fixed exchange rate in Canada would immediately bring Canadian interest rates to the level of those in the United States, as it did for several small European economies when they pegged their currencies to the deutschemark.

Third, with the European single currency in sight, the Canadian dollar might become one of the last small currencies that can absorb the anxiety of the world's financial markets. If our dollar becomes the favourite target of the world's financial crises, the cost of supporting it could become prohibitive.

Fourth, and finally, in pursuing this policy, the Bank of Canada could truly contribute to the nation's effort to regain control of public finances by being reduced itself to a nominal size.

References

Acheson, Keith, and John Chant. 1973. Bureaucratic Theory and the Choice of Central Banks' Goals: The Case of the Bank of Canada. *Journal of Money, Credit and Banking* 15: 637–55.

Akerlof, George A., Willam T. Dickens, and George L. Perry. 1995. The Inflation Unemployment Trade-Off at Low Rates of Inflation. Working Paper. The Brookings Institution.

Bank of Canada. 1990. Technical Report No. 54:3.

Bank of Canada. 1994. Annual Report: 5.

Bank of Canada. 1997. Monetary Policy Report. November 1997.

Buchanan, James M., and Marylin R. Flowers. 1980. *The Public Finances: An Introductory Textbook.* 5th ed. Homewood, Ill.: Irvin.

Cooper, Sherry, and Alex Araujo. 1997. *Regional Diversity: The Canadian Unemployment Story.* Special Report. NB Economic Research.

Fortin, Pierre. 1995. Nominal Wage Growth at Low Rates of Inflation in Canada. Working Paper. Université du Québec à Montréal.

Niskanen, William. 1971. *Bureaucracy and Representative Government.* Chicago: Aldin-Atherton, Inc.

Organization for Economic Cooperation and Development (OECD). 1990. *Economic Surveys: Canada.* November.

Social Policy, Macro Policy and the Debt[1]

Lars Osberg

Can the unemployment problem be solved by reforming social policy? Lars Osberg of Dalhousie University notes that there is little point in improving training programs or increasing "work incentives" if there are no jobs available for the retrained and remotivated. The federal government controls macroeconomic policy, while provincial governments administer social assistance and deliver most training programs. In the absence of a commitment to full employment by the federal government, social policy reform at the provincial level is doomed to failure.

In the ongoing debate on what to do about Canada's deficits, debts and high unemployment, one often hears the assertion that the source of our problems lies in bad social policy, and any hope for salvation lies in social policy reform. If unemployment can be blamed on excessive "generosity" of unemployment insurance, and if the deficit can be blamed on excessive social spending, then the answer may appear to be simple. Those who shoot from the hip say "kick the bums off UI and reduce both the deficit and the unemployment rate," while more sophisticated analysts may mumble generalities about work disincentives and budgetary imperatives. The essential message is the same — social policy is both the problem and the solution.

This perspective may be simple, but it does not fit the facts. In 1990, approximately 90 per cent of Canada's unemployed received

UI benefits. Since then, a series of cuts to UI, and its transformation into EI, has produced a dramatic change — by June 1997 recipients of regular benefits numbered only 33.6 per cent of the unemployed — somewhat less than the UI recipiency rate in Alabama of 37.6 per cent (CANSIM D980712 and D730603). As well as current and projected cuts to UI/EI, social assistance support levels have also been cut substantially in most provinces, most notably in Ontario and Alberta. By any criterion, the decrease during the 1990s in the eligibility, duration and rate of unemployment benefits in Canada has amounted to a huge cut in "generosity," but unemployment has remained high. Furthermore, as the chapters in this volume by Gillespie, Fortin and McCracken demonstrate, social spending played a very minor role in the creation and the escalation of Canada's debt and deficit problems. But if social spending did not cause the deficit, and if cuts to social spending do not solve the unemployment problem, why has social policy received so much attention?

In part, an emphasis on social policy arose because the priority of deficit reduction seemed to rule out the option of stimulating the economy by increasing the demand for labour and thus reducing unemployment. Improved social policy was advocated as a way to increase the potential output of the economy, with the hope that a more productive labour force would lead to faster economic growth, a larger primary surplus and faster elimination of Canada's debts. Social policy practitioners did protest that the deficit reduction agenda produced program cut-backs that reduced the accessibility of training and postsecondary education, and that macroeconomic policy produced a labour market in which there are no jobs for the retrained or remotivated. However, such objections appear to have had little influence on policy, partly because the frames of reference of macroeconomic analysts and social policymakers differ so dramatically.

When the current generation of macroeconomic policy analysts in Ottawa discuss unemployment and economic growth, they are likely to use econometric techniques such as vector auto regression to analyze highly aggregated time series data. They often do not mention how individual firms or workers would behave; at best, they consider the behaviour of a single "representative agent." At the Bank of Canada, the "calibrated" type of economic model, which depends heavily on "judgement," has become common.[2] The world of economic decision makers has thus become rather distant from concrete economic phenomena.

Social policy practitioners, on the other hand, speak a very different language. Because they often come from an academic tradition that favours case studies and because they focus on the casualties of society, they are concerned with why the particular characteristics of some individuals put them at the margins of mainstream society. As a result, models of how a "representative agent" might behave are of little interest. As well, designers[3] of social policy interventions (such as training programs for the unemployed) tend to adopt a microeconomic orientation, since their interest lies in learning which *types* of interventions, for which types of clients, can increase the chances of moving from transfer dependency to paid employment. As a result, the debates of social policy designers tend to emphasize the determinants of the skills and motivation of workers; that is, they focus almost exclusively on the supply side of labour markets.

All too often, discussions between social policy advocates and macroeconomists rapidly descend into mutual incomprehension. This essay, however, emphasizes the interactions between macroeconomic policy, social policy, and the debt and deficit. It does so because deficit reduction has forced major changes on social policy and because a prime objective of social policy is to move individuals from dependence on social assistance to paid employment. However, despite the financial and social benefits of getting people off welfare and into jobs, it is obvious that, whatever their motivation or training, individuals cannot make such a transition if no jobs are available. To be more precise, if there are not *enough* jobs available, social assistance clients will remain on social assistance, because available vacancies will be filled by those who are favoured by age, gender, race, class, education or experience. Cuts to social assistance payments will increase the depth of poverty, but such cuts do not create jobs.

Although it is sometimes asserted that better training or education can reduce unemployment, such policies cannot, by themselves, do the job. An analogy may help make the point. In many ways, having a job in today's labour market is like having a seat in a lifeboat. Although there are a number of lifeboats in the water, there are many people trying to get into them. Since the sea is storm-tossed, some lifeboats occasionally sink, and their occupants have to swim for safety. (Indeed, lifeboats which are in danger of sinking have been known to throw some of their occupants overboard.) Once in the water, people have to swim for the nearest available boat; some people make it, some people don't and some keep treading water, in the hope that a lifeboat will appear.

To extend the analogy to labour markets, we have to allow for the idea that new entrants to the labour force are continually trying to find a seat, and new lifeboats (that is, firms) are always being launched. The number of lifeboats varies, since bad weather (e.g., a recession) means that more lifeboats sink and that fewer are launched, and the total number of available seats (that is, jobs) shrinks. Some lifeboats have higher sides than others and are much safer, but they are also harder to get into. To get into the best lifeboats, people have to have special training and strength or a helping hand from someone inside.

At any given time, what kind of people get a seat? Basically, those who make it to safety are the individuals who are stronger, who had swimming lessons or who knew someone who threw them a line and pulled them in. In the labour market, analysts have long stressed the importance of ability, training and personal contacts for getting ahead. However, although it is true that better swimmers have a better chance of getting lifeboat seats, it does not necessarily follow that more swimming lessons will decrease the number who drown.

If there are plenty of lifeboats, swimming lessons will help. The faster swimmers will fill up the closer lifeboats first, but even slow swimmers will eventually make it to safety. Analogously, if job vacancies are available, training programs have powerful social pay-offs. However, if there are not enough lifeboats, there simply will not be enough spaces available. Swimming lessons (job training) can help some individuals get to safety faster than others. But if there are not enough spaces available, those who are relatively slow cannot make it. The key issue then is how many places are available, that is, how many jobs the labour market is producing.

This essay summarizes the existing state of Canadian labour markets and medium-term projections of macroeconomic performance in Canada. The continued implementation of a macroeconomic policy that focuses on zero inflation and deficit reduction implies continuous high unemployment rates; the next section discusses the implications of this situation for social policy. High unemployment, especially for long periods of time, adversely affects the abilities of individuals to cope in society and in the labour market. High unemployment diminishes the probability that remedial programs, or altered incentives, will be effective in assisting individuals to find employment, and the resulting loss in economic output constrains the fiscal resources available for social services or remedial programs.

Figure 31

Unemployment Rate

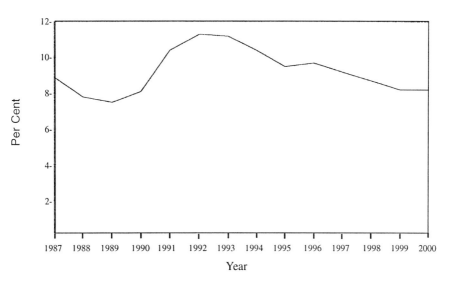

Source: 1987-1994 Statistics Canada *Historical Labour Force Statistics* Cat.
No. 71-201.
1995-2000 Informetrica Limited *The National Forecast* — July 1995.

Given that most social policy is implemented at the provincial level, while macroeconomic policy is set by the federal government, we then consider the consistency and the coordination of policies in a federal system. In Canada, the objective of zero inflation has taken precedence over other objectives and produced a rate of unemployment in labour markets that dooms long-run structural adjustment policies, like retraining, to failure. Provincial governments cannot deliver, in the short run, the jobs which their electorates demand, while the federal government continues to bewail the failure of provincial social assistance reform and training policies which stems from its own macroeconomic policies.

The Labour Market in the Nineties

In June 1997, after allowing a decline in interest rates that had produced a period of growth in the Canadian economy, the Bank of

Canada signalled that the party — such as it was — was over, and began raising interest rates again. Although unemployment in Canada was still over 9 per cent and the inflation rate was below the midpoint of its target band (and declining), the Bank moved "pre-emptively" to slow the economy and head off future danger of inflation. Fear of inflation remains the overriding determinant of macroeconomic policy in Canada. Consequently, growth is expected to slow to 3.0 per cent in 1998 and 2.3 per cent in 1999. Since labour productivity is expected to grow at 1.1 per cent per annum, the increase in employment (at 1.9 per cent in 1998, declining to 1.4 per cent from 1999 to 2001) only marginally exceeds growth in the labour force. As a result, unemployment decreases at a painfully slow rate to 8.2 per cent at the turn of the century. Only when the model is extended to 2020 does the slower rate of growth of an aging labour force eventually produce a decline in unemployment rates.

This forecast is shown in Figure 31, which is taken from the September 1997 National Forecast of Informetrica Ltd. All forecasts are conditional, and changes in economic policy or in the international economic environment could produce different outcomes. However, the National Forecast assumed a continuation of the macroeconomic policy then in place.

If unemployment continues at these levels, there will be so much excess supply in labour markets that there is no danger of inflation. Although there is substantial uncertainty about the exact rate of unemployment at which inflation might re-emerge (see Setterfield, Gordon and Osberg 1992), this chapter adopts the estimate of researchers at the Department of Finance[4] of the long-run, natural rate of unemployment in Canada as about 6 per cent (see Sargent, 1996: 32). This estimate reflects the efficiency of current training and educational programs and the incentives to individual behaviour which are implicit in existing social programs. If Canada adopts more effective educational, training and social policies, the natural rate of unemployment will fall, since the potential capabilities of unemployed individuals will more accurately match the needs of employers. However, without an improvement in the aggregate demand for labour, such policies will only add to the gap between the natural and the actual rates of unemployment.

When aggregate demand increases and the unemployment rate is reduced, firms move closer to full utilization of their capital stock. Greater efficiency in the utilization of capital equipment and the workforce means that productivity increases as unemployment falls.

Okun (1981) argued that the output gap (the percentage difference between potential and actual output) could be approximated as 2.5 times the difference between the actual and natural unemployment rates. In Canada in 1997, this calculation is 2.5 per cent x (9.0 - 6.0) = 7.5 per cent of GDP. Since GDP in Canada was approximately $861 billion in the third quarter of 1997, this type of rough calculation produces a current estimated output gap of about $65 billion per year. There is good reason to believe that the output gap was larger than this in 1997, because Sargent's 1996 estimate of 6 per cent as the long-run natural rate of unemployment referred to 1995. Since then the determinants of the natural rate that he identified (such as UI/EI generosity) have changed somewhat as the downward trend in UI/EI generosity has continued. Unemployment benefits in Canada are now quite comparable to those in the U.S. which by late 1997 had experienced a long spell of unemployment below 5 per cent with no resurgence of inflation. Sargent states, "As those who have recently tried to estimate equations of the natural rate will know, it is truly hard to come up with respectable variables that can explain why the natural rate would be much higher now than it was in the 1960s." (1996: 28). (Fortin [1994] surveys other methods of calculating the output gap and reaches approximately the same figure.) The slow decline in unemployment over the next four years means that the output gap will not shrink appreciably for the rest of the nineties.

Implications of High Unemployment for Social Policy

High unemployment means that household income decreases because of job loss, the increasing number of individuals outside the labour force and downward pressure on wage rates in depressed labour markets. In addition, the availability of a queue of qualified potential employees has made it easier for employers to shift to a "just-in-time" labour strategy, in which they hire part-time, casual or contract workers when necessary to accommodate peaks in labour demand.[5] The Economic Council of Canada (1991, 81) estimated that "nonstandard" forms of employment accounted for 44 per cent of the growth in employment in the eighties. As a result, the workers who shift to the casual sector because they cannot find permanent employment face greater insecurity of income flows, as well as depressed expectations of earnings. Both the instability and the lower level of labour earnings increase the demand for social services.

In the short run, each household faces an increased risk and the chance of a greater depth of poverty. Despite UI and social assistance payments, the National Council of Welfare (1997) estimated that the poverty gap (the difference between an income at the poverty line and actual incomes, summed over all low-income households) increased from $11.167 billion in 1990 to $16.305 billion in 1995. As a percentage of GDP, the poverty gap (at 1.6 per cent in 1990 and 2.1 per cent in 1995) is far smaller today than the output gap, but much of the poverty gap can be attributed to high rates of unemployment. When the national unemployment rate is 7.5 per cent (as in 1981 or 1989), the poverty gap is about 1.3 per cent of national GDP, but the reductions in social assistance rates and the UI/EI coverage of the nineties have undoubtedly widened this gap.

In the long run, high unemployment increases the demand for social services because the characteristics of households change. Prolonged unemployment does bad things to people. It is well established that high unemployment produces higher rates of mental and physical illness, suicide, crime, drug abuse, child abuse and divorce.[6] These problems increase the probability that individuals will have to rely on social assistance and decrease the probability that they will be able to move off it. As a consequence, the health care and criminal justice systems face increased demands. And because more people are sick and in trouble with the law, greater expenditures on hospitals, prisons, physicians and police officers swell the deficit, while illness and incarceration diminish the productivity of the labour force.

In the sixties, the War on Poverty in the United States adopted the maxim "a rising tide lifts all boats." At that time, the U.S. government decided to stimulate the macroeconomic demand for labour in order to ensure the availability of jobs for the graduates of new training programs for the disadvantaged. The sixties consensus on the efficacy of macroeconomic policy became unfashionable in the seventies and eighties, when, with hindsight, it became apparent that although a rising tide may lift many boats, some boats will still need repairs. But in the nineties, it has become clear that without enough water, even the best-repaired boats do not float. Emphasis on the supply side of labour markets — on education, training and the incentives of social policy — is important, but when jobs are not available, policies to increase the supply of trained labour are pointless.

Government policies affect the amount of training delivered in the government sector and influence the level of training provided in the private sector. Many commentators (e.g., Betcherman 1992) have noted the relatively low levels of investment in training by Canadian employers; what should be stressed are the reasons for this strategic choice by Canadian firms and the influence of unemployment. Employers who face depressed conditions in product markets and who are laying off skilled workers have no need for training programs to increase their supply of skills. Employers who have a queue of qualified workers available in the labour market have no incentive to bear the costs of training programs.

Although it may be widely recognized that, in the long run, productivity and jobs in Canada depend upon the skill level of the labour force and the quality of training programs, lamenting the lack of a "training culture" in Canadian industry is pointless if long periods of high unemployment imply that it is irrational for employers to invest heavily in training. It is not surprising that employers do not bother with training programs, when an excess supply of labour means that the skills which they need are readily available on the open market. As Sharpe (1993) has noted, a mismatch between labour market demands and available candidates may have been an important source of unemployment in 1988–89 in Canada, but continued high unemployment has created a generalized surplus of labour in almost all skill categories.

Government provides training directly to individuals through the standard system of primary, secondary and postsecondary education and through the specialized set of remedial programs provided to social assistance clients and, increasingly, to EI recipients. The proportion of students who stay in school and levels of enrolment in university and community colleges increased substantially in Canada during the eighties. (Between 1980 and 1992, for example, the proportion of students who attended grade 12 in Nova Scotia increased from 57 to 94 per cent; see Osberg, Wien and Grude 1995). Economists have always emphasized that foregone wages are one of the major costs of continued education, and one implication of high unemployment is that the opportunity cost of staying in school falls. In a relative sense, this investment in higher education is a successful strategy for individuals, as evidenced by the continued differential in unemployment rates and income levels between university and high school graduates.

However, the other side of the coin is that the increasing educational qualifications of the mainstream population do not make it easier for the disadvantaged to succeed in the competition for jobs. Fewer years of education can also make it increasingly difficult for the disadvantaged to gain access to job training. For example, although one of the intended functions of the community college system was to service the need for job-relevant training of high school drop-outs, the abundance of well-qualified applicants means that grade 12 graduation is now the de facto entry requirement for almost all training programs.

In addition to the standard courses available at secondary schools, community colleges and universities, government finances a wide range of special remedial services targeted at those on social assistance. Counselling, supported work and life skills programs help individuals acquire the self-esteem, interpersonal skills and attitudes which are even more fundamental to employability than cognitive skills. Remedial literacy programs raise the educational level of individuals to one at which they can begin to assimilate training, and customized training modules teach job-relevant skills, such as word processing. And for the fastest-growing segment of the social assistance population — the "Steady Eddies" who have decades of work experience, a stable family life and no disabilities, but who also have no job and who have run out of EI — there are "job-finding clubs" to help with the unfamiliar skills of searching for a job.

In the United States, there have been a number of careful econometric analyses of the effects of job search assistance and training on displaced workers (which often use control groups of nonparticipants). This literature is not entirely negative: job search assistance can yield benefits, and carefully designed programs, with effective integration of remedial education, vocational training and job placement, can make a difference. However, these positive effects occur only if the number of jobs in the local labour market is expanding rapidly. Evaluation surveys of training interventions are, in the main, fairly depressing reading, since so many training experiments have had statistically insignificant results for later income levels or for chances for employment (e.g., Decker and Corson 1993; Leigh 1993).

As part of a larger research project that examined this phenomenon, I interviewed some of the people who administer these remedial programs in Canada. Although many of these programs seem to be well conceived and well executed and have a history of previous success, the administrators' depression and sense of futility in facing today's labour market is tangible. After all, their "graduates" have to compete in the labour market with the unblemished new graduates of universities, community colleges and high schools, many of whom will take almost anything today.

When the advertisement of a low-level clerical position produces upwards of 100 applications, it is not surprising that the skills taught in remedial programs (and the work history of their clients) are less attractive than the qualifications of other applicants. Although remedial training programs may well provide the skill set which is actually required for the job, and many of the other applicants for the same position are overqualified and would, essentially, be "underemployed," in today's tough economic times, we can hardly criticize employers for hiring the applicant with the best possible qualifications.

One of the main lessons from the evaluation literature is the diversity of needs of the social assistance population. For example, the needs of teenaged, single parents are very different from those of mature, displaced workers, and the overlap of social, psychological and educational disadvantages is far from perfect. People with multiple, severe problems are at great risk of long-term welfare dependency, while others' receipt of social assistance can be very short term.

This diversity implies that while many people touch the social assistance system for a brief period, only a small proportion is dependent for longer periods of time, and thus accounts for most of the costs. In social assistance, as in health care, a few people incur the bulk of the costs, and prevention is often *much* cheaper than the cure (see ECC 1992).

However, in a high-unemployment environment, the few tend to become many. As mentioned above, high unemployment results in more single-parent families, abuse victims, psychologically disabled individuals, and so on, who are at great risk for long-term dependency. Furthermore, both preventing the problem and implementing the cure become much more difficult, since it becomes harder for training programs to actually lead to employment.

Clearly, any society that foregoes $65 billion of potential income will have difficulty satisfying competing demands for resources. As noted earlier, the poverty gap in Canada has been about 1.3 per cent of GDP when the rate of unemployment was in the range of 7 to 7.5 per cent. However, the output gap is currently almost six times this value. A tax of 17 per cent on the increase in output, if we moved to 6 per cent unemployment, would entirely finance the transfer payments required to eliminate poverty in Canada. The remaining funds would be sufficient to significantly reduce the budget deficits of provincial and federal governments, as well as to increase aggregate consumer expenditure.

In the popular press, we sometimes hear of "jobless growth" in reference to firms which have increased output while decreasing employment. However, growth in labour productivity is not a new phenomenon. Since the Industrial Revolution over two centuries ago, firms have been replacing workers with machines. Greater productivity means that more output can be produced by fewer workers, but if demand is growing fast enough, firms will also want to hire new workers, to satisfy that demand. The output gap and the rate of job creation depend primarily on the growth rate of aggregate demand. If aggregate demand grows fast enough, unemployment will decline.

As the recent history of employment in Ontario manufacturing illustrates, high real interest rates can produce capital inflows and an overvalued exchange rate (averaging U.S.$.86 in 1990), which will price firms out of export markets — as we saw from 1988 to 1991. However, prices in general (and exchange rates in particular) do matter, even if they operate with a lag. In 1993, the Bank of Canada lowered interest rates, and the resulting drop in the exchange rate to U.S.$.72 produced a resurgence in exports and in manufacturing employment during 1994. This flurry of activity was stifled in 1995 by a surge in interest rates — in 1997 the pattern was repeated. One of the advantages of being a small country is that Canada could let short-term interest rates decline and allow further decreases in the exchange rate, without major international retaliation.

We must recognize that a strategy of declining exchange rates and "export-led growth" would have costs. There would be implications for income distribution, since a lower exchange rate means higher prices of imported goods and services and, effectively, a cut in real incomes. However, if the alternative to cutting real wages quickly in this way is to cut wages slowly and unevenly through the cumulative pressure of long-term, mass unemployment, it seems fairer and more efficient to use the exchange rate mechanism. Historically, Canadian governments have often made use of exchange rate flexibility to produce periods of sustained growth (e.g., from 1962 to 1970). Higher growth rates of GDP and lower unemployment rates are entirely feasible.

Furthermore, depressed tax revenues and the higher EI and social assistance payments that accompany slow growth continue to sabotage Canada's attempts to reduce the debt. Faster growth is essential for reducing the debt-to-GDP ratio, and panic over this ratio is now the main constraint on the available funding for social assistance and for remedial social policies.

Although, in a financial sense, Canadians could "solve" the poverty problem with resources equivalent to a small proportion of the output gap, this chapter is not arguing for "cheque-book social work." Even though individuals on social assistance live well below the poverty line in all provinces in Canada, and many of these people need primarily more income (preferably through employment), there remains a significant group who need more than money. For those people who have been damaged by abuse or handicapped by psychological problems or substance dependency, counselling, retraining and supported work initiatives are essential supplements to cash payments. However, if the number of such casualties is to stop increasing, or if their training programs are to have a hope of success, lower unemployment is essential.

The Interdependency of Macro and Micro Policy

According to the Constitution of Canada, provincial governments control:

- the labour legislation, which frames the industrial relations system;
- the primary, secondary and postsecondary education system, which trains the labour force;
- the health care system, which keeps the population healthy; and
- the social assistance system.

Although Human Resources Development Canada contributes sizable funds to training, provincial government community colleges actually deliver most of the training.[7] The "structural policies" of government, which help to ensure that a healthy, well-trained and highly motivated labour force is available for business, are, in Canada, provincial responsibilities.

In the long term, structural policies are crucial to the health of the Canadian economy, and provincial government decisions do make a major difference. However, it is simply not possible for structural policies to have rapid results. Recently, much attention has been given to failures in the education system, and since the issue is fairly easily quantified, we will use education as an example.

Even if the best possible education system in the world could be implemented in time for the first day of school next year, the immediate implications of education reform for the quality of the labour force would be rather small because:

- the number of people who graduate from high school each year is a small percentage of the labour force (approximately 2.5 per cent);
- most students have already gotten most of their education under the old system; it would take twelve years for a reform of primary and secondary education to have its full effect on graduates;
- the potential benefit of education reform is the difference between current educational achievement in Canada and that in other countries. Although some other students do better than Canadian students in international comparison testing, the difference is not huge.[8]

Believers in "quick-fix" social policies, who have an exaggerated idea of the size of labour supply elasticities, want to think that changes in the implicit incentives of social policies can have immediate, significant effects. As Phipps has shown (1993), there is a large body of econometric literature which demonstrates that labour supply elasticities are typically quite small, even for individuals who are not constrained by the availability of employment hours.[9] Changing the incentives implicit in social assistance policies will affect the hours people want to work, but only slightly. Furthermore, whatever the size of the effects of greater financial incentives to work, these policy measures affect only the desired hours of work of individuals (i.e., the supply side of labour markets). They have no direct consequences for the desired employment levels of firms. However, getting a job is a joint event: an individual must want a job *and* a firm must want to hire him or her. In a market with an excess supply of labour, greater incentives only add to the excess of supply.

Over time, the health care, counselling, retraining and educational policies of provincial governments can have significant implications for labour force productivity by changing the characteristics which the clients of these programs bring to the labour market. Since it takes a long time to affect the average characteristics of the labour force stock, however, these policies can only have long-term pay-offs. Provincial governments control most of the policy levers which affect lasting structural change in the labour market, but these policies cannot be expected to have more than marginal significance for unemployment within a single electoral mandate. By contrast, it is clear that the fluctuations of the business cycle can create or destroy hundreds of thousands of jobs within a one- or two-year period. The federal government can influence the timing and intensity of the recessions and recoveries of the macroeconomic business cycle through its control over fiscal, monetary and exchange rate policies, but it can do much less to influence long-term structural policies.

In adjusting to structural change, Canada has the significant advantage of a relatively mobile and well-educated population. As the majority has adapted, however, it has left behind an increasingly large minority. High unemployment impedes structural adaptation by "chilling" the labour market; it reduces the number of people who voluntarily change jobs or relocate and increases the difficulties of the disadvantaged in gaining access to the labour market (Osberg 1991; Picot and Pyper 1993). High unemployment therefore hinders structural adjustment.

Short-term and long-run unemployment also interact, since workers who have been unemployed for long periods of time bear the social costs in health and family life and the economic costs of obsolescence of their skills. In recent years, the term "hysteresis" has been coined to describe the idea that high unemployment feeds on itself; those who have been unemployed for a long time eventually become unemployable. However, the debate on hysteresis in unemployment has, in Canada, a particular federalist wrinkle. Federal government decisions on fiscal and monetary policy can quickly influence the rate of unemployment, and this higher unemployment creates social casualties, firm closings and depreciation of human capital, which contribute to long-term unemployment. Provincial governments' social policies then have to react to an increased demand for social services, fewer financial resources and a diminished probability of program success, due to the unavailability of jobs. The failure of these provincial policies increases the rate of inflation associated with any given level of unemployment, worsening the trade-off between inflation and unemployment which faces federal decision makers.

Conclusion

A long-term objective of social policy is to help Canada adapt to structural change and to integrate those who now depend on EI and social assistance into employment. The day-to-day reality is a generalized surplus of labour. This surplus makes getting ahead in the competition for jobs extremely difficult for the disadvantaged. How can the socially disadvantaged be integrated into employment if they face, year after year, a labour market crowded with an excess supply of qualified new graduates? In this situation, how can prolonged high unemployment *not* generate more long-term candidates for social assistance?

When the economy grows slowly and interest rates are kept high, reducing the debt-to-GDP ratio requires governments to make massive cuts to social assistance payments and to the programs that try to move people off social assistance. Meanwhile, the social costs, in health care and crime, of intensifying competition for jobs, less job security and high unemployment simultaneously increase the deficit pressures facing governments.

In Canada, the failure of one level of government reduces the likelihood that the other level can be successful. The policy levers which might influence the rate of structural change in labour markets are almost entirely under provincial jurisdiction, but the success of these policies depends heavily on whether there are any jobs available for the clients of counselling, retraining or mobility programs. In other words, provincial success depends on federal macroeconomic policy. Although macroeconomic policies are firmly under federal control, their long-term success depends on the effectiveness of the provincial policies which might help to prevent increases in the natural rate of unemployment. Federal government decision makers seem, however, either unable or unwilling to recognize the interdependence between short-term macro-economic policy and structural change, or the implications of their decisions for provincial governments.

In a very real sense, however, macroeconomic policy is implicit social policy. Macroeconomic policy has profound social implications and social policy has serious macroeconomic implications in the long run. But if both types of policies are to be successful, they have to be coordinated, both across levels of governments and in time, and the crucial ingredient for success is recognition, by *all* policy actors, of the paramount importance of full employment.

References

Bartolini, L., and S. Symansky. 1993. Unemployment and Wage Dynamics in Multi-Mod. In *Staff Studies for the World Economic Outlook*, International Monetary Fund, Washington, D.C., December.

Betcherman, G. 1992. Are Firms Underinvesting in Training? *Canadian Business Economics* 1, no. 1: 25–33.

Brenner, H.M. 1973. *Mental Illness and the Economy.* Cambridge, Mass.: Harvard University Press.

Coletti, D., D. Muir, and R. Tetlow. 1995. Measuring Potential Output in the Presence of Model Mis-Specification — A Stochastic Simulation Approach. Research Department Bank of Canada, Ottawa. Mimeograph.

Decker, P.T., and W. Corson. 1993. International Trade and Worker Displacement: Evaluation of the Trade Adjustment Assistance Program. Mathematica Policy Research, Princeton, New Jersey, June. Mimeograph.

Economic Council of Canada (ECC). 1991. Employment in the Service Economy. Supply and Services, Ottawa.

Economic Council of Canada (ECC). 1992. The New Face of Poverty: Income Security Needs of Canadian Families. Supply and Services, Ottawa.

Fortin, P. 1994. A Diversified Strategy for Deficit Control: Combining Faster Growth with Fiscal Discipline. Department of Economics, University of Quebec at Montreal.

Fougère, M. 1995. Why the Unemployment Rate is Higher in Canada Than in the United States. Paper presented at the annual meeting of the Canadian Economics Association, Montreal, Quebec, June.

International Association of Educational Progress (IAEP). 1992. Learning Science Report No. 22-CAEP-02. Educational Testing Service, Princeton, New Jersey.

James, S. 1991. Hysteresis and the Natural Rate of Unemployment in Canada. Paper presented at the meeting of the Canadian Economics Association, Kingston, Ontario, June. Mimeograph.

Kelvin, P., and J.E. Jarrett. 1985. *Unemployment — Its Social and Psychological Effects.* Cambridge: Cambridge University Press.

Ketso, V.L. 1988. Work and the Welfare Costs of Unemployment. PhD diss., Dalhousie University, Halifax, Nova Scotia.

Killingsworth, M. 1983. *Labor Supply.* Cambridge: Cambridge Unversity Press.

Leigh, D.E. 1993. Effective Retraining for Displaced Workers: The U.S. Experience. Paper presented at Canadian Employment Research Forum Workshop, Ottawa, Ontario, 24 September.

National Council of Welfare. 1992. Poverty Profile 1980–1990. Supply and Services, Ottawa. Autumn.

———. 1997. Poverty Profile 1995. Supply and Services, Ottawa.

Okun, A.M. 1981. *Prices and Quantities — A Macroeconomic Analysis.* Blackwell.

Osberg, L. 1986. Behavioral Response in the Context of Socioeconomic Microanalytic Simulation. Research Paper No. 1, Analytical Studies, Statistics Canada, Ottawa.

———. 1991. Unemployment and Inter-Industry Mobility of Labour in Canada in the 1980s. *Applied Economics* 23, no. 11: 1707–1718.

———. 1993. The Role of Education in the Economic Development of Atlantic Canada. Dalhousie University, Halifax, Nova Scotia. Mimeograph.

———. 1995. Concepts of Unemployment and the Structure of Employment. *Économie Appliquée* 48, no. 1: 151–181.

————. 1996. Unemployment Insurance and Unemployment — Revisited. Chap. 5 in *The Unemployment Crisis: All for Naught?* Kingston: McGill-Queen's University Press.

Osberg, L., and S. Phipps. 1993. Labour Supply with Quantity Constraints: Estimates from a Large Sample of Canadian Workers. *Oxford Economic Papers* 45 (April): 269–291.

Osberg, L., F. Wien, and J. Grude. 1995. *Vanishing Jobs: Canada's Changing Workplaces*. Toronto: James Lorimer.

Pencavel, J. 1986. Labour Supply of Men: A Survey. Chap. 1 in *Handbook of Labour Economics*, edited by O. Ashenfelter and R. Layard. Elsevier: North Holland Press.

Phipps, S. 1993. Does Unemployment Insurance Increase Unemployment? *Canadian Business Economics* 1, no. 3: 37–50.

Picot, G., and W. Pyper. 1993. Permanent Layoffs and Displaced Workers: Cyclical Sensitivity, Concentration and Experience Following the Layoff, Research Paper No. 55, Business and Labour Market Analysis Group, Analytical Studies, Statistics Canada, Ottawa.

Sargent, Timothy C., and Munir S. Sheikh. (1996) *The Natural Rate of Unemployment: Theory, Evidence And Policy Implications*. Economic Studies and Policy Analysis Division, Department of Finance, Ottawa, August 1996.

Setterfield, M., D.V. Gordon, and L. Osberg. 1992. Searching for a Will O' The Wisp: An Empirical Study of the NAIRU in Canada. *European Economic Review* 36 (January): 119–136.

Sharpe, A. 1993. The Rise of Unemployment in Ontario. Paper presented at conference, Unemployment: What Is to be Done? at Laurentian University, Sudbury, Ontario, 26–27 March.

Business Cycles and Economic Growth: Current Controversies about Theory and Policy

James Tobin

What can governments do about employment and economic growth? What should governments try to do? In this chapter, Nobel Laureate James Tobin of Yale University discusses two opposing views. The classical perspective argues that market forces will automatically produce an optimal economic outcome. Hence, governments should follow a "do nothing" macroeconomic policy. Tobin argues that this analysis fundamentally misunderstands the nature of modern economies and that when total unemployment is high and the economy is producing below its potential, governments can and should intervene to stimulate demand.

The crucial issue of macroeconomics today is very much the same as it was in the thirties when John Maynard Keynes revolted against the "classical" orthodoxy of the day. Today's weapons may be more powerful and sophisticated, but the issues are pretty much the same. It does not speak well for the supposed "science" of economics that there are still doctrinal "schools." But perhaps controversies are inevitable when the issues are so close to policy, politics and ideology, and are so difficult or impossible to resolve by controlled experiments. I am quite dismayed by the prevalence in my profession today, in a particularly virulent form, of the macroeconomic doctrines against which I as a student enlisted in the Keynesian revolution. The high priests of the counterrevolution call themselves new classicals and refer to their explanation of fluctuations in economic activity as "real business cycle theory." I guess "real" is intended to mean "not monetary" as well as "not false."

Keynesian versus Classical Macroeconomic Theory

I am going to discuss these differences in theory, Keynesian versus classical, both then and now. The main purpose and preoccupation of macroeconomic theory is to guide fiscal and monetary policies. Therefore, theoretical disagreements imply important differences in policy. These disagreements are not confined to economists. They seep gradually into the ways students, pundits, politicians, bureaucrats, financiers, business executives and the general public view the world.

The doctrinal differences stand out most clearly in the opposing diagnoses of the fluctuations in output and employment to which democratic capitalist societies like ours are subject, and in the remedies, if any, that are prescribed. Keynesian theory regards recessions as lapses from a desirable state — full employment equilibrium. The lapses are massive failures in the performance of the market economy, resulting from shortages of spending on goods and services, and consequently shortages of jobs for workers who produce them.

The opposing theory interprets those fluctuations, recessions and booms, as moving equilibria — not pathological departures from an optimal healthy state, just changes in the state itself. In this view, business cycles are individually and socially rational responses to inevitable changes in the economic environment.

Keynesian logic leads its adherents to advocate active fiscal and monetary policies to restore and maintain full employment. But the logical implication of new classical theory is that no policy interventions are either necessary or desirable.

Should we describe the macroeconomy by two regimes or one? The old Keynesian view favours two regimes. In one, the Keynesian regime, aggregate economic activity is constrained by demand but not by supply. That is, if there were additional effective demands for goods and services, more of those commodities could and would be produced to satisfy those demands. An apt aphorism is Demand Creates Its Own Supply. The necessary inputs of labour, capital, capacity and other factors of production are available, ready to be employed at prices, wages and rents that their productivity would earn. Only customers are missing.

The alternate regime, which Keynes called classical, is supply-constrained. Extra demand cannot be satisfied at the economy's existing capacity to produce. Workers or other inputs needed are not available at affordable wages and rents. New demands on those resources can be met only if they displace old ones. These supply limits bring about prices and incomes that restrict aggregate demand to capacity output. At those prices and incomes, people neither can nor want to buy more. As capacity increases over time, thanks to investments in new capacity and to technological progress, market prices and incomes will automatically generate just enough additional purchasing power to buy the extra output. The aphorism is Supply Creates Its Own Demand.

The two polar regimes are oversimplifications, but I will stick with them in this article. Keynesians believe that the economy is sometimes in one regime and sometimes in the other. New and old classical models depict the economy as always supply-constrained, always in an equilibrium where demand and supply are equal to each other at existing prices. In the real business cycle model, the shocks that move economic activity up and down are essentially supply shocks, changes in technology and productivity or in the bounty of nature or in the costs and supplies of imported products.

Growth Trends and Short-Run Cycles: Potential and Actual GNP

The distinction between regimes is concretely illustrated in Figures 32 and 33. Charts of this kind, meant to depict a Keynesian view of the economy, were originated by President John F. Kennedy's Council of Economic Advisers in 1961. Here, real GNP (i.e., inflation-corrected, measured in 1987 prices) is plotted quarterly from 1950 through 1992; the vertical scale is logarithmic. The wiggly track is the actual GNP reported by the Commerce Department. The smooth track is the real Potential Gross National Product (PGNP), a hypothetical estimate of the growing capacity of the economy to produce goods and services.

PGNP approximates the supply constraint on GNP. This definition cannot, of course, be taken literally. "Capacity" means what can be produced by the normal peacetime operations of a market economy, not what can be done in an emergency mobilization like a world war.

Figure 32

**Real GNP: Actual and Potential
Quarterly, 1950–92**

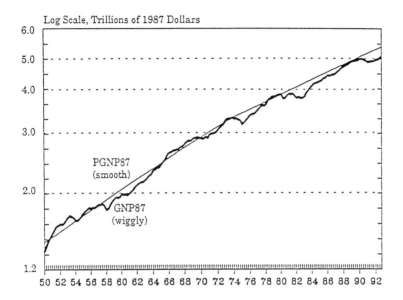

Note: Shown in quarterly figures (1987 dollars) on a logarithmic scale.

In some periods, Figure 32 shows, actual GNP exceeds PGNP. These are periods of labour shortage and unsustainably low unemployment; the economy is overheated and inflation is increasing. The Vietnam War period of the late sixties is an example.

Conceptually, PGNP is meant to correspond to full employment, indicated by a balance between unemployment and vacancies and by stable prices, or at least by stable rates of inflation. In practice, the unemployment rate when GNP coincides with PGNP rises gradually from 4 to 5.5 per cent (see Figure 32).

The proximate determinants of the growth of PGNP are the growth of employment — which is, for roughly constant unemployment rates and hours of work, that of the labour force — and the growth of the productivity of labour. Both of these growth rates slowed down around 1973. In Figure 32, the slope of PGNP (shown on a log scale) is reduced from 3.5 to 2.5 per cent in that year. The disappointing slow-down is that of the productivity of labour. Its growth depends largely on technology, on the education and training of the labour force, and on the quantity and quality of the tools and machinery that augment human powers to produce.

The sources of PGNP growth are supply phenomena, which by their very nature, change slowly. Actual GNP is more variable; it wanders around PGNP. Keynesian theory is that those fluctuations are demand-generated, caused by the ups and downs of spending, which is much more volatile than capacity. When GNP falls below PGNP, the economy is in the Keynesian demand-constrained regime. When it is equal to or above PGNP, the economy is supply-constrained. Those statements are overprecise. Regime shifts are not so abrupt, and there are many times when diagnosis is uncertain.

Keynesian regimes are maladies confined largely to market capitalism. Throughout most human history, and for most of the world's population today, fluctuations in production, short-run as well as long-run, have been usually supply-generated — by weather, harvests, and natural catastrophes. Today, in a big economy like ours, such natural disasters are just small wiggles in national capacity, whose trend is quite smooth.

The fluctuations shown in Figure 32 are the eight recessions and business cycles of the U.S. economy since 1950. If you look at them relative to the PGNP trend, you will not use the conventional criterion used by the National Bureau of Economic Research (NBER) in declaring and dating recessions and recoveries. Their criterion for recession is essentially negative growth of GNP for at least two quarters. The recession criterion suggested by Figure 32 would be two quarters of growth slower than potential. Par these days would be not zero growth but 2.5 per cent. By that standard, the economy has been in recession or incomplete recovery a much greater share of the time than the official calls of the NBER arbiters imply. The difference is striking for the last four years, during which the economy rarely declined in absolute terms but was growing more slowly than its potential almost all the time.

Figure 33 charts the percentage gap between PGNP and GNP, together with the national unemployment rate. Clearly they go up and down together. However, the amplitude of the gap is much the greater. A one-point increase or decrease in the unemployment rate is associated with a 2.5 or 3 per cent change in the same direction in actual GNP and thus in the gap. This phenomenon is one of the most reliable and important regularities in empirical macroeconomics. It is known to economists as Okun's law, because the late Arthur Okun quantified PGNP and the relation of the gap to unemployment for Kennedy's Council of Economic Advisers. The council wanted to demonstrate to the president and Congress that the economic pay-offs of fiscal and monetary stimuli to reduce unemployment went far beyond the benefits to the unemployed themselves.

It may seem paradoxical that a reduction of one percentage point in unemployment would raise output by more than 1 per cent, indeed by a great deal more. The answer is that the same spending that reduces unemployment rates raises labour inputs to production in other ways: increased work hours, movement of discouraged workers into the labour force and more efficient use of redundant workers kept on payrolls in hard times.

Apostles of the new classical macroeconomics reject this Keynesian interpretation. For them, there is no PGNP path distinct from actual GNP. Fluctuations of actual GNP are also fluctuations of PGNP, caused by shocks to the economy's productive capacity. Interpretations of unemployment measures likewise differ radically. The Keynesian view is that the increases in unemployment in recessions are involuntary. Idle workers would like to have jobs at prevailing wages and are capable of doing the work, but the jobs don't exist. Market demands and supplies at existing wages are not clearing. There is excess supply.

For their part, new classicals regard all unemployment as voluntary; workers choose to withdraw from or enter or re-enter the labour force as the advantages of employment change relative to those of other uses of time.

The Framework Applied to the Current Scene

Our economy has been suffering from two maladies at the same time. One has afflicted us since 1973. It is that the growth of potential output is too slow. We'd like the potential line to be both higher and steeper. The problem is the labour productivity component. Real wages reflect productivity growth; their stagnation has disappointed and alienated most workers. Government seeks measures to increase productivity over the long run. Public infrastructure, education and skill training, science and technology, and business plant and equipment — investments in those areas are all intended to lift PGNP.

The second malady, of more recent origin, is the large gap between actual and potential GNP, of which persistent high unemployment is one big symptom. The remedy for that is more spending, regardless of whether it is for investment or consumption or something else.

Figure 33

GNP Gap and Unemployment Rate
Quarterly, 1950–92

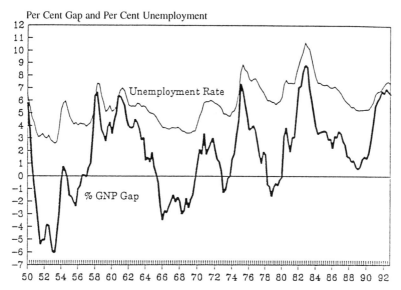

Per Cent Gap and Per Cent Unemployment

The coincidence of these two maladies, for which remedial prescriptions are quite different and even contradictory, has created confusion and ambiguity in federal policy making. If federal deficit reduction is a solution to anything, it is to the longer-run problem of capacity growth. Under favourable circumstances, deficit reduction would channel more of the country's resources into investment for the future. But deficit reduction can only be accomplished by reducing spending by somebody, government or taxpayers. With respect to demand deficiency, our short-run problem, deficit reduction works in the wrong direction.

Public opinion and the political process find it difficult to cope with two macroeconomic problems at once, especially when the indicated therapy for one appears to be the opposite of the prescription for the other.

Keynes's Principle of Effective Demand

Keynes said that the most important principle in his 1936 book was what he called the principle of effective demand. By *effective* demand, he meant, for example, the demands of unemployed workers for goods and services given that they are not earning wages, as distinct from the demands they would have if they had jobs and earnings to spend. In this way, demand limits the performance of the economy and is itself constrained by the economy's subpar performance.

Practical people are instinctively Keynesian, especially during recessions. They realize that companies lay off workers and shut down production lines when sales fall off. They realize that the effects multiply as workers who lose jobs and suppliers who lose orders cut back their own spending. They see what cut-backs in defence spending, despite their potential long-run benefits to the nation, do to New London-Groton, St. Louis and San Diego. But the dominant theory in academic macroeconomics today has no room for economy-wide spending shocks and demand-side recessions.

Market-Clearing and Price Flexibility

At the centre of the controversy is "market clearing," specifically the role of prices in equating demand and supply. Figure 34 is the economics teacher's all-time favourite diagram for beginning students, and it is unquestioned reality for graduate students. The quantity of some commodity is on the horizontal axis, and its price is measured vertically. If the demand curve is D_0 and the supply curve is S_0, the market-clearing price is p_0 and the quantity bought and sold is x_0. Should demand shift back to D_1, the market would clear at p_1, x_1.

But does a price adjustment like this occur instantaneously, so that there is no real time when the market fails to clear? Is there no real time when price stays at p_0 and sellers can sell only x_{01}? More generally, should we model the economy as if all markets, labour markets as well as product markets, are cleared by prices at every moment in time? If so, we are assuming away excess supplies and excess demands altogether, assuming that all prices and quantities we observe reflect demand=supply equalities, assuming that no non-price rationing of sales among buyers or sellers occurs. This argument is the core of the dispute between Keynesians and new classical theorists.

This discussion is not entirely new. The same controversy occurred in the thirties. Then, as now, the issue was whether a market economy possessed reliable, automatic adjustment mechanisms that would return it to full-employment equilibrium reasonably fast, if

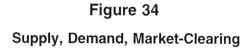

Figure 34

Supply, Demand, Market-Clearing

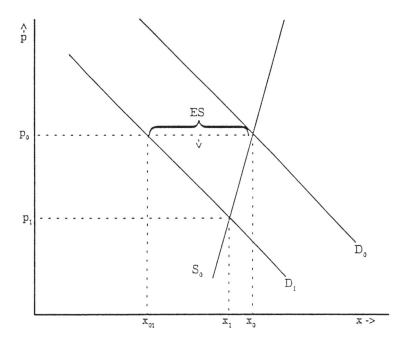

D, demand; S, supply; p, market-clearing price; x, quantity bought and sold; ES, excess supply

ever. The essential stabilizing mechanisms were, then as now, flexible prices.

Yet the classical economists of Keynes's day were more moderate than their latter-day successors. They did not argue that a model of *perfect* price flexibility, in which prices clear all markets at every instant in time, was a realistic approximation of actual economies or a practical guide to government policies. They did not deny that demand shocks might occur and would temporarily create excess supplies of labour. The debate was about the efficacy and speed of natural recuperative mechanisms. Specifically, will deflation or disinflation, the wage and price declines that naturally result from excess supplies (like ES in Figure 34) do the job? Will they do it without help from stimulative fiscal and monetary policies? Keynes said, "No, or anyway not always, and if ever, not soon enough." His friend and Cambridge colleague, Professor A. C. Pigou, said, "Yes, surely yes, eventually anyway." He objected as a matter of theoretical principle to Keynes's *General Theory* and its pretentious title. As a practical matter, however, he agreed that public works spending to reduce unemployment would be worthwhile.

In contrast, new classical theorists today do not allow excess supplies and demands ever to arise in the first place. Thus they finesse the Keynes-Pigou issue, the efficacy and speed of wage and price movements in eliminating discrepancies between demand and supply. In their view, Keynes arbitrarily assumed that wages and prices were rigid, irrationally unresponsive to demand and supply shocks. Without that assumption, they say, there is no case for demand constraints on GNP or for involuntary unemployment or for activist demand management policies.

They misread Keynes and misunderstand Keynesian macro-economics. Price flexibility is not a yes-or-no circumstance. Consider instead a spectrum of the degree of price flexibility, from perfect flexibility at one extreme to perfect rigidity at the other. Perfect flexibility means instantaneous adjustment: prices always clear markets, jumping sufficiently to absorb at once all demand or supply shocks. Perfect rigidity means that prices do not change at all during the period of analysis. In between are various speeds of adjustment, various lengths of time during which markets are not clearing.

Who owns the middle ground? We Keynesians do, despite assertions to the contrary. Keynes and Keynesians did not assume perfect rigidity, nor did they need to. Any degree of price stickiness that prevents complete instantaneous and continuous price adjustment has the same qualitative implications, bringing into play Keynes's multipliers and other demand-determining processes (including the IS/LM curves taught to generations of college students.)

In Figure 34, it is easy to believe that price reductions triggered by the excess supply, ES, will be equilibrating. But jumping from a small single market in a large economy to economy-wide price adjustments brings a host of difficulties.

Think of a diagram like Figure 34 as referring to an economy-wide labour market, abstracting from the reality of numerous diverse but interconnected labour markets. Then the demand curve would reflect employers' offers of jobs, and the supply curve, workers' willingness to take them.

The price on the vertical axis, the price that might clear the market, would be the wage — actually the *real* wage, measured in terms of goods that workers both produce and consume.

But there's a big difference between a local bagels market and an economy-wide labour market, a difference which Keynes emphasized in 1936. The instinct of classical economists then and now is to say that the solution for unemployment is for the price of labour to drop, just as the solution for an oversupply of bagels in a local market is for the price of bagels to fall. As the dollar price of bagels falls, bagels become cheaper relative to workers' earnings and to the prices of other consumer goods. It's safe to ignore the impact of events in this local bagels market on the rest of the economy.

An economy-wide labour market is a different ball game. One big reason is that, as Keynes stressed, we live in a monetary economy. Money is the medium in which prices, including wages and salaries, are quoted. In insisting that this is a consequential fact, Keynes was deviating from a cherished classical (and new classical) principle, the proposition that "money is a veil," behind which everything works out as it would in a miraculously efficient barter economy. In other words, money is neutral. It affects nominal prices (prices in dollars) but not real prices (prices in other goods) or real quantities. In very many economic contexts this is the right presumption. But in business cycle dynamics it is misleading. The facts that prices are quoted in the monetary unit of account and that transactions involve payments of money are consequential. It is not a vulgar "money illusion" to recognize those facts.

It is dollar prices that initially respond to excess supplies and demands, not real or relative prices. Employers' demands for labour and workers' supplies basically depend on real wages, but bargains are made in money wages, like dollars per hour. When excess demand or supply develops, if a wage responds it will be dollar wages. Are other dollar prices, in particular the prices of the products workers make and those they consume, going to remain invariant as that happens? The answer is clearly not. Real wages are going to move less than money wages, perhaps not at all. Employers' incentives to hire more labour are dulled when the prices of the products they sell also decline. The intuition drawn from the microeconomic example does not carry over to the macroeconomic context.

Prices and Effective Demand

The macroeconomic question is whether the demand for GNP goods and services as a whole and consequently for the labour force as a whole will respond positively to economy-wide reductions in money wages and money prices.

The crucial issue is the following: Suppose all dollar prices and wages are lower by x per cent. Will aggregate demand for products and for labour be greater? Maybe, because with the same quantity of currency and bank reserves, interest rates could be lower and encourage businesses and households to spend. But in depressions, interest rates may be already as low as they can be; after all, the interest rate on currency cannot be less than zero. Anyway, as Keynes observed, lowering the overall price level cannot reduce interest rates more than the central bank could on its own, with much less social trauma.

Another possibility, stressed by Professor Pigou, is that owners of assets denominated in dollars feel richer after the purchasing power of the dollar has increased; therefore they buy more goods. The trouble is that debtors with dollar obligations are correspondingly poorer. There is a small excess of privately owned credits over private debts, the monetary issues and near-money obligations of the central government. But this net credit may not be sufficient to offset the likelihood that increased private debt burdens deter spending more than the corresponding gains in the purchasing power of creditors encourage it. So argued Irving Fisher, my revered predecessor at Yale. Even if Pigou, rather than Fisher, is right, the direct effect of the price level on demand is not an equilibrating mechanism of any practical importance. Certainly the big deflation during the Great Depression did no good.

A serious drawback to deflation (or disinflation) as an adjustment mechanism is its perverse effect on aggregate demand. Even if lower prices stimulate demand once prices have fallen, the process of falling prices is destabilizing. If you expect falling prices, you will postpone purchases, preferring to hold money rather than buy goods. For this reason, Keynes and Fisher rejected concerted deflation as a remedy for depression and unemployment.

These perverse effects arise when price changes occur in real time. Not surprisingly, the new classical theorists take the easy way out of this embarrassment. They assume perfect flexibility, instantaneous and complete; responding to surprise shocks, prices jump to the new supply=demand equilibria without passage of time. The new classicals' semantic trick is to pretend that the only alternative assumption is complete rigidity of prices. But there is a lot of room in the spectrum between the extremes, and the Keynesians own that middle ground. Their propositions do not require extreme price rigidity, only imperfect flexibility.

Policies and Effective Demand

An economy in a demand-constrained regime can benefit from policies that augment effective demand. Fiscal policies can add to demand in three ways: by increasing government purchases of goods and services; by increasing transfers to private individuals and businesses, enabling and inducing beneficiaries to raise their demands for goods and services; and by reducing taxes, enabling and inducing taxpayers to raise their demands for goods and services. These policies can be designed to target different categories of public and private expenditures on GNP. Their consequences for long-run growth of potential output will depend on the composition of the additional demand, as between public investment, private investment and current consumption.

Monetary policies augment effective demand by lowering interest rates, raising market prices of stocks, bonds and other assets, and relaxing restrictions on availability of credit to borrowers. These financial effects of the central bank's expansionary policies encourage individuals and enterprises to spend more on goods and services. An important additional channel of stimulative monetary policy occurs in an economy — especially a small economy, such as Canada's, in a big world — that is open to foreign trade and capital movements, with a foreign exchange rate allowed to respond flexibly to market conditions. As local interest rates tend to fall relative to world interest rates, outflows of funds depreciate the exchange rate and — at least after some lag — raise exports relative to imports. The result is a net increase in effective demand. Just as much of the domestic demand induced by monetary policy takes the form of domestic investment, so the increment in net exports is an increase in the nation's foreign investment.

Obviously these demand policies can and should be put in reverse if the economy is threatened by aggregate demand in excess of potential, with inflationary consequences.

Empirical Evidence

Fancy econometrics is not needed to mobilize evidence against the real business cycle view that observed fluctuations in output and employment are movements in price-cleared equilibrium. Here are a number of regularities of U.S. business cycles that falsify the implications of the new classical hypothesis. For most of them I am indebted to the last paper of the late Arthur Okun.

- Unemployment itself. If people voluntarily choose not to work at prevailing wages, why do they report themselves as unemployed, rather than as "not in labour force"? Real business cycle theory explains unemployment as voluntary intertemporal choice. Workers drop out when they perceive that real wages, the opportunity costs of leisure, are temporarily low. This might be a possible explanation of cyclical movements in employment if real wages were strongly procyclical. But there is no such systematic regularity. Nor is there empirical evidence of high sensitivity of the labour supply to current and expected real wages.

- Unemployment and vacancies. New classical theorists ask us to believe that the labour market is in equilibrium at 9 per cent unemployment just as truly as it is at 5 per cent. If so, there would be no reason to expect the balance between unemployment and job vacancies to differ between these two cases. Both unemployment and vacancies would be more numerous in recessions. However, a strong negative association between unemployment and vacancy rates, as would be expected in Keynesian theory, is obvious in the U.S. and other market capitalist economies.

- Quits and lay-offs. If recessions and prosperities are both supply=demand equilibria, there is no reason to expect the relative frequencies of voluntary resignations and involuntary separations from jobs to vary over the business cycle. But, of course, there are regularly many more lay-offs, relative to quits, when unemployment is high and vacancies are scarce. There are many more "job losers" relative to "job leavers" in recessions.

- Excess capacity. Utilization of plant and equipment varies cyclically parallel to utilization of labour. Presumably, machines do not choose leisure voluntarily.

- Unfilled orders and delivery delays. These move procyclically, again suggesting strongly that demand is much higher relative to supply in prosperities than in recessions.

- Monetary effects on output. According to the classical "money is a veil" principle, monetary events and policies should affect only nominal prices. Real outcomes should be independent of them. The evidence that this is not true is overwhelming.

The list could go on. Why do so many talented economic theorists believe and teach elegant fantasies obviously refutable by plain facts? Trying to answer that question would take us on an excursion into the sociology of my profession, beyond the scope of this paper.

References

Fisher, Irving. 1933. The Debt-Deflation Theory of Great Depressions. *Econometrica* 1 (October): 337-57.

Keynes, John Maynard. 1936. *The General Theory of Employment, Interest, and Money*. New York: Harcourt Brace.

Okun, Arthur M. 1980. Rational Expectations-with-Misperceptions as a Theory of the Business Cycle. Part 2. *Journal of Money, Credit, and Banking* 12 (November): 817-25.

Pigou, Arthur Cecil. 1943. The Classical Stationary State. *Economic Journal* 53 (December): 343-51.

Tobin, James. 1975. Keynesian Models of Recession and Depression. *American Economic Review (Papers and Proceedings)* 55 (May): 195-202.

———— 1993. Price Flexibility and Output Stability. *Journal of Economic Perspectives* 7 (Winter): 45-65.

Credibility Mountain

Lars Osberg
Pierre Fortin

How can Canada avoid a repetition of the policy errors that have produced such an enormous increase in Canada's debt burden? In their concluding chapter, Pierre Fortin and Lars Osberg note that although the contributors to this volume differ somewhat in their opinions on the proper role and size of government, they all agree that monetary policy has been a critical determinant of the increase in Canada's national debt in the 1980s and 1990s. The Bank of Canada's decision in 1988 to try to eliminate inflation entirely has had especially large consequences for the national debt in the 1990s. Since there was, and is, very little empirical evidence available to support the wisdom of this decision, Fortin and Osberg argue for fundamental reform of the Bank of Canada. They note that the federal government is now collecting far more in taxes than it spends on programs and that current policy settings will bring the debt/GDP ratio down substantially over the next dozen years. The level of interest rates will, however, heavily influence the size of the debt that remains.

Let's imagine that the waste of unemployment in Canada is visible, rather than invisible. Let's imagine that Canada has in place a system of "workfare" so that, rather than sitting around at home feeling useless, the unemployed are put to work doing something useless. Let's imagine, for example, that Canada's unemployed are put to work building "Credibility Mountain."

Let's think of Credibility Mountain as an enormous construction project, aimed at building a mountain of sand just outside Ottawa to symbolize our national willingness to tolerate high unemployment in the hope that inflation will disappear. We would not use in this construction project any of the resources that aren't normally unemployed in a market economy. We would only use unemployed labour and capital in excess of the rate of unemployment which prevailed in 1989 (7.5 per cent). Since the construction of Credibility Mountain uses only unemployed resources, it would not compete with private sector output (unlike most actual workfare projects), and the income of all other Canadians would remain unchanged. However, since the cumulative amount of output foregone due to excess unemployment over the period from 1989 to 1997 was approximately $475 billion,[1] by now Credibility Mountain would be rather large and growing.

Built as it is of sand, Credibility Mountain is continually subject to erosion, and therefore requires ongoing expenditure of resources for its maintenance. Since it is huge and impressive, its designers are proud (although a little sensitive about cost overruns) and resent any criticism. However, imagine how different the debate on deficits and debt in Canada would be if the cost of excess unemployment were visible and assembled in one place, rather than being invisibly dispersed across the nation.

The size of Credibility Mountain would certainly be a highly visible indicator to the international financial community of the seriousness with which the government of Canada approaches the crusade for zero inflation. However, the visibility of Credibility Mountain would also lead many Canadians to question whether there is a connection between the fact that we have built a huge mountain of sand and the fact that, at the same time, we have added enormously to our mountain of debt.

At a minimum, the building of Credibility Mountain would attract the attention of journalists, parliamentary committees and investigative agencies, such as the Office of the Auditor General, all of whom would want to know what evidence there was to support the decision to engage in its construction. They would naturally ask:

- Was a careful study of the costs and benefits of this decision done beforehand?
- How reliable was the evidence on which this decision was based?
- Were there cost overruns during construction?

- What have the benefits of building Credibility Mountain actually been?

People ask these sorts of questions of public officials in a democracy because they are interested in governance and competence. In a democracy, the expectation is that substantial expenditures of public resources require public consent — specifically, through a referendum, or indirectly, through the election of a government pledged to a particular course of action. If decision making is delegated to civil servants, the democratic expectation is that they should be responsible to elected officials and competent in the exercise of their duties.

If these issues of competence and governance are crucial to the debate about Credibility Mountain, they are also crucial to the debate about Canada's "debt mountain," because these two monuments are connected. As Fortin and Kneebone's chapters in this volume document, we can divide the construction of the debt mountain into three distinct phases: 1975 to 1980, 1981 to 1988 and 1989 to 1997. Over the first period, the debt-to-GDP ratio rose because governments ran a series of deficits, as the result of a succession of tax policy changes which decreased the tax share of total GDP. Although the second period saw a rapid rise of the debt-to-GDP ratio due to the collapse of output and the rise in interest rates of the recession of the early eighties, it can be argued that during this recession, Canada actually followed the United States in a high interest rate policy, in order to control inflation. By the late eighties, Canadian governments had raised taxes considerably, and despite high real interest rates, they were running a sufficiently large surplus on their primary balances to begin to reduce the debt-to-GDP ratio by 1989.

In 1988, although the Canadian inflation rate had stabilized at approximately 4 per cent, the Bank of Canada embarked on a new policy that aimed to eliminate inflation entirely. Since this policy was not imitated by other countries, it produced a "Made in Canada" recession. By raising interest rates and thereby engineering a 21 per cent increase in the exchange value of the Canadian dollar,[2] monetary policy precipitated a collapse in aggregate demand. Excessively tight monetary policy worsened the severity of the recession from 1989 to 1992 and destroyed the debt stabilization plans of Canadian governments. The debt-to-GDP ratio soared to new heights, and by 1995, Canadian governments perceived no alternative but to cut program expenditures severely.

Among the contributors to this volume, there is substantial disagreement about whether Canadian governments should have taken action earlier to control their aggregate expenditures. There is also disagreement as to whether or not, and to what extent, further increases in taxation are desirable or feasible. However, there is no disagreement about the implications for the national debt of the 1988 decision to use monetary policy to attempt to achieve a zero inflation rate. As the debt stability equation implies, when the debt-to-GDP ratio is at its 1988 level, any increase in interest rates has profound effects on the national debt, effects that are much more serious than those of social programs.[3]

Since the increase in interest rates was large, and the consequent recession was severe, substantial increases in the national debt and the debt-to-GDP ratio were the result. In his chapter, McCracken estimates that the change in monetary policy between 1988 and 1995 is essentially responsible for the increase in the debt-to-GDP ratio. All these changes occurred despite the fact that, during the eighties, elected Canadian governments had adjusted their taxation and expenditure decisions to generate, by 1989, a *surplus* on their primary balances.

However, the policy initiative of an unelected agency — the Bank of Canada — has produced such a large increase in the debt-to-GDP ratio that deficit reduction became the overriding objective of all Canadian governments. Deficit reduction forced a substantial retreat of the federal government from areas, such as health care and social policy, that it had influenced since World War II. Deficit reduction also transformed the services that both provincial and federal governments provide to their citizens. The result was a drastic reorganization of federal and provincial roles within the Canadian federation and a profoundly different social role for government. Surely there are no issues in politics more important than the structure and role of government, but these changes were driven by an economic policy choice — the decision to use monetary policy to achieve zero inflation.

There are two logical possibilities. When the decision was made in 1988 to begin raising interest rates in order to eliminate inflation, it was either (a) foreseen or (b) not foreseen that such decisions would seriously affect the national debt and the role of government in Canadian society.

If these effects were foreseen, then *governance* is the issue. Since the experience of the 1981–82 recession clearly showed that higher interest rates would produce a substantial increase in the debt-to-GDP ratio and since the debt stability equation was already well known, it should have been easy to predict the consequences of such a tight monetary policy. And if the full political and economic consequences of the zero inflation policy were foreseen, the fact that the Bank implemented the policy implies that an agenda for substantial political change that was never mandated democratically was successfully imposed on Canadian society.

Some people applaud the trend towards reducing the role of government in general, and of the federal government in particular. Some people oppose the trend to provincialism and a more market-dominated society. However, whatever our opinions about whether "less government" is "good" or "bad," a fundamental principle of our legal system is the rule of law: elected officials can only instruct appointed officials to perform actions that are within their legislatively authorized terms of reference. Moreover, a fundamental democratic value is that decisions of this order of importance should be publicly debated and should receive public consent. Since officials at the Bank of Canada are not elected, it would not be appropriate for such officials, on their own initiative, to embark on a policy which redesigns the Canadian political system. Since the legal mandate of the Bank of Canada does not include any mandate to implement political and economic change of this magnitude, the approval of the finance minister is not enough. Either the mandate of the Bank of Canada should have been amended, or the specific policy should have been approved, by an explicit act of the elected legislature. Hence, the possibility that the full consequences of the Bank of Canada's monetary policies were foreseen, and implemented anyway, raises important issues of governance in a democracy.

The alternative is that the consequences were not foreseen. This hypothesis gains some support from Kneebone's review of the published discussions of the period, but it raises important issues of *competence*. In the literature on monetary policy, there is frequent reference to the importance of central bank credibility in the pursuit of anti-inflation objectives. "Credibility" has two possible interpretations. In theoretical economics literature, credibility is said to exist when the public believes in the firmness of the anti-inflation resolve of the central bank, but in day-to-day life, credibility is usually interpreted in terms of competency, and there is a significant difference between believing in the firmness of anti-inflation resolve and the competency of the analysis that underlies it.

Although Canada has invested a huge amount of resources in the implementation of the Bank's monetary policy, anyone who probes the issue will rapidly discover that there is far less documentation[4] to support assertions about the benefits of the policy than we routinely demand of other major expenditures of public resources. Furthermore, the vast majority of studies that had been published in 1988, when the decision was made, were entirely theoretical in nature and were contradicted by other studies. Since that time, a significant body of work has tried to find some empirical evidence for the supposed benefits of zero inflation, but has come away empty-handed. As Ragan (1997: 2) puts it, "The current state of economic knowledge provides no compelling basis for expecting significant *observable* benefits of low inflation, such as a higher level of real GDP or a higher growth rate of real GDP. Moreover, what observable benefits do exist do not justify a policy of disinflation, even if the short-run costs of disinflation are assumed to be quite moderate." In other words, this policy choice was advocated by a segment of the theoretical economics profession,[5] on the basis of very little empirical evidence, and has not been vindicated by any subsequent empirical work.

We prefer to believe the Bank simply did not foresee the full consequences of its policy choice. If this hypothesis is true, how do we avoid similar errors in the future?

Since we prefer the "not foreseen" hypothesis, we are not impugning the motives of officials at the Bank of Canada or suggesting that they did not inform officials at the Finance Department of their analysis. We are also not questioning the wisdom of the legal mandate of the Bank of Canada. What we *are* questioning is the narrowness of economic perspective that informed that analysis and the failure to foresee a very important implication of monetary policy choice.

The law now requires the Bank of Canada "to regulate credit and currency in the best interest of the economic life of the nation, to control and protect the external value of the national monetary unit and to mitigate by its influence fluctuations in the general level of production, trade, prices and employment, so far as may be possible in the scope of monetary action, and generally to promote the economic and financial welfare of Canada."

In our view, a capitalist market economy needs some assurance of stability in a macroeconomic context if it is to function effectively. If individuals and firms have reasonable grounds to believe that there will be large fluctuations in the general level of production, trade, prices and employment, they will try to insure themselves against the risk of resulting losses, in ways that are often socially costly. We are questioning the wisdom of the decision made by the Bank to narrow its chosen policy mandate to that of price stability alone, at the cost of greater instability in production, trade and employment.

We recognize that not everyone agrees with us. On issues of this importance, there is now a vigorous debate among economists, based on differences in analysis and emphasis. However, we think that it is crucial that such a debate should occur and that all relevant evidence is considered, before policy decisions are made. We also think that it is desirable that such a debate be open, both because open, informed debate is politically essential in a democracy and because errors that are often missed in closed gatherings of the like-minded may be spotted in an open debate.

Structural reform of the administration of the Bank of Canada might increase the likelihood that alternative interpretations of the economic evidence will be seriously considered. We feel confident that if the evidence on the potential output capacity of the Canadian economy is rigorously assessed and if the economic costs of unnecessarily low growth and high unemployment are dispassionately considered, the unavoidable conclusion will be that the Bank of Canada should use its control over short-term interest rates to encourage economic growth. We think that unemployment in Canada could be safely brought down below 7 per cent, without fear of producing a resurgence of inflation. Macroeconomic policy[6] which reduced the output gap gradually, would substantially reduce the deficit.

We therefore emphasize the importance of monetary policy in solving Canada's debt problem. We do not advocate further cuts to program expenditures because the cuts that have already been made have been massive, and because we think the debate on "big government" has become rather misleading.

In thinking about the costs and benefits of "big" or "small" government, Ruggieri and Hermanutz (1995) argue that it is crucial to distinguish between the resources which governments *use* (e.g., in building schools or roads) and the resources which governments *transfer* between households (e.g., by making payments to bondholders or to Canada Pension Plan recipients). They note that the resources used by Canadian governments increased very little over twenty-two years (1970–1992), if measured as a percentage of GDP or relative to total employment or total consumption in the private sector.[7] What did increase was the share of GDP going to transfers to individuals and to businesses, as well as the taxes needed to pay (partially) for such transfers. They note that transfers to persons and businesses grew at similar rates between 1961 and 1993 but with different patterns. As Rosenbluth points out in his chapter, high unemployment has played a crucial role in increasing the need for social transfers to individuals, and high interest rates have increased transfers to bondholders. Since there has been no increase in the percentage of resources used by government, but there has been an increase in the resources transferred by government, Ruggieri and Hermanutz argue that the current debate on "big government" and how to control the deficit is really a debate on income distribution.

Since careful analysis of the winners and losers of the disinflationary process shows that, not surprisingly, the unemployed tend to be poor while the beneficiaries of high real interest rates tend to be rich (see Erksoy 1994), the anti-inflation crusade has already redistributed a great deal of income from poor to rich. We think it would be unfair, as well as inefficient, to both continue with a high-unemployment policy and slash the budgets of programs that have partially mitigated the burden of unemployment.

Furthermore, additional cuts are not necessary to reduce the debt ratio, *if* monetary policy allows real interest rates to decline to their historically normal levels and growth to resume.

Figures 35 and 36 compare two scenarios with alternative interest rate assumptions. In both scenarios we assume no further cuts to federal government program spending. The top line in each chart is a projection of the implications of a continuation of the 1995 interest rate (7.3 per cent). The bottom line projects an alternative scenario of the implications of a 5.3 per cent interest rate and a short-run continuation of modest growth, followed by sustained 2.7 per cent annual real growth.

In both scenarios, it is assumed that the federal government keeps federal revenues at the same percentage of GDP that they were in 1997 (17.6 per cent — i.e. "no new taxes").

We assume throughout that the growth in federal government program expenditures parallels the growth of the economy, and remains a constant 12.5 per cent of GDP. In dollar terms, federal program expenditures will therefore grow from $104.5 billion in 1997 to approximately $186 billion in the year 2010. However, since taxes are assumed to be 17.6 per cent of GDP and program expen-

Figure 35

Federal Debt/GDP Ratio — Two Interest Rate Scenarios

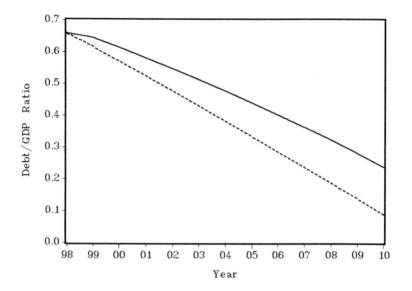

Note: Along the solid line, the interest rate is 7.3%. Along the dotted line, the interest rate is 5.3%. Under both scenarios, the trend growth rate of real GDP is 2.7%, the global tax rate is constant at 17.6% (no new taxes), and government program expenditures are set at a constant 12.5% of GDP.

ditures are assumed to be 12.5 per cent of GDP, the primary surplus of the federal government is now a very large 5.1 per cent of GDP, or $43 billion in 1997. With a primary surplus of this magnitude, the federal government eliminates the deficit in 1997. Furthermore, as GDP grows, the dollar value of a primary surplus of 5.1 per cent of GDP grows with it. As the debt begins to decline, the cost of interest payments also shrinks. Hence, even with an increase in federal expenditures that amounts to over $80 billion by 2010, the overall budget balance of the federal government is strongly positive from 1997 on. As a consequence, under both interest rate scenarios, total federal debt declines substantially.

Since both these scenarios freeze the current share of taxation and program expenditure in GDP, neither builds in political initiatives to

Figure 36

Federal Debt — Two Interest Rate Scenarios

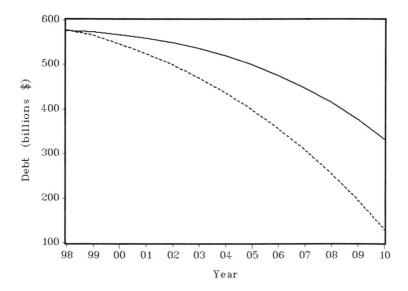

Note: Along the solid line, the interest rate is 7.3%. Along the dotted line, the interest rate is 5.3%. Under both scenarios, the trend growth rate of real GDP is 2.7%, the global tax rate is constant at 17.6% (no new taxes), and government program expenditures are set at a constant 12.5% of GDP.

spend the "fiscal dividend." We are not claiming that this is realistic — in fact, Canadian political discourse is already dominated by the competing claims of tax cuts and spending plans. What we want to show is the implication of a continuation of current policy settings — how the deficit and debt would evolve in the absence of decisions to spend the primary surplus on tax relief or major new program initiatives.

The two scenarios of Figures 35 and 36 embody real interest rates that are high by historic standards. As Chapter 2 indicated, from 1962 to 1981, the real interest rate on government debt in Canada averaged 0.9 per cent. However, the low interest rate scenario of Figures 35 and 36 embodies an average interest rate on the federal debt of 5.3 per cent per year, while the high interest rate scenario is based on an interest rate of 7.3 per cent. Clearly, if the government of Canada paid a lower rate of interest on its debt, the debt would compound at a slower rate. (Currently, the government of Canada refinances its maturing debt with a mixture of long-term and short-term bonds. However, since the rate of interest it must pay on long-term bonds is significantly higher than that paid on short-term bonds, the total interest burden could be reduced if all maturing debt were refinanced with debt of short maturities. We do not claim to understand why the Department of Finance persists in paying more than is necessary to finance the debt, but for the purposes of these calculations, we just assume that it continues to do so.) Although neither of these two scenarios assumes a decline to the level of real interest rates that fuelled the robust growth of the Canadian economy during the 1960s and 1970s, they do differ in how high they assume real interest rates will be. A decision to move interest rates up by 2 per cent could be expected to produce a significant slowing of economic growth in 1999. As well, over the next dozen years, the cumulative impact of such a decision on the public debt amounts to over $200 billion — a total debt of $333 billion in 2010, compared to $130 billion if the lower interest rate is assumed.

A difference of 2 per cent in nominal interest rates does not sound like much, but when it is applied to an amount as large as Canada's public debt, it adds up to a lot. On a per capita basis, the difference between these two scenarios in public debt in the year 2010 is about $3,800 — or approximately $15,200 in greater debt liability for the average four-person, tax-paying family. Because the federal government is running such a huge primary surplus, the debt problem is "under control" in both scenarios. However, monetary policy remains a very important determinant of the size of the debt and of the distribution of wealth between bond holders and tax payers.

Appendix B provides the details of our calculations. We want to stress that we have tailored our assumptions to err on the conservative side. Although we think that unemployment could be safely reduced below 7 per cent without danger of sparking any resurgence of inflation, the growth assumptions underlying Figures 35 and 36 are much more modest. In both scenarios, unemployment declines only marginally — i.e., we take no chances with inflation. Although an interest rate of 5.3 per cent, together with an inflation rate of 1.8 per cent, provides a real return to capital that compares extremely well with historic norms, we have not assumed that interest rates are lowered below this level (although such a decrease occurred during 1993). Although the rate of growth of GDP was greater than the interest rate in the seventies, and these conditions greatly assisted the effort to reduce the debt ratio in those years, we have not assumed that this fortunate situation returns. And although we think that the Canadian economy can do substantially better, in real economic growth and in unemployment, than it has done in the past, these calculations adopt the consensus forecast for 1998–99 and only 2.7 per cent growth thereafter. Relaxing any of these assumptions would make it easier to control the debt. Yet, even with these pessimistic assumptions, and even if the federal government allows expenditure to resume growing, the debt-to-GDP ratio declines substantially. Under the lower interest rate scenario, the debt is only about 9 per cent of GDP in a dozen years, while the higher interest rate scenario projects a debt to GDP ratio of 24 per cent in 2010.

Picking a set of conservative assumptions on interest rates and growth has the advantage of showing that forecasts of massive decline in the federal debt are not dependent on a highly optimistic projection of Canada's growth potential. However, conservative assumptions may have the disadvantage of lacking in pessimism. In fact, we are highly optimistic about Canada's growth potential. We think that the overriding priority of Canadian economic policy in the short term should be elimination of excess unemployment. In the long term, we see no fundamental reason why the Canadian economy should not perform somewhat better than the U.S. economy, since for some years Canadian youth have been coming into the labour market with a higher level and quality of education than American youth.

We therefore advocate a policy of reducing the output gap and encouraging growth at a rate that is closer to the potential of the Canadian economy. Why is this not happening? In our view, the answer is a combination of vested interests in the wisdom of past policy decisions, flawed methodology in the estimation of potential output and a blinkered vision of the costs and benefits of zero inflation in the long term. The builders of Credibility Mountain have an understandably human desire to minimize their perception of its costs and to overstate its importance to the international financial community. Since the Bank of Canada has always followed a policy of promoting candidates from within, and since control over monetary policy essentially rests in the hands of the governor of the bank, each new governor comes to office having participated in previous policy decisions.

What incentives do participants in the monetary policy debate have to accept or reject evidence on the costs and benefits of the zero inflation strategy? As the authors of many scholarly articles, both of us have argued against the policy of zero inflation in the past. Therefore, we face the potential barrier of ego — the difficulty everyone has in admitting that he or she was possibly wrong. This barrier may cloud our judgements in assessing the strengths of new arguments and new evidence on the issue. On the other hand, as professors of economics, we are expected to examine the evidence dispassionately. If we were to convert to monetarism, we would gain new friends (and lose old ones), but we could expect to receive increased status within the economics profession as people who are scientifically objective in their consideration of the evidence. However, whatever happens, we have tenure. Our current jobs would remain, and nothing very important in our personal lives would change.

On the other hand, senior officials of the Bank of Canada face great incentives to deny new evidence and to encourage the continued implementation of previously announced policy. After inducing the most severe recession in fifty years, destabilizing the national debt and forcing momentous political and social changes on the entire country, the Bank could not conceivably appear before the Commons Committee on Finance and say, "Oops — we got it wrong." All incentives — personal, professional and financial — point to maintaining the status quo.

On a personal level, most people would find it hard to admit that they were responsible for a policy that had caused enormous pain to many thousands, to no good purpose. To the ordinary barriers of ego, one must add the sense of personal responsibility which goes with the power of the Bank of Canada. As well, it is inconceivable that senior officials of the Bank could admit misjudgement on such a fundamental policy and expect to retain their jobs; thus, income, prestige and power are on the line, over and above any personal misgivings. These conditions make it highly unlikely that the senior staff of the Bank of Canada will admit to such an error. After all, there is always the option of reinterpreting the evidence to see the benefits which are "just around the corner," if only Canada stays the course for just a bit longer.[8]

In the current system, therefore, each new governor comes to office having been a part of the policy team that produced past decisions. As governor, he becomes a personal embodiment of the Bank's policy, with enormous power and responsibility. In the fall of 1993, when the Chrétien government was considering whether or not to reappoint Governor Crow, dire predictions were made of financial instability in international capital markets if Crow was not reappointed. These predictions proved false, but they raise the point that it is not reasonable to place such great importance on one individual (who could, after all, get run over by a bus at any given time).

A new model of governance for the Bank of Canada might be to replace the governor with a governing council. In place of a single, full-time governor with executive decision-making powers who reports to a part-time, nominal Board of Directors, the day-to-day operation of monetary policy could be under the control of a committee of full-time governors, which operates by a majority vote and whose members rotate as chair of the committee. If a seven-member governing council were appointed with overlapping seven-year terms of office, there would be substantial continuity in membership, hence financial markets would be assured that monetary policy would not change radically in the short term. On the other hand, the gradual replacement of the membership of the governing council would ensure that new perspectives have a chance to appear and be considered in decision making, and that members would be able to examine dispassionately the lessons of past policy decisions. To ensure a genuine sharing of responsibility for monetary policy, it would be essential that the chair of the governing council rotate, by seniority, among its membership.

The members of such a council should be recruited from outside the permanent staff of the Bank of Canada, and they should assume full-time appointments, each supported by a research staff of economists. It would make sense, in a regionally diverse country such as Canada, to ensure regional representation in membership: for example, two members from Ontario, two from Quebec, two from Western Canada and one from Atlantic Canada. The members should reside in their regions of appointment, and their research staff should likewise be regionally based.

With electronic mail and telephone conferencing, a geographically dispersed council could easily consult daily, if not more frequently, on monetary policy issues. This interaction could be supplemented by weekly meetings in Ottawa with the minister of finance. However, the geographical separation of research staffs, reporting to their own member of the operational committee, is crucial both in order that monetary policy researchers see, in their day-to-day lives, the world outside Ottawa, and in order to increase the chances of an informed diversity of approaches and analyses.

Many readers may realize that this structure of decentralized governance and majority decision making is very similar to the current structure of the U.S. Federal Reserve Board system. Although the U.S. Federal Reserve Board can be criticized, its system has generated a more reasonable mix of policy choices over the last few decades than the Bank of Canada has in recent years.

In Canada's parliamentary system, responsibility for fiscal policy rests with the minister of finance, and it is crucial that fiscal and monetary policy be coordinated. Furthermore, the government's position on macroeconomic policy should be clearly and credibly announced to all. Hence, we urge that, on a quarterly basis, the minister of finance and the Bank of Canada should issue a joint policy statement on fiscal and monetary policy and the macroeconomic outlook for the coming year, which should include medium-term forecasts of economic outcomes.

When a major national institution, such as the Bank of Canada, makes a systematic series of decisions which substantially decrease the economic well-being of Canadian society, calls for radical change are to be expected. Marc Van Audenrode's article in this volume is an example. He essentially rejects the possibility of reforming the Bank of Canada, and advocates that Canadians import the better monetary policy decisions of the U.S. Federal Reserve Board system, by tying the Canadian dollar to the U.S. dollar and forswearing independent monetary policy of any kind.

When we wrote the first edition of this book in 1995, we felt that this idea went too far. We said that although we have seen in the nineties the costs of implementing an ill-advised independent monetary policy adventure, there are still some potential benefits to the capacity for independent monetary policy choices (even if such benefits are not now being realized). As Goodhart (1994) has argued, central banks influence the real economy through their near-total control over the level of short-term interest rates. Interest rate policy regulates the level of economic activity through its effects on business investment, on purchases of consumer durables and (as higher interest rates impinge on mortgages coming up for renewal) on general consumption expenditure. Acting indirectly through the exchange rate, short-term interest rates influence exports and imports. (For a summary diagram, see Rosenbluth's article in this volume.) These tools could be used to generate more rapid economic growth and a more rapid reduction in the deficits and debts of Canadian governments.

We still believe that monetary policy could be used to improve the performance of the Canadian economy, but we are increasingly convinced that it will not happen. Over the past few years, the performance of the U.S. economy has shown that it is quite possible to have low inflation while pushing unemployment well below the 6 per cent level, which used to be thought "dangerous" in terms of inflation. Despite this evidence, the Bank of Canada decided in June of 1997 to begin raising interest rates again, although the inflation rate was near 1 per cent and the unemployment rate remained around 9 per cent. There appears to be little chance the Bank will change its fixation with avoiding any possible risk of inflation, at whatever cost that implies for the real economy.

If a monetary policy that emphasizes growth and employment is not attainable, what is the second-best alternative? If Canada were to adopt Marc Van Audenrode's suggestion of moving to full monetary union with the United States, we would give up independent monetary policy decision making, but there would be real benefits. Trade and investment would flow more easily, and Canadians would save the cost of foreign exchange transaction fees on $500 billion per year in trans-border trade, and even more in investment transactions. As well, Canada would no longer be exposed to the possibility of uncertainty in international financial markets forcing us into inappropriate interest rate increases (as happened in the Mexican currency crisis of 1994 and, to some extent, in the Asian currency crisis of 1997).

In this scenario, although Canada would be giving up its independence in monetary policy, and the potential benefits for employment and growth of good monetary policy decisions, we would be avoiding the possibility (amply demonstrated during the 1990s) that bad monetary policy choices could produce a decade of lost opportunities. As the debate on the European monetary union demonstrates, the adoption of a common unit of account is about politics as well as economics. However, as the "Euro" also demonstrates, it is not necessary to give up national currency notes and coins in order to acquire the advantages of a common international unit of account. Monetary union does not require the surrender of national symbols, but would have practical economic benefits. Since the benefits of monetary union are fairly clear, while the benefits of continuing with the current management of monetary policy are difficult to pinpoint, full monetary union with the United States deserves serious consideration.

References

Bank of Canada. 1995. Monetary Policy Report. May.

Cozier, B., and J. Selody. 1992. Inflation and Macroeconomic Performance: Some Cross-Country Evidence. Working Paper No. 92-6, Bank of Canada, Ottawa, November. Mimeograph.

Ericsson, N.R., and J.S. Irons. 1995. The Lucas Critique in Practice: Theory without Measurement. International Finance Discussion Paper No. 506, Board of Governors of the Federal Reserve System, March. Mimeograph.

Erksoy, S. 1994. The Effect of Higher Unemployment on the Distribution of Income in Canada 1981–1987. *Canadian Public Policy* 20, no. 3: 318–328.

Fortin, Pierre. 1996. Presidential Address: The Great Canadian Slump *Canadian Journal of Economics* Vol. XXIX No. 4 November 1996, Pages 761 to 787.

Goodhart, C.A.E. 1994. What Should Central Banks Do? What Should Be Their Macroeconomic Objectives and Operations? *The Economic Journal* 104, no. 427: 1424–1436.

Howitt, P. 1990. Zero Inflation as a Long-Run Target for Monetary Policy. In *Zero Inflation: The Goal of Price Stability*, edited by R.G. Lipsey. Toronto and Calgary: C.D. Howe Institute.

Jarrett, J.P., and J.G. Selody. 1982. The Productivity-Inflation Nexus in Canada 1963–1979. *The Review of Economics and Statistics* 44 no. 3: 361–367.

Johnson, D. 1995. Review of "Economic Behaviour and Policy Choice under Price Stability: Proceedings of a Conference Held at the Bank of Canada," *Canadian Journal of Economics* 28, no. 3: 723–726.

Laxton D., and R. Tetlow. 1992. A Simple Multivariate Filter for the Measurement of Potential Output, Technical Report No. 59, Bank of Canada, Ottawa, June.

Levine R., and S. Zervos. 1993. What We Have Learned about Policy and Growth from Cross-Country Regressions? *The American Economic Review (Papers and Proceedings)* 83 (May): 426–430.

Lucas, R.E. 1976. Econometric Policy Evaluation: A Critique. in K. Brunner and A. Meltzer, eds. *The Phillips Curve and Labor Markets.* Carnegie Rochester Conference Series on Public Policy, Vol. 1, *Journal of Monetary Economics* supplementary issue: 19-46.

MacLean, B., and M. Setterfield. 1993. Nexus or Not? Productivity and Inflation in Canada. *Canadian Business Economics* 1, no. 2: 44–52.

Ragan, Chris. 1997. "On the Believable Benefits of Low Inflation" paper presented at the 1997 meetings of the Canadian Economics Association, June 1997, St. John's Nfld., Mimeo, McGill University, March 1997.

Ruggieri, G.C., and D. Hermanutz. 1995. Leviathan Revisited — The Growth of Government Spending since 1961. Alberta Treasury, July. Mimeograph.

Selody, J. 1993. Comment on "Nexus or Not? Productivity and Inflation in Canada. *Canadian Business Economics* 1, no. 2: 53–60.

Appendix A:
The Debt Stability Equation

Economists of all political persuasions agree on the debt stability equation, because it is based on established accounting identities.

Let's start with the accounting identity that the amount the government can pay back on the national debt in any year is the difference between taxes raised and program expenditures. This amount is usually referred to as the "primary balance," (which conveniently has the same initials as "pay-back").

Primary Balance = Taxes – Expenditures

We can shorten this to

$PB = T - X.$

The second accounting identity states that the debt in any particular year is equal to the debt in the previous year plus the interest which has to be paid on the debt minus the amount that has been paid back. Subscripts denote the "first" and "second" year's debt.

Debt$_2$ = Debt$_1$ + (Average rate of interest) x Debt$_1$ – Primary Balance

In short form,

$D_2 = D_1 + rD_1 - PB.$

The third identity simply says that national income (GDP) in any year is equal to national income in the previous year plus the amount by which national income has grown. The change in national income is equal to the growth rate multiplied by the level of national income.

Income$_2$ = Income$_1$ + Change in income
=Income$_1$ + (Growth rate) x Income$_1$

Again, it is convenient to shorten this to

$$Y_2 = Y_1 + g \times Y_1 = Y_1 (1 + g).$$

We are concerned with change in the debt-to-income ratio.

Change in debt-to-income = $\dfrac{\text{Debt}_2}{\text{Income}_2} - \dfrac{\text{Debt}_1}{\text{Income}_1}$

In shorter notation,

$$\Delta(D/Y) = \frac{D_2}{Y_2} - \frac{D_1}{Y_1}.$$

Since the national income accounting identity states that $Y_2 = Y_1 (1+g)$, then

$$\Delta (D/Y) = \frac{D_2}{Y_1(1+g)} - \frac{D_1}{Y_1}.$$

To bring a common denominator to this equation, we rewrite it as

$$\Delta (D/Y) = \frac{D_2 - D_1 (1+g)}{Y_1(1+g)} = \frac{D_2 - D_1 - gD_1}{Y_1 (1+g)}.$$

The accounting identity for national debt states that

$$D_2 = D_1 + rD_1 - PB,$$

and if we now substitute for D_2, then

$$\Delta (D/Y) = \frac{D_1 + rD_1 - PB - D_1 - gD_1}{Y_1 (1+g)}.$$

The D_1 terms cancel out, and since we can express $rD_1 - gD_1$ as $(r - g)D_1$,

$$\Delta (D/Y) = \frac{(r - g) D_1 - PB}{Y_1 (1 + g)}.$$

And since, $Y_2 = Y_1 (1+g)$,

$$\Delta \, (D/Y) = \quad (r - g) \; \frac{D_1}{Y_2} \quad - \; \frac{PB}{Y_2} \, .$$

In words,

(change in debt-to-income ratio) = (interest rate — growth rate) (debt-to-income ratio) — (primary balance as a percentage of national income)

Appendix B:
A Compromise Scenario
for Debt Reduction

Table 7 below provides the details of the calculations used to obtain the "low interest" scenario of Figure 35 and Figure 36 in Chapter 9. Although the calculation of the trend of the debt-to-GDP ratio could be made much more complex, the key ideas are straightforward: Table 7 presents the details of the calculations in order to demystify, as much as possible, the determinants of the trend in total debt of the federal government. The level of GDP and the federal gross debt are measured in billions of dollars (as are all dollar figures). Inflation, taxation, expenditure and growth figures are for the year as a whole while debt figures follow the financial year. The figures for 1993 to 1996 are actual data, taken from CANSIM, while later years are calculated from the assumptions listed in the text.

The existence in the federal debt portfolio of longer-term debt, issued at higher interest rates in the past, means that, even if short-term interest rates are lowered rapidly, the average interest rate on outstanding debt declines more slowly. This worksheet assumes that the consensus forecast of private sector analysts of 3.9 per cent growth in 1997 will hold true, and that the effect of higher interest rates during 1997 would appear only partly in 1998, producing 3.4 per cent real growth in 1998 and 2.7 per cent real growth in 1999 and thereafter.

The assumption of a sustainable long-term growth rate of 2.7 per cent is taken from the Royal Bank of Canada, and is consistent with a labour force that grows at 1.5 per cent (as some discouraged workers reenter the labour force and as the population of working age continues to grow), and a productivity growth rate of 1.2 per cent (which is low by historical standards). (See also Thomas 1995.)

Growth in excess of 2.7 per cent in 1997 and 1998 reduces the output gap, but only by a cumulative total of 1.9 per cent of GDP; that is, under these assumptions, excess capacity remains a feature of the Canadian economy. More robust growth would greatly increase the speed with which the debt-to-GDP ratio declines and is both possible and desirable.

In this scenario, setting total federal program expenditures at $104 billion (the actual 1996 and 1997 levels) means that expenditure on programs (including transfers to the provinces) has dropped by 12.0 per cent, compared to 1994. Measured as a percentage of GDP, the relative size of government shrinks from 15.8 per cent of GDP in 1994 to 12.5 per cent of GDP by the turn of the century.

The key assumption in this scenario is the moderate level of interest rates, which are still high by historical norms of the rate of return after inflation and still greater than the long-term growth rate of GDP, but which are lower than the interest rates that deepened the recession of the early nineties.

With the use of a spreadsheet program, it is relatively easy to calculate the implications, for the deficit and the debt, of alternative assumptions about future economic trends. Table 7 should not, however, be interpreted as either a forecast or as desirable policy. Interest payments on the debt will remain higher than they need be, and the Canadian taxpayer will not receive the full benefit of any decline in short-term interest rates if maturing debt is not refinanced at the lowest interest rate available. The Department of Finance signalled, in the fall of 1995, its intention to *increase* the percentage of the federal debt which is held in more expensive long-term maturities (see *Report on Business*, the *Globe and Mail,* 6 December 1995), and we have assumed it will do so, despite the increased costs of this policy to taxpayers.

Readers may also want to test the sensitivity of these sorts of calculations to alternative assumptions. Table 7 simply works out the implications of two identities:

GDP =   (previous year's GDP) x (1 + inflation rate + real
            growth rate)

Debt =   (previous years's debt) + Deficit
       =   (previous year's debt) – (average tax rate) x (GDP)
            – (program expenditure) – (average interest rate) x (debt)

In the discussion of the national debt, it is often not recognized that since federal program expenditures have already been cut substantially, the underlying primary balance of the federal government

Table 7

Stable Fiscal Policy and Moderate Growth and Interest Rates

YEAR	GDP	INFLATION	REAL GROWTH	NOMINAL GROWTH	DEBT
1994	747.26	0.007	0.0407	0.048	545.70
1995	776.30	0.015	0.0233	0.038	574.30
1996	797.79	0.013	0.0147	0.028	583.20
1997	836.88	0.01	0.039	0.049	583.20
1998	877.89	0.015	0.034	0.049	577.50
1999	920.90	0.018	0.027	0.045	565.19
2000	962.35	0.018	0.027	0.045	546.06
2001	1005.65	0.018	0.027	0.045	523.71
2002	1050.91	0.018	0.027	0.045	497.88
2003	1098.20	0.018	0.027	0.045	468.25
2004	1147.61	0.018	0.027	0.045	434.54
2005	1199.26	0.018	0.027	0.045	396.41
2006	1253.22	0.018	0.027	0.045	353.51
2007	1309.62	0.018	0.027	0.045	305.45
2008	1368.55	0.018	0.027	0.045	251.85
2009	1430.14	0.018	0.027	0.045	192.26
2010	1494.49	0.018	0.027	0.045	126.23

Table 7 (con't)

INTEREST RATE	INTEREST PAID	TAX RATE	REVENUE	PROGRAM EXPENDITURE	BUDGET BALANCE	PRIMARY BALANCE
0.083	42.000	0.165	123.300	118.700	-37.400	4.600
0.086	46.900	0.1678	130.300	112.000	-28.600	18.300
0.078	45.000	0.1766	140.900	104.800	-8.900	36.100
0.074	43.000	0.1762	147.500	104.500	0.000	43.000
0.067	39.074	0.176	154.508	109.736	5.698	44.772
0.06	34.650	0.176	162.079	115.113	12.316	46.966
0.053	29.955	0.176	169.373	120.293	19.125	49.080
0.053	28.941	0.176	176.995	125.706	22.347	51.288
0.053	27.757	0.176	184.959	131.363	25.839	53.596
0.053	26.387	0.176	193.282	137.274	29.621	56.008
0.053	24.817	0.176	201.980	143.452	33.711	58.528
0.053	23.031	0.176	211.069	149.907	38.131	61.162
0.053	21.010	0.176	220.567	156.653	42.905	63.914
0.053	18.736	0.176	230.493	163.702	48.055	66.791
0.053	16.189	0.176	240.865	171.069	53.607	69.796
0.053	13.348	0.176	251.704	178.767	59.589	72.937
0.053	10.190	0.176	263.031	186.812	66.030	76.219

Table 7 (con't)

YEAR	PB/GDP	DEFICIT AS %GDP	DEBT/GDP RATIO	UNEMPLOY.	EXPENDITURE AS %GDP	INTEREST% AS % OF EXPENDITURE	TREND GROWTH
1994	0.006	-0.050	0.730	0.103	0.159	0.261	0.027
1995	0.024	-0.037	0.740	0.100	0.144	0.295	
1996	0.045	-0.011	0.731	0.095	0.131	0.300	
1997	0.051	0.000	0.697	0.090	0.125	0.292	
1998	0.051	0.006	0.658	0.087	0.125	0.263	
1999	0.051	0.013	0.614	0.086	0.125	0.231	
2000	0.051	0.020	0.567	0.086	0.125	0.199	
2001	0.051	0.022	0.521	0.085	0.125	0.187	
2002	0.051	0.025	0.474	0.085	0.125	0.174	
2003	0.051	0.027	0.426	0.085	0.125	0.161	
2004	0.051	0.029	0.379	0.084	0.125	0.147	
2005	0.051	0.032	0.331	0.084	0.125	0.133	
2006	0.051	0.034	0.282	0.083	0.125	0.118	
2007	0.051	0.037	0.233	0.083	0.125	0.103	
2008	0.051	0.039	0.184	0.083	0.125	0.086	
2009	0.051	0.042	0.134	0.082	0.125	0.069	
2010	0.051	0.044	0.084	0.082	0.125	0.052	

is strongly positive. With growth in the economy, the primary surplus grows rapidly if expenditure continues to be restrained.

Although the scenario reported here is one of steady-state growth, experimentation shows that it is only slightly affected by a "normal" recession (i.e., one that is not precipitated by a policy of extremely high real interest rates, as that from 1988 to 1990). Normally, the output loss of a recession is followed by the recovery of lost ground as growth surges to a rate significantly higher than long-term potential, before declining to a sustainable level. In the sixties and seventies, the recovery phase of recessions was usually assisted by monetary policy, and the lower interest rates of relaxed monetary policy helped to keep the national debt from compounding. If the recovery phase of a future recession is not impeded by an excessively tight monetary policy, (as that between 1990 and 1992), the long-term decline of the debt-to-GDP ratio is not affected much by a normal recession.

The nineties' recession produced an escalation of the debt-to-GDP ratio because that recession was induced by high interest rates. As the debt stability equation of Appendix A makes clear, when interest rates are going up at the same time as growth is going down, the debt ratio becomes unstable — it is the *difference* between the interest rate and the growth rate that is crucial.

A recession would produce a blip in the downward trend of the debt-to-GDP ratio, but *if* monetary policy keeps interest rates low, the rapid growth which follows a recession would make up the lost ground. The key point is that, as long as the Bank of Canada does not exacerbate Canada's debt problem by restrictive monetary policy, the federal government is running a large enough surplus of revenue over program expenditure to bring the debt ratio down substantially over the next dozen years.

References

Thomas, Alun. 1995. *Canada — Economic Developments and Policies.* IMF Staff Country Report No. 95/46, International Monetary Fund, Washington, June.

Notes

Introduction

1. The charter expressed in the Bank of Canada Act charges the Bank of Canada to "regulate credit and currency in the best interest of the economic life of the nation, to control and protect the external value of the national monetary unit and to mitigate by its influence fluctuations in the general level of production, trade, prices and employment, so far as may be possible within the scope of monetary action, and generally to promote the economic and financial welfare of the Dominion." In practice, however, the Bank of Canada has reinterpreted its mandate since 1988 as focusing solely on "price stability."

2. Since the recession in the early nineties in the United States would have hurt Canadian export sales, even without a high interest rate policy in Canada, we could not have escaped recession entirely in Canada. However, the decline in output and rise in unemployment would have been far smaller, and would not have lasted as long had Canada followed its traditional policy of tracking the United States' interest rates, as McCracken demonstrates.

3. See M. Setterfield, D. Gordon and L. Osberg, 1992, Searching for a Will o' the Wisp: An Empirical Study of the NAIRU in Canada, *European Economic Review* 36: 119–136, and P. Fortin, 1993, The Unbearable Lightness of Zero Inflation Optimism, *Canadian Business Economics* 1, no. 3: 3–18.

Chapter 1

1. From *Tax, Borrow and Spend: Financing Federal Spending in Canada, 1867–1990*. Ottawa: Carleton University Press, 1991, based on excerpts from pp.5–12, 48–55, 66–71, 145–153, 210–217 and 234–242.

2. The charts in this chapter are based on information from a new database for federal government expenditures, tax revenues by revenue source, deficit financing and the national debt, presented in Appendices B and C of Gillespie (1991). These data are comprehensive in measurement and consistent in definition for the years 1868–1990. The database for national income begins in 1870 and continues through 1989, the last year available at the time of the study. It is unlikely that, when the database is extended to include the years 1990 to 1994, the analysis and discussion of this chapter will significantly change.

3. The data for government spending and financing on a fiscal year basis (derived in Appendix B of Gillespie 1991) are used for discussions of (1) changes in absolute levels, and (2) changes in the share of one revenue source in total financial requirements. The data for government spending and financing on a calendar year basis (derived in Ap-

pendix C) are used, along with GNP data (also in Appendix C), for discussion of changes in spending, financing and the various revenue sources relative to the size of the economy. Canadian data on national income do not exist until 1870.

4. The level of Dominion spending rose, fell and underwent virtually no change in years 33, 12 and 4 respectively, in the fiscal period 1868–1917 (see Appendix Tables B-2 and B-3 of Gillespie 1991).

5. I am designating these sources as the Confederation revenue sources, because they are the most important sources of revenue initially used by Dominion governments under terms of the Confederation agreements. The other revenue sources during this period include post office revenues, miscellaneous revenues, miscellaneous indirect taxes (later referred to as excise taxes), and special receipts and other credits (see Appendix Table B-3 of Gillespie 1991).

6. See Rich (1988, 206). Domestic borrowing accounted for at least 45 per cent of total Dominion borrowing until the mid-1880s; thereafter, domestic borrowing declined rapidly to less than 10 per cent of the total (until 1913).

7. In 1907, the fiscal year change resulted in a nine-month year for 1907 and a fifteen-month year for 1908; the uneven timing of revenues and expenditures most likely accounts for the modest surplus in 1907 and part of the substantial deficit in 1908.

8. Fiscal years 1903 and 1904 had surpluses; the remaining seven surpluses occurred in 1871, 1882, 1900, 1907, 1913, 1957 and 1970 (see Table B-2 of Gillespie 1991).

9. During the five fiscal years between 1921 and 1925, Dominion spending fell by 54.5 per cent, with most of the decrease occurring during the first two years. The five years of reductions in spending after World War II actually began in 1945, with most of the 61.3 per cent reduction occurring during the fiscal year 1947–1948. See Appendix Tables B-2 and B-3 of Gillespie (1991).

10. Dominion total tax revenues increased by 24 per cent over the fiscal year 1920–1921, and then declined, with some fluctuation to 17 per cent by 1925. Revenues increased again by a trivial 2 per cent over the fiscal year 1946–1947, and then declined 16 per cent until 1950. See Appendix Tables B-2 and B-3 of Gillespie (1991).

11. For growth rates in real national income, see Appendix Table C-1 of Gillespie (1991).

12. For the derivation of the theory of optimal provision and financing of a collective consumption good, see Musgrave (1958, Chapters 1 and 4), Samuelson (1954) and such recent references as Musgrave, Musgrave and Bird (1987, Chapters 3 and 4) and Boadway and Wildasin (1984, Chapter 4).

13. See Appendix C of Gillespie (1991) for several measures of the magnitude of the national debt: the current dollar value of the debt, the current dollar annual increase in the value of the debt and the value of the debt relative to GNP, annually, from 1870 through 1989.

14. It also provides no support for the displacement hypothesis, in any of its three variants. See Peacock and Wiseman (1967) and Bird (1970, 107–117).

15. The fiscal years 1950–52 comprised a unique period of Canadian fiscal history. The pressures of war-related expenditures and a buoyant economy allowed the finance minister to increase tax rates on many revenue sources, finance the Korean War entirely on a pay-as-you-go basis, and generate surpluses that were used to reduce the debt. The key difference between this period of surpluses and other periods is that the surpluses were the outcome of increased tax rates, imposed across the board, that generated revenues in excess of spending.

16. The measure of sales tax as a proportion of revenue illustrates these policy choices clearly for the first postwar period, the thirties and the second postwar period. In each period, it peaked, respectively, at 29 per cent (in 1924), 26 per cent (in 1938) and 18 per cent (in 1950) of total financial requirements (see Table B-3 of Gillespie 1991).

17. For the growth in government expenditures and total spending relative to GNP, see Tables B-3, C-1 and C-3 of Gillespie (1991).

18. The proposal was not passed before the October election which resulted in a minority Liberal government, and it was repackaged in Mr. Turner's 1973 budget. When the proposal was finally passed, the depreciation write-off was effective from May 8, 1972, and the tax rate reduction was effective from January 1, 1973. In November 1974, with a majority government, Mr. Turner made the depreciation write-off permanent and exempted manufacturing and processing firms from his 10 per cent corporate surtax.

19. The investment tax credit also covered petroleum, minerals, logging, farming and fishing, and was extended to research and development expenditures by Finance Minister MacDonald in his 1977 budget.

20. Mr. MacDonald's proposal to allow 3 per cent of inventories to be deductible before calculation of corporate income tax reduced the effective tax rate further in 1977. Specifically, changes in the petroleum sector reflected the federal government's attempts to share in the windfall, attributable to the worldwide rise in oil prices, and aggravated the friction between Alberta and Ottawa.

21. The share of corporate income tax revenues in total tax revenues in the United States demonstrates a pattern similar to that in Figure 5 for Canada. See J. Pechman's posthumous presidential address to the American Economic Association (1990).

22. See MacDonald (1977, 12) and Chrétien (1978, 9, and 1978, 7 and 11); see also Turner (1975, 21).

23. See Winer and Hettich (1988, 413–14) and Maslove (1989, 10–11 and 16–19).

24. See Gillespie (1978, 28–39) and Doman (1980) for a summary of the details of these tax choices of the seventies.

25. The indexation of the personal income tax in 1974 and some of the transfer-payments to persons in the seventies did not contribute to this

relative decline in personal income tax revenues as a source of total financing (see Chapter 9 of Gillespie 1991, 189–194 and 226–227).

26. See Turner (1974, 19) and Chrétien (1978, 19). Turner also exempted clothing and footwear from the tax (1974, 17).

27. The oil export charges were born in 1974 and died in 1986; the excise tax on gasoline was born in 1976 and is the most substantial energy tax today; the petroleum and gas revenue tax and the natural gas tax were born in 1981 and died in 1987 and 1985, respectively, (although some revenues are still collected on previous sales); the Canadian Ownership special charge was born in 1982 and died in 1986; and the excise tax on aviation gas and diesel fuel, born in 1986, still exists today.

28. See Crosbie (1979, 3). See also MacEachen (1980, 4; 1981, 1, 2 and 5; and 1982, 1), Lalonde (1983, 20 and 21; and 1984, 5) and Wilson (1985, 5 and 15; 1986, 1, 5 and 23; 1987, 2, 6 and 13; 1988, 2 and 5; and 1989, 1, 3, 4, 10 and 15). In addition, see the separate studies of the deficit and the debt in Lalonde (1983) and Wilson (1989).

29. See MacDonald (1989, 7). See also Toulin (1988), Simpson (1989) and the *Globe and Mail* (1990), which refers in alarmist tones to "the crushing burden of the federal debt," the slow progress in "taming the unruly federal debt" and the "stock pile of debt."

30. Angus Reid Associates Inc. found that the deficit was second on the list of the public's concerns, and Environics Research Group found that the percentage of Canadians who saw the deficit as an important problem had risen over four months from 50 to 60 per cent (Kohut, 1989).

Chapter 2

1. "Net debt" means the excess of liabilities over financial assets on a national accounts basis. This is a smaller number than net debt on a public accounts basis, mainly because public accounts include liabilities toward government employees' pension funds, whereas national accounts do not. However, up to a vertical translation, the two series display almost identical trends over time. Hence, for the analysis of change, either will do. I use national accounts stock and flow concepts throughout to ensure overall consistency.

2. To illustrate, in 1993, program spending (PX) totalled $288.8 billion and the GDP (Y) was $711.7 billion. Thus, the actual program spending ratio was PX/Y or 40.6 per cent. But the cyclically adjusted values for PX and Y were $278.8 billion and $783.8 billion, respectively, giving a cyclically adjusted ratio (PX*/Y*) of 35.5 per cent. These calculations are based on estimates of 7.5 per cent for the nonaccelerating inflation rate of unemployment or NAIRU (Fortin 1994) and 9.2 per cent for the output gap in 1993 (Dungan and Wilson 1994).

3. Also noticeable is the brief attempt by the Trudeau government to redress the financial situation in 1981–1982, which was followed by a reversal of policy between 1983 and 1985 in the wake of the recession.

4. Of course, the net result of the shift in the structural balance on the debt ratio from 1974 to 1981 (i.e., the impact relative to the no-shift situation instead of relative to zero) was, cumulatively, eighteen points; without the shift, the debt ratio would have declined by twelve points instead of increasing by six.

5. See Crow (1988) for a clear policy pronouncement and Bank of Canada (1991) for the specification of operational inflation reduction targets.

6. The 1994 average unemployment rate in Canada (10.3 per cent) was about three points above the NAIRU. With such a high rate of unemployment in the United States in 1994, GDP would have been about $450 billion lower (following Okun's law), and the public sector deficit would have been at least $200 billion higher. The U.S. fiscal deficit would have then exceeded $400 billion, or 6.3 per cent of the smaller GDP. This figure exceeds the 5.6 per cent projected for Canada in 1994, based on a $42 billion deficit in public sector national accounts and a $745 billion GDP.

7. The average real rate is defined as the average nominal rate minus the current annual GDP deflator rate. The average nominal rate on the debt in a given year is calculated as the ratio of interest payments for that year to the level of net debt at the end of the previous year.

8. See Laidler and Robson (1993) for a favourable detailed account of the Canadian disinflation experiment.

9. Such a quantitative assessment overestimates the effects of the interest-growth spread and underestimates those of the operating balance. This is because the current implications of the interest-growth differential factor on the rate of change of debt depend on the current stock of debt (last equation), which in turn results from the past effects of both the interest-growth differential and the operating balance. The intertemporal nonlinear interaction between these two causal factors makes a precise assessment of their respective contributions difficult.

10. See Fortin (1994). The potential growth rate and output gap estimates are taken from the Conference on the Gap between Actual and Potential Output, held at the University of Toronto in August 1994. Under these assumptions, five years of 5 per cent growth will send the actual-to-potential output ratio to $91.8 \times (1.05/1.031)^5 = 100$ per cent and the output gap to zero. Note that the consensus estimate for the output gap is based on the medium-term inflation outlook. It is (as it should be) larger than those estimates recently produced by the Bank of Canada, the International Monetary Fund and the OECD, which are based on short-term inflation prospects.

11. On the assumptions that the average real interest rate on the public debt would decline permanently from 7.5 to 6 per cent as the difference with U.S. interest rates would fall, and that the potential growth rate would remain at around 3 per cent.

12. If program spending is initially equal to 35 per cent of GDP and if the potential growth rate of real GDP is 3 per cent per year, then freezing program spending will send its ratio to GDP to $35/1.03 = 34$ per cent after one year, $35/(1.03)^2 = 33$ per cent after two years, and so on.

Chapter 3

1. Subject to the usual caveat, I would like to thank Lars Osberg for helpful suggestions. I would also like to thank Alex Araujo of Nesbitt Burns Inc. and John Sheriff of Midland Walwyn Capital Inc. for providing data on provincial bond yields.
2. This system differs from that in the United States, where tax and expenditure limits and constitutional restrictions on state budget deficits are widespread.
3. In all provinces but Quebec the personal income tax rate is defined as a percentage of the federal rate. Thus changes in the federal tax rate have a direct effect on revenues in these provinces.
4. The value of the relevant nominal interest rate was determined by matching the average term of maturity of federal debt (see Bank of Canada) to the interest rate paid on Government of Canada bonds of that maturity. The real interest rate was calculated using the rate of change in the current period GDP implicit price deflator.
5. Laidler and Robson (1993) note that, at this point, the Bank of Canada was not a leader in adopting monetary restraint. The Bank imported the strict money policy of the U.S. Federal Reserve rather than accepting the depreciation of the dollar that would have resulted.
6. Provinces pay higher interest rates on their debts than does the federal government, with the amount varying by province. To get an idea of the rates involved, in July 1989, the yields on Ontario and Quebec government ten-year bonds exceeded that on the ten-year Canada bond by forty-two and seventy-three basis points, respectively (Data supplied by Alex Araujo of Nesbitt Burns Inc.).
7. The figures in columns four and five are derived using the arithmetic of the government budget constraint reviewed in Appendix A. The figures in column four show, given the value of the debt-to-GDP ratio in column one, the growth rate of GDP in column three and assuming a real interest rate of 5 per cent, the value of the primary balance as a percentage of GDP sufficient to hold the deficit-to-GDP ratio constant. The figures in column five are derived by subtracting from column one the difference between columns two and four.
8. In fact, Quebec has been subject to larger interest rate fluctuations than other governments, owing to political uncertainties. Thus, in the three months leading up to the 1980 referendum, the yield on ten-year Quebec government bonds jumped by thirty-five basis points relative to the ten-year Canada bond (Data supplied by John Sheriff, Midland Walwyn Capital Inc.). To the extent that these shocks affected the Quebec government's debt servicing costs, the point made in the text is reinforced.
9. Another lesson is worth mentioning. The hypothesis that those governments in a monetary union without the power to print money would, if faced with serious debt problems, try to avoid the costs of imposing large primary surpluses on their citizens and simply wait to be bailed out by the other members of the union receives little support from our

review of the budgetary responses of provincial governments in Canada. The province which entered the turbulent eighties with the largest debt, Newfoundland, responded to the disastrous combination of high interest rates and lower economic growth by increasing the size of its primary surpluses beyond the already high levels set during the late seventies. Rather than await rescue, the government of Newfoundland imposed significant costs on its citizens in the form of very large primary surpluses. Partly due to concern that highly indebted member states might wait to be bailed out, the Maastricht Treaty requires that applicants for entry into the proposed European Monetary Union satisfy certain standards of fiscal prudence. The Canadian experience suggests that these rules may not be necessary.

10. See Laidler and Robson (1993) for an excellent discussion of the Bank of Canada's monetary policies during this period.

11. All data presented in this paragraph are from the Department of Finance (1995).

12. Tables 2 and 3 present the most up-to-date data available (as of June 1995) that facilitates comparisons of budget figures across time and across governments using a common accounting convention. The budget figures reported for fiscal years 1993–94 and 1994–95 are taken from provincial budget papers. Thus, while data in budget papers might suggest a balanced budget by a certain year, data obtained using the accounting conventions applied by Statistics Canada (in Tables 2 and 3) would not necessarily reflect the same situation.

13. Saskatchewan's rate of 7.4 per cent also deserves mention. This province operated under the constraint of a very large debt-service-to-GDP ratio and an economic slow-down persisting since 1987. British Columbia did not suffer either of these handicaps, so its performance is far less impressive.

14. In July 1995, the newly elected government reduced welfare rates by 21.6 per cent, leaving them at 110 per cent of the average in the other provinces.

15. This figure is based on the calculation of the government budget constraint introduced earlier.

16. Data on bond yield spreads are supplied by Midland Walwyn Capital Inc. with the exception of data for Alberta's spread, which is from the Alberta government publication, *Measuring Up*. Further shrinking in bond yield spreads is apparent from data for March 31, 1995. However, as this period also saw the credit rating on federal bonds fall, it is unclear whether the reason for the shrinking yield spread is the financial markets' response to that downgrade or to further improvements in provincial finances.

Chapter 4

1. Gorbet, F.W., 1973. Econometric Models: Some Comments on Their Use in Policy Analysis. *Bank of Canada Review* (October): 3–13.

Chapter 5

1. For this figure, I measure price changes in terms of the prices of the goods households buy in Canada, as recorded by Statistics Canada's Consumer Price Index. This differs from the GDP Deflator, which measures price change for the goods we produce. Use of the GDP Deflator would have produced an even greater rise in real GDP per head.
2. We have not subtracted net government interest payments to Canadian residents, because these payments are not a drain on the Canadian economy. They shift purchasing power between Canadian residents.
3. The government debt figures used here are Statistics Canada's "national accounts basis" figures. They include the net debt of federal, provincial, territorial and local governments, as well as the Canada and Quebec Pension Plans. An accounting system is employed that is uniform across jurisdictions and that does not change over time. For details, see Moore (1994).
4. The term "primary balance" is often used for the negative primary deficit: revenues minus "program expenditures." While the deficit, the GDP and interest paid can be taken directly from the National Accounts, interest received, and hence net interest and the primary deficit, have to be calculated from detail in the tables of government investment income.
5. This includes cross-border shopping and trips abroad.
6. Treasury bills are essentially government IOUs of less than one year's duration.
7. For those interested in economic theory: The conservative theories of central bank impotence assume that the right model for the world market in debt instruments is that of perfect competition, but the realistic and relevant model is that of product differentiation and imperfect competition. Floyd (1995) gives a recent example of the implicit use of the model of perfect competition to argue that the Bank of Canada is impotent.
8. The statistical analysis corrects for the influence of the inflation rate, U.S. interest rates and monetary policy.
9. Another conservative theory is that unemployment can be "voluntary," meaning that some of the unemployed do not want to work. But the statistical surveys on which our count of the unemployed is based define the unemployed as either looking for work or on temporary layoff, so the "voluntarily" unemployed are not included when the unemployment rate is calculated.
10. "Actions by the Bank to force interest rates lower would require us to pump more liquidity into the financial system. Such actions would raise worries about inflation and a declining trend in the Canadian dollar. This is a recipe, not for low interest rates, but for higher rates" (Thiessen 1995).
11. See Alan Freeman and Barrie McKenna's article, "Banks Ask Millions in R&D Credits," The *Globe and Mail,* 15 December 1994.

Chapter 6

1. This text is a translated and revised version of a talk entitled "La lumière au bout du tunnel" given at the conference "Révolutionner l'état ... Est-ce possible?" organized by Quebec's Conseil de la santé et du bien-être in Montreal, on April 28, 1995.
2. This measure essentially excludes payment of interest on the debt.
3. By the term "money illusion," economists mean that people do not always correctly comprehend the implications of inflation. People, for example, are more likely to agree to freeze their nominal wages despite a 10 per cent inflation rate, while they would never agree to a 10 per cent wage cut in a situation of zero inflation. These two situations, however, are identical from an economic point of view, and people should not differentiate between them.

Chapter 7

1. This article is a substantially revised version of a paper published in Canadian Business Economics, Fall 1993, pp. 36–45. I would like to thank Shelley Phipps, Andrew Sharpe, David Slater and two anonymous referees for their helpful comments. Any remaining errors are my own.
2. Coletti, Muir and Tetlow (1995) provide an excellent and very interesting example, with a comprehensive list of references.
3. Social policy designers are often quite different, in background and experience from social policy practitioners, but both focus on the disparate individuals who would like to supply labour, not on the firms which supply jobs.
4. See Fougère (1995) and Bartolini and Symansky (1993, 79).
5. For a formal model, see Osberg (1995).
6. See, for example, Brenner (1973) and Kelvin and Jarrett (1985). Ketso (1988) examined a simultaneous equation model in which the relative influence of unemployment on illness and illness on unemployment could be assessed. Unemployment plays an unambiguous causal role in increasing the probability of illness.
7. Of course, the road network, electrical power distribution and municipal services on which business depends are also provided at the local level. Local governments also compete for grants, tax concessions and specialized public services for marginal "footloose" investments. Although highly visible politically, these initiatives affect only a small percentage of all jobs.
8. The differential in test score achievement among senior high school students is heavily influenced by the degree of selectivity of the school systems. At the age when comparable populations are being tested (in junior high), the highest achieving country (South Korea) has an average test score in science achievement that is 13 per cent above the Canadian average, (nine percentage points — 78 compared to 69, IAEP, 1992,18). The difference in average mathematics scores was 17 per

cent. If educational reform could improve Canadian students' test scores by 15 per cent, it would take at least twelve years before education reform could have its full impact on the skill level of high school graduates. By the end of that period, new graduates would have come to make up about 30 per cent of the labour force, but, on average, only half their schooling would have been under the new system; that is, the impact on the average quality of the labour force as a whole would be, at the end of twelve years, an improvement of about 2.25 per cent in educational quality. Although, in the long run, education reform can have significant effects on the workforce, the basic point is that reform in educational policy takes a very long time to have a major effect. For a detailed discussion, see Osberg (1993, 1995).

9. A large number of studies concur in estimating the wage elasticity of labour supply at 0.1 or less. For a recent study that uses a large, Canadian data set, see Osberg and Phipps (1993). Surveys of the literature are also given by Osberg (1986), Pencavel (1986) and Killingsworth (1983).

Chapter 9

1. Fortin (1996:761) calculates lost output in Canada up to 1996 as $400 billion, and still growing at an annual rate of $75 billion per year.

2. From an average of U.S.$.72 in 1986, the dollar went to $.754 in 1988 and peaked at an average of $.867 in the third quarter of 1990.

3. In 1988–89, the federal debt-to-GDP ratio was .539. Between March 1988 and March 1990, the Bank of Canada raised the bank rate from 8.7 per cent to 14.05 per cent, (an increase of 5.27 per cent) and other short-term interest rates followed in rough parallel. This increase cannot be explained by international trends. The comparable U.S. interest rate (the Federal Reserve Bank discount rate) was 6.0 per cent in March 1988 and 7.0 per cent in March 1990; that is, the Canada-U.S. interest rate differential widened to an unprecedented level. Nor can the increase in interest rates be explained by trends in core inflation (4.7 per cent in the second quarter of 1988, 4.4 per cent in the second quarter of 1990); real short-term interest rates were raised to dramatic levels.

     The impact of such a rise in interest rates on the deficit depends in part on the term structure of the federal debt and the percentage of the federal debt that has to be refinanced during the period in which interest rates are kept high (quite a while, in this case). The importance of a 5 per cent hike in interest rates can be partly gauged from the fact that, if applied to the entire debt when the debt-to-GDP ratio is .539, this rate would amount to an increase in the deficit equal to 2.84 per cent of GDP, or over $13.9 billion (in 1988). This increase in interest costs can be compared to the total expenditure of the federal government on social assistance under the Canada Assistance Plan ($5.108 billion in 1988–89).

4. See the references in Selody (1993) for evidence on the empirical content and date of publication of support for the zero inflation argument. The only existing empirical study of the productivity benefits to Can-

ada of zero inflation that existed in 1988 (Jarrett and Selody 1982) was widely referred to by advocates of the zero inflation initiative at the time (e.g., Howitt 1990) but has since been largely discredited. (See MacLean and Setterfield 1993). It is crucial to emphasize that one can agree that high and variable inflation rates have substantial social costs, yet disagree with the 1988 decision to try to go from a low and stable inflation rate to zero. There is little evidence on the benefits of zero inflation for the simple reason that no country has managed to come close to zero inflation for long enough for the policy to pay off (see Cozier and Selody 1992, Footnote 7, which indicates that the lowest long-run inflation rate 1960–1985 was 3.6 per cent annually). However, by 1993, Bank of Canada researchers preferred to ignore the issue of the productivity benefits of zero inflation on the grounds that estimates are "fragile" (see Johnson 1995). More disinterested observers are less ambiguous in their conclusions. Levine and Zervos (1993, 428) conclude that "inflation is not significantly negatively correlated with long-run growth. More impressively, we could not find a combination of variables that produced a significant negative association between growth and average inflation over the 1960 to 1989 period."

5. By way of comparison, we can ask whether it would have been considered reasonable, for example, to embark on the construction of a $50 billion cold-fusion reactor, based on the theoretical writings of several university professors and the empirical results of a single research project.

6. Some readers may have been taught the "Lucas critique": that macroeconomic policy is ineffective because optimizing agents will incorporate anticipated policy responses into their decision making. Ericsson and Irons (1995) have convincingly demolished this perspective by examining all the published economics articles (513) which made reference to Lucas (1976) between 1976 and 1990, and categorizing them by whether or not they were purely theoretical, they assumed the truth of the Lucas critique, they tested the Lucas hypothesis or they tested some other, unrelated hypothesis. Their conclusion is unambiguous: "Virtually no evidence exists that empirically substantiates the Lucas critique. Numerous studies refute the Lucas critique for various empirical macroeconomic relations."

7. Ruggieri and Hermanutz add the numbers of federal, provincial and local government employees, teachers and professors, employees of armed services and institutions (excluding medical doctors) and calculate public sector employment as a percentage of total employment to average 22.01 per cent between 1961 and 1970, 24.24 per cent from 1971 to 1980 and 22.58 per cent from 1981 to 1992 (1995, 46). Total purchases by all levels of government of goods and services rose between 1961 and 1971 from 24.14 per cent of net national income to 31.13 per cent (as the national health care system was phased in) but fell to 30.05 per cent of net national income in 1981 and 30.31 per cent in 1991 (Table 2-2).

8. An example of the opportunity for data reinterpretation is the Bank's method of calculating potential output (see Bank of Canada 1995, 8 and Laxton and Tetlow 1992), which relies heavily on the "Hodrick-Prescott filter," to estimate the trend in potential output. Since this measure is really a type of weighted average of past output levels, the calculation has two implications: (1) With the estimation of output potential as a weighted average of past actual output, past actual economic performance heavily influences estimates of potential performance (and when the past is redefined as being "as good as it could get" the Bank and other macro policymakers are implicitly absolved of responsibility for bad macroeconomic performance). (2) In order to keep inflation from ever increasing, the economy is never allowed to exceed this estimate of potential output, which tends to guarantee, since current unemployment is always kept above a moving average of past unemployment, that unemployment will rise over time.

Glossary
of Economic Terms

Automatic stabilizers: Tax and expenditure programs that tend to reduce the magnitude of fluctuations in output and employment. For example, tax collections tend to fall during a recession and rise during a boom, slowing the change in disposable incomes and total demand. When the economy goes into a recession and people become unemployed, their receipt of UI benefits enables them to maintain expenditures, preventing a further drop in output and employment.

Balanced budget: A budget with revenues equal to expenditures. Often, a budget with revenues equal to or *greater than expenditures* is referred to as "balanced," but strictly speaking, it is "in surplus."

Balance of payments: A country's record of international trading, borrowing and lending.

Bank of Canada: Canada's central bank, which controls the supply of money and sets short-term interest rates.

Bank rate: The interest rate at which the Bank of Canada stands ready to lend to the chartered banks.

Consumer price index (CPI): A weighted average of the prices of goods and services consumed by an average household, as calculated by Statistics Canada.

Debt: The debt (in the form of bonds, Treasury Bills, Canada Savings Bonds) owed by governments as a result of previous borrowing to finance budget deficits.

Budget deficit: A government's budgetary balance that is negative — total expenditures exceed tax revenues.

Deficit: The amount by which expenditures exceed revenues.

Deficit financing: The financing of government programs out of borrowings rather than from tax revenues.

Demand management policy: A change in monetary and/or fiscal policy aimed at affecting total demand.

Exchange rate: The price of one national currency in terms of another (e.g. if the price of the Canadian dollar is 73 cents U.S., the Canadian/U.S. exchange rate is .73)

Fiscal policy: The adjustment of tax rates or government spending in order to affect total demand in the economy.

Frictional unemployment: The unemployment that arises due to the time it normally takes for new entrants to the labour market and those changing jobs to locate employment.

Global tax rate: The total fraction of national income taxed by governments.

Gross domestic product (GDP): The value of all final goods and services produced in Canada in a year.

Gross national product (GNP): The value of all final goods and services produced in a year by Canadians or by Canadian-owned factors of production (differs from GDP by the net earnings of foreign investment in Canada).

Inflation: The rise in the average level of prices — often measured by the percentage change in the *consumer price index* but also measured (if the intent is to measure the change in costs of *production* of *all* goods rather than just consumption goods) by the percentage change in the GDP deflator (the average level of *all* prices).

Macroeconomic policy: Policy (e.g. a change in interest rates) that affects the overall aggregates of the economy, such as total employment, the unemployment rate, GDP or the rate of inflation.

Microeconomic policy: Policy that affects the decisions of individual households and firms and the way in which individual markets work (e.g. taxes and government regulation affecting the allocation of labour and of goods and services).

Monetary policy: The Bank of Canada's manipulation of interest rates to influence total demand in order to control inflation and the foreign exchange value of our currency and to moderate the business cycle.

Money illusion: The perception that economic welfare is changed, when money wages and prices all change by the same percentage.

NAIRU: The non-accelerating inflation rate of unemployment. That rate of unemployment at which inflation is constant (lower unemployment would cause inflation to accelerate, while higher unemployment would reduce inflation). It is not necessarily the same as the "natural" rate of unemployment. It may vary over time (i.e., because long spells of unemployment may make some people unemployable).

"Natural" rate of unemployment: That rate of unemployment which one would expect to observe, if the economy were growing at its long-run potential, given the labour market institutions and labour force characteristics that influence the rate of unemployment (i.e., given the characteristics of the UI system, the percentage of the labour force that is under 25, and so on).

Nominal interest rates: Interest as a percentage per annum of the amount borrowed.

Output gap: The difference between the total output the economy is *actually* producing, and the total output the economy *could* produce, without causing an increase in inflation.

Real GDP: The level of GDP measured in constant prices.

Real GNP: The level of GNP measured in constant prices.

Real interest rates: The nominal rate of interest less the expected rate of inflation.

Recession: A downturn in the level of economic activity in which real GDP falls in two successive quarters.

Stagflation: The coexistence of a high rate of unemployment (stagnation) and inflation.

Structural unemployment: The unemployment that arises because jobless workers are in the wrong place or have the wrong skills to fill available job vacancies; that is, there is a mismatch between the requirements of available vacancies and the characteristics of available workers.

Supply-side economics: The view that it is supply factors — such as the quantity and productivity of capital and the willingness to work — that are always the principal constraints to growth. According to this view, a lack of aggregate demand is not the main constraint, and government policy should emphasize the establishment of appropriate incentives to greater supply of labour and capital.

Transfer payments: Payments, usually made by the government to individuals, that do not result from the purchase of goods or services. Old age pensions, unemployment insurance and welfare are examples.

About the Contributors

Pierre Fortin holds degrees in classical humanities, mathematics and economics. He received his PhD in economics from the University of California at Berkeley in 1975. He has since taught economics at various institutions, including the University of Quebec at Montreal since 1988. He is a Fellow of the Royal Society of Canada and the Canadian Institute for Advanced Research. He was the 1988 President of the French Canadian Economics Association, the 1991 Innis Lecturer of the Canadian Economics Association, and the 1995 President of the CEA. In the last twenty years, he has been the author of about 100 scholarly publications in Canada and abroad. His research interests include wage and employment dynamics, economic fluctuations and growth, adolescent behaviour, taxation, fiscal and monetary policies, and social policy. In the 1980s, he was chief economic advisor to a Quebec premier and a member of the Economic Council of Canada.

W. Irwin Gillespie is a professor in the Department of Economics at Carleton University, Ottawa, where he has taught since 1964. He has worked with the Royal Commission on Taxation as a research member and the Ontario Fair Tax Commission as an advisor and has written several books on the redistribution of income in Canada and government taxing, spending and borrowing policies. He is continuing his work on income redistribution through the tax system and the financing of provincial government spending.

Ronald Kneebone is an associate professor of economics at the University of Calgary. He received his PhD from McMaster University. He has published articles dealing with the consequences for government finances of multiple levels of governments and with the implications of alternatives to deficit financing. Other publications have been in the areas of regional labour markets and public choice. He is currently involved in a large research project examining efforts by the Alberta government to balance its budget and eliminate its debt through large cuts in its expenditures.

Michael C. McCracken is a senior economic advisor to government agencies, corporations and associations. His areas of expertise include current and long-term economic policy, energy policy, economic forecasting and the use of quantitative methods in economic analysis. He is founder, chairman and chief executive officer of Informetrica Limited. Since 1972, this Ottawa-based economic research and information company has provided comprehensive support to corporations, governments and other organizations. Informetrica produces forecasts on the Canadian economy, specific industries, and the provinces for clients in public benefit/cost studies, and other quantitative economic research. Related outside activities include participation in the Statistics Canada National Accounts Advisory Group, the Campaign for Open Government, and the Canadian Employment Research Forum (CERF). He is past president and Honorary Member of the Canadian Association for Business Economics in the United States. Other major accomplishments include remaining married for more than thirty years, seeing three children graduate and reaching a golf handicap index of 13.4.

Lars Osberg was born and raised in Ottawa, Ontario. As an undergraduate, he attended Queen's University, Kingston, and the London School of Economics and Political Science: he graduated from Queen's with an Honour's BA in economics and politics in 1968. From 1968 to 1970, he served as a CUSO volunteer in Tanzania, working initially with the National Insurance Corporation but primarily with the Tanzania Sisal Corporation. From 1970 to 1973, he attended Yale University, receiving his PhD in economics in 1975. His first academic appointment was at the University of Western Ontario, but in 1977 he moved to Dalhousie University, where he is now McCulloch Professor of Economics. He is the author or editor of eight books, and numerous articles, reviews, reports and miscellaneous publications. His main fields of research interest have been the determinants of poverty and economic inequality, with particular emphasis in recent years on the effects of unemployment, structural change in labour markets and social policy. He is president-elect of the Canadian Economics Association.

Gideon Rosenbluth, F.R.S.C., Professor Emeritus, Department of Economics, University of British Columbia, is author or co-author of six books, many articles in professional journals and other media, and several reports commissioned by government agencies. He studied economics at the London School of Economics, the University of Toronto, and Columbia University. Before joining the University of B.C. in 1962, he had worked as a Federal civil servant and taught at Princeton University, Stanford University, and Queen's University. He is a past president of the Canadian Economics Association and of the Canadian Association of University Teachers. Since his retirement in 1986, Dr. Rosenbluth has worked mainly on the problems of macroeconomic policy confronting Canada's federal and provincial governments.

James Tobin is Sterling Professor of Economics Emeritus at Yale University and has been on the Yale faculty since 1950. He retired from his teaching position in 1988. He graduated from Harvard College summa cum laude in economics in 1939. He received a PhD in economics from Harvard in 1947 and was a junior fellow of the Society of Fellows for three years (1947 to 1950), the last of which he spent at the Department of Applied Economics at the University of Cambridge, England. In 1961–62, on leave from Yale, he was a member of President Kennedy's Council of Economic Advisers in Washington. He was president of the Econometric Society in 1958, of the American Economic Association in 1971, and of the Eastern Economics Association in 1977. In 1955, the American Economic Association awarded him the John Bates Clark Medal, which is given to one economist under age forty. He has been a member of the National Academy of Sciences since 1972. In 1981, he received the Nobel Prize in Economic Science, established by the Bank of Sweden in Memory of Alfred Nobel. He is author or editor of thirteen books and more than four hundred articles. His main areas of interest have been macroeconomics, monetary theory and policy, fiscal policy and public finance, consumption and saving, unemployment and inflation, portfolio theory and asset markets, and econometrics. He has written for both academic and general audiences.

Marc Van Audenrode is a professor at the Economics Department of Laval University, in Quebec City. He has an MA from the University of California at Los Angeles and a PhD from the University of California at Berkeley. He specializes in labour economics. He was an economist in the research department of the Belgian Central bank. His current research interests deal with questions related to the influence of unemployment insurance and other institutions on the functioning of the labour market. He has several academic publications in highly regarded international reviews, but also conducts applied research. He has, among other things, recently collaborated in several studies on the reform of unemployment insurance in Canada and a study on Quebec's public finances.